W9-ACC-406

81-01457

DEMCO

THE VONNEGUT STATEMENT

Edited by

JEROME KLINKOWITZ & JOHN SOMER

A DELTA BOOK

A DELTA BOOK
Published by
Dell Publishing Co., Inc.
New York, New York 10017

All of the essays in this book were written for *The Vonnegut
Statement;* some have also appeared in the following publications:
Critique: Studies in Modern Fiction,
for "Kurt Vonnegut, Jr. and the Crime of his Times"
by Jerome Klinkowitz, copyright © 1971 by Critique;
Fusion, for "Kurt Vonnegut: The Sound of Two Hands Clapping"
by Dan Wakefield, copyright © 1972 by Dan Wakefield;
and *Summary,* for "Chasing a Lone Eagle" by Robert Scholes.

Published by
DELL PUBLISHING CO., INC.
1 Dag Hammarskjold Plaza
New York, N.Y. 10017

Designed by Joel Schick

Delta ® TM 755118, Dell Publishing Co., Inc.
ISBN: 0-440-59236-4
Reprinted by arrangement with Delacorte Press, New York
A Seymour Lawrence Book
Printed in the United States of America
Third Printing—April 1978

FOR
BOB TATALOVICH
AND
JIM MELLARD,
WHO TOLD US, YEARS AGO,
TO READ VONNEGUT

"I love you sons of bitches . . ."
—ELIOT ROSEWATER

CONTENTS

CONTENTS

THE LITERARY FIGURE

THE LITERARY ART

CONTENTS

ACKNOWLEDGMENTS
AND
A NOTE ON
THE TEXT

———•◦•———

WE WISH TO THANK several persons for their help with *The Vonnegut Statement:* Scott Bryan and Jack Fritscher for reading and making suggestions for parts of the manuscript; Don Fiene, whose work with J. D. Salinger has become the model for international bibliographies of contemporary writers, for advice about items for our appendix, and Mary Burns for additional fugitive items; Knox Burger, William Cotter Murray, Jordan Pecile, and Max

Wilkinson for notes on Kurt Vonnegut, Jr.'s literary and academic career; Bantam Books and Fawcett Publications, and especially Jim Trupin, for information on the early paperbacks; our chairmen, Charles W. Hagelman, Jr., and Charles E. Walton, for departmental support of our research; Seymour Lawrence, for editorial help and encouragement; and Elaine Klinkowitz and Connie Somer, for assistance too comprehensive to list.

Chapters Five and Eleven of *The Vonnegut Statement* received their first publication in the pages of *Summary* (I.2; 1971) and *Critique* (XII.3; 1971) in somewhat different form; we are grateful to editors Andrew Mylett and James Dean Young for permission to reuse this material.

All quotations from the works of Kurt Vonnegut, Jr., in *The Vonnegut Statement* are taken from the standard edition, as established by Mr. Vonnegut's publishers, Seymour Lawrence/Delacorte Press. This edition consists of *Player Piano, The Sirens of Titan, Mother Night, Cat's Cradle,* and *God Bless You, Mr. Rosewater* (1971); *Welcome to the Monkey House* (1968); *Slaughterhouse-Five* (1969); and *Happy Birthday, Wanda June* (1971). Page numbers will be indicated parenthetically, and all material is quoted by permission.

PREFACE

—————•·•—————

ONCE UPON A TIME artists were people; that is, they were for the people, by the people, and of the people. In the seventeenth century, for example, Urian Oakes could write a fine poem (considering he was a Puritan and an American), an elegy, expressing not only his own grief over the death of a fellow minister, Thomas Shepard, but the grief of the entire community. Oakes had performed an important service for the community by giving it a means of participating in the general sorrow. Even late into the nineteenth century Rudyard Kipling, in such poems as "Recessional" and "The White Man's Burden," could express sentiments held commonly by his culture. But Kipling was among the last of the great public poets.

Between Oakes and Kipling something happened. Some intellectuals and artists started to read books by Descartes, Darwin, Kant, Comte, Taine, Weston, and Frazer. These books had a strange effect upon artists and intellectuals. They decided the common culture, the popular culture, was not all it was cracked up to be. They began to sense that mankind was living in a spiritual wasteland, and they began to fall back into themselves with the hope of finding there, in private visions, an elixir that would restore life to man. They tried very hard to tell the common man of his plight, but they had read so many more books than he that they forgot his language. What the artist considered to be his most profound expression appeared to the common man as the babbling of an incoherent child. The artists became very lonely. Not only were they cut off from a mythic past, but they were also cut off from common humanity. The intellectuals called this state "alienation." That idea was frightening, but the word was consoling. It gave definition. Artists knew what they were; they were alienated. Soon artists began to equate the two words—artist and alienation. In fact, it became popular to be unpopular.

Then came Kurt Vonnegut, Jr. He was weird. He wrote book after book, and people seemed to like them. Cheers. Critics were confused. Obviously anybody who wrote science fiction "buggered the truth for money" and could not be trusted. Anybody who competed with comic books and television and came in a close second could not be profound. And yet a distinguished member of the literary

Establishment (who shall remain nameless to protect his professional reputation) had the audacity and honesty to say, in print, "I loved *The Sirens of Titan* when it came out. I still do and wish someone would tell me why." Many serious critics felt the same way. They hated to admit they were common because they dug Vonnegut, especially since they could not understand him. So, while the critics were confused, Vonnegut scored a victory for the people. Art Power. Art Power, he was the president of the first Vonnegut fan club. He lives in Wellington, Kansas, and bowls an impressive 240. He thinks the Buddha is the name of a bubble gum, and when he picks up a handful of Kansas soil he can tell you whether the fields need to be harrowed or not. He has a mystical understanding of the plains. To him, the heavens over the plains are as majestic and awesome as the mountains of Colorado. He never left Wellington, Kansas. We did. The three of us used to read Captain Marvel comic books when we were kids together there on the plains. Because he knows we are interested in life and literature, too, even though we have doctorates in English literature, he wrote and asked us to tell him why he loves Kurt Vonnegut's books the same way he loves Kansas. Thus, *Shazam,* this book for a distinguished literary critic and Art Power—*The Vonnegut Statement.*

J. K.
J. S.

Chapter 1

THE
VONNEGUT
STATEMENT

———•·•———

JEROME KLINKOWITZ
AND JOHN SOMER

ALL THIS HAPPENED, more or less. Kurt Vonnegut, Jr.,
who in the 1950's had been barely known as the writer of
obscure science-fiction paperbacks, had by the late 1960's
rolled up an impressive series of credits: a brilliant res-
idency at the Iowa Writers Workshop, a Guggenheim
grant to Germany, the reputation as a national spokesman
for the values of "youth," a guest lectureship at Harvard,
and a hit play on Broadway. Moreover, his novels, many
of which were virtually ignored at their first publication,

1

were all back in print, selling millions; *Slaughterhouse-Five,* his most recent book, was a popular, literary, and academic success, and graduate schools across America were accepting dissertations on his work. Even Vonnegut's publisher, Seymour Lawrence, seemed interested in reading a critical manuscript on the whole phenomenon. Vonnegut had arrived.

It is a delicate matter to deal with the works of a living, producing writer. But people do it nevertheless: popular audiences, more educated and media-ized than ever before, read with a critical eye; contemporary literature is widely taught and analyzed at universities; and carefully written books have already appeared on major writers attaining such status only a few years before Vonnegut— among them Saul Bellow, Norman Mailer, and John Updike. Modest Vonnegut studies have been published, as pamphlets, symposia, and special numbers of critical journals. To transcend the limitations of these forms, yet to retain the virtue of a relativistic approach, we have prepared *The Vonnegut Statement.* Our plan was that, for such a difficult contemporary subject, a particular authority consider Vonnegut in relation to each specific interest: popular acceptance, counterculture style, fictional form, and so forth; and that the whole project be directed by a common purpose: studying a salient literary event of our times, the emergence of Kurt Vonnegut, Jr., as a significant American writer.

The chapters which follow were completed with an eye to each other; indeed, they may be among the first essays in criticism written in part and revised by long-distance telephone. For a broad study of Kurt Vonnegut and his work, three divisions obtained: "The Public Figure," "The Literary Figure," and "The Literary Art." Within these topics we agreed to cover his popular acceptance as a paperback writer, as a nationally prominent figure, and as a hero of college youth; his literary experiences dating from his own college days through his academic acceptance and popular acclaim; and, finally, the treatment of his six novels and countless short stories. As our work proceeded, a thesis developed: that *Slaughterhouse-Five* constituted a resolution of sorts to themes and techniques developing throughout his previous work; and that although he was certainly producing more—*Happy Birthday, Wanda June* right before our eyes—it seemed safe to offer analysis of this first, twenty-year phase of Vonnegut's career. Although more work is certainly forthcoming, the period from 1949 through 1969 is settled enough that we can now, as D. H. Lawrence said, "trust the tale" even as the teller prepares new stories. *The Vonnegut Statement,* then, begins with a consideration of Kurt Vonnegut himself, the artistic canary in a cathouse; and it concludes with a study of his cry, on the last page of his most recent novel—"Poo-tee-weet?"

THE
PUBLIC
FIGURE

Chapter 2

KURT VONNEGUT, JR.: THE CANARY IN A CATHOUSE

JEROME KLINKOWITZ

IT IS A MIRACLE that the books were written, that Kurt Vonnegut, Jr., ever survived. His novels, which in 1970 sold over one million copies, have of all contemporary classics the shakiest of histories: misconceived by their publishers and sometimes stillborn in the press, the six novels (and early story collection, *Canary in a Cathouse*) present the strangest picture of an "emerging novelist" to be found in modern literature. Vonnegut is our first major writer to have begun and sustained his career in the paperback industry, and the ramifications of such a career, in the days when even *Moby Dick* was put between soft covers and dressed with a lurid jacket, make the unpuzzling of his several novels all the more bizarre.

Kurt Vonnegut has been a writer since 1949. "When I write," he tells us in the preface to *Welcome to the Monkey House,* "I simply become what I seemingly must become." Before 1949 Vonnegut had come to frustration: he attended four colleges in four years, interrupted by a hitch in the Army which was itself interrupted by the Germans, who captured Vonnegut at the Battle of the Bulge and interned him as a prisoner. After the war and some time in graduate school he worked at a series of odd jobs and small businesses, such as selling the Saab automobile years before imports became popular. His last job, the most stable, was as a public-relations man for General Electric in Schenectady, New York—the job he suddenly walked out on, like Sherwood Anderson, to become a writer. Remaining one was not easy. " 'Publishers always explained very carefully that I wasn't worth any money. They would publish me almost as they did poetry—as a public service.' "[1] What appeared first as a major assault on the reading public became, for his publishers, at least, a frustrating series of campaigns to introduce Vonnegut to America. *Player Piano,* dustjacketed as "America in the Coming Age of Electronics," over-anticipated by a decade the college popularity of its anti-utopian cousins, *Brave New World* and *1984;* and through its marketing, as a Science Fiction Book Club edition and then in a retitled and futuristically designed Bantam paperback, Vonnegut, who wanted only to write about implications of real life in the G. E. family, was labeled a science-fiction hack. After that, Kurt Vonnegut followed a peculiar course for an "emerging novelist"—he didn't write a novel for seven years, and might not have for even longer had not a paperback editor casually asked at a party, "Why don't you write another book?" and be told in return, quite as casually and impromptu, the story of *The Sirens of Titan*. *Sirens*, now regarded as one of Vonnegut's most sophisticated experiments in literary art, was cataloged as a science-fiction title and fitted with a suggestively lurid cover, even though part of its thrust was as a satire of the genre. Quickly out of print, it sold for fifty dollars in the college underground until Dell reissued it several years later, with a toned-down cover and minus the original advertisement:

MALACHI CONSTANT WAS THE RICHEST
MAN IN AMERICA. . . .

All of his life there had been nothing on earth that was not his for the asking. Since attaining manhood, there was no woman he desired who had not succumbed.

Why should such a man, all America wondered, give up a life of unequaled indulgence to risk the unknown? Why should Malachi Constant venture into the dangers of Eternity in an untested spaceship?

But all America could not know that Malachi Constant had no choice. They did not know about the Sirens of Titan, begging him to come to them, beckoning him on, with their unearthly, irresistible beauty. . . .

Sirens did, however, make of Vonnegut a paperback writer, who within a year had a two-book contract with Fawcett. But he perplexed America again: *Mother Night*, confusingly presented as "The American edition of the confessions of Howard W. Campbell, Jr.," late of the Nazi party and the O.S.S., was lost among a spate of war books flooding the drugstores at the same time (a sample: "*Hitler's Secret Service,* told by his spy chief, Walter Schellenberg, 35¢"). Moreover, its companion collection of stories from *Collier's* and the *Post, Canary in a Cathouse,* gave few clues to the correlation Vonnegut was making between the mad, absurdist realms of science fiction or Nazi Germany and American middle-class life. "I sometimes wondered what the use of any of the arts was," Vonnegut later pondered; "The best thing I could come up with was what I call the canary in the coal mine theory of the arts. This theory says that artists are useful to society because they are so sensitive. They are super-sensitive. They keel over like canaries in poison coal mines long before more robust types realize that there is any danger whatsoever."[2] "Poo-tee-weet," the cry of a canary in a cathouse, or in a coal mine, or in a slaughterhouse, becomes clear to the public only on the last page of his last novel. In the meantime, Vonnegut continued his only dependable means of support, writing stories for the slick magazines. As is detailed in Chapter Three, these pieces were reflective of the middle-class audiences of *Collier's,* the *Post,* and *Cosmopolitan,* and were sold, says the author, to buy time for the writing of his novels. Although Vonnegut himself added some gum to the sci-fi label by sending stories to *Galaxy, Worlds of If,* and the *Magazine of Fantasy and Science Fiction,* Knox Burger, who was then an editor at *Collier's,* has confided that most of them were written for but rejected by the better-paying markets where Vonnegut's other material was appearing. In the 1950's and early 1960's Kurt Vonnegut wrote just about every type of popular story, even doing a satire on the Kennedys which was, as ill fortune would have it, killed by the *Post* in galleys because of the President's assassination.

Mother Night and *Canary in a Cathouse* were floundering as paperbacks when Vonnegut's luck turned; Samuel Stewart of the Western Printing Company, which had produced the first edition of *Sirens,* moved to Holt, Rinehart and Winston, and from his new position arranged another two-book contract for Vonnegut—but this time in hardbound. *Cat's Cradle* was published in 1963, the year of Vonnegut's abortive Kennedy story and probably at the low point of his popular reputation; *God Bless You, Mr. Rosewater* followed in 1965. In discussing such matters as the destruction of the world and the reconstitution of society, Vonnegut was again close to the realities of his culture—but too close, since America, as indexed by the presidential campaign of 1964, was too near the living of these events to entertain the satire of them. Both books were shelved as "science fiction," meriting few reviews and no Dewey Decimals at all. But on this fourth time around with the reading public Vonnegut made some headway, for in the year following *Rosewater,* 1966, two publishers, Dell and Avon, reissued the full canon of his works in paperback. For the first time readers could examine all his books—take them home for less than five dollars, read them in perhaps as many hours, and consider the full extent of Vonnegut's vision. A similar phenomenon had occurred in 1946 when Malcolm Cowley assembled the loose strands of the Yoknapatawpha saga into *The Portable Faulkner;* in the four years following, Faulkner went from an out-of-print Hollywood hack to a position as America's major writer, the recipient of the Nobel prize for literature. For Vonnegut, Holt, Rinehart and Winston reissued *Player Piano,* and Harper & Row published a hardbound edition of *Mother Night* and made tentative plans to do the same for a story collection similar to *Canary in a Cathouse.*

For the first time in fourteen years, all his works were in print, and within another year (as described by Dan Wakefield in Chapter Six), Seymour Lawrence would be signing Vonnegut to a three-book contract.

Vonnegut's 1966 re-publication, with its attendant retrospective reviews, led to his solid collegiate popularity. The writer who for years had written notes from underground was now being read by an "underground" itself about to be exploited and fanfared as the new generation, "Youth." Yet Vonnegut remained perplexing. Unlike the rush to capture Salinger a decade before, academic critics kept their distance; and except for a piece by his friend Robert Scholes, no scholarly articles on Vonnegut appeared in American academic journals until 1971. "Youth" itself misunderstood this man; freaks and hippies would camp on his lawn, only to be chased off by an irate author, looking more like their parents than the guru they thought he was. Approached by the Jefferson Airplane with regard to their fantastical "starship" program, Vonnegut (in his wing-tip shoes and Brooks Brothers suit) was put off, regretting that naïve youth culture should expect him to endorse many things he did not favor or even understand.[3]

Vonnegut's favor with youth increased steadily through the late 1960's, until CBS News was driven to ask him, "What do you think it is about what you've done that makes you so highly respected by young people who don't go around idolizing a lot of men your age?" His answer was simple:

> Well, I'm screamingly funny, you know, I really am in the books. I think so. And that helps because I'm funnier than a lot of people, I think, and that's appreciated by young people. And I talk about stuff Billy Graham won't talk about, for instance; you know, is it wrong to kill? And

what's God like? And stuff like that. And they like to hear talk like that, because they can't get it from the minister; and I show what heaven is like, you know, which you can't get a minister to talk about. . . . They want to know what happens after you die. And I talk about it. That's a very popular subject.[4]

Yet most people were amazed at Vonnegut's background: tolerantly atheistic parents, a solid middle-class upbringing in the Middle West, college study in chemistry, mechanical engineering, and anthropology, plus several years in the Army and in the structure of a large American corporation. But at a certain point along the way, something had changed Kurt Vonnegut, as he explained to the graduating class at Bennington in 1970:

> Scientific truth was going to make us *so* happy and comfortable.
> What actually happened when I was twenty-one was that we dropped scientific truth on Hiroshima. We killed everybody there. And I had just come home from being a prisoner of war in Dresden, which I'd seen burned to the ground. And the world was just then learning how ghastly the German extermination camps had been. So I had a heart-to-heart talk with myself.
> "Hey, Corporal Vonnegut," I said to myself, "maybe you were wrong to be an optimist. Maybe pessimism is the thing."
> I have been a consistent pessimist ever since, with a few exceptions.[5]

The publication in 1969 of *Slaughterhouse-Five* was in many senses the culmination of Vonnegut's novelistic career. In its first chapter he revealed that it was the book he had been working on all those years, and after its publication he remarked, "Now that I've expiated it, life is always pleasant."[6] In late 1970 he announced that he was delaying publication of his next work, *Breakfast of Champions*, and would at least for a time write no more novels.[7] In the preface to his play, *Happy Birthday, Wanda June*, he complained that the year after publishing *Slaughterhouse-Five*—his forty-seventh year—was "a time of change." Suddenly rich, but with his brood of children grown and dispersed, his own life was taking a new shape:

> I was supposedly a right-handed person, but I found myself using my left hand more and more. It became the hand that did most of the giving and taking for me. I asked my older brother what he knew about this. He said that I had been an ambidextrous infant. I had been *taught* to favor my right hand.
>
> "I'm left-handed now, and I'm through with novels," I told him. "I'm writing a play. It's plays from now on" (p. vii).

Especially in terms of this first phase of Vonnegut's career, *Slaughterhouse-Five* is a very conclusive work. Nominated for the National Book Award and missing it, according to rumor, only because "the award committee was looking for realism,"[8] it brought Vonnegut before the public in a totally respectable, and ultimately understandable, way. For his whole career Vonnegut had been drawing upon his pre-1949 life experiences. General Electric's slogan, "Progress Is Our Most Important Product," gave him the mood for stories about science and people's lives; he remarks of those times that it seemed any day somebody was going to take a photograph of God and sell it to *Popular Mechanics*.[9] He recalled his middle-class, Middle Western background in *Rosewater*. But the most commonly repeated topic of his novels could be traced back to his experience when a prisoner of war in Germany, as related in the Introduction to *Mother Night:*

> There were about a hundred of us in our particular work group, and we were put out as contract labor to a factory that was making a vitamin-enriched malt syrup for pregnant women. It tasted like thin honey laced with hickory smoke. It was good. I wish I had some right now. And the city was lovely, highly ornamented, like Paris, and untouched by war. It was supposedly an "open" city, not to be attacked since there were no troop concentrations or war industries there.
>
> But high explosives were dropped on Dresden by American and British planes on the night of February 13, 1945, just about twenty-one years ago, as I now write. There were no particular targets for the bombs. The hope was that they would create a lot of kindling and drive firemen underground.
>
> And then hundreds of thousands of tiny incendiaries were scattered over the kindling, like seeds on freshly turned loam. More bombs were dropped to keep firemen in their holes, and all the little fires grew, joined one another, became one apocalyptic flame. Hey presto: fire storm. It was the largest massacre in European history, by the way. And so what?
>
> We didn't get to see the fire storm. We were in a cold meat-locker under a slaughterhouse with our six guards and ranks and ranks of dressed cadavers of cattle, pigs, horses, and sheep. We heard the bombs walking around up there. Now and then there would be a gentle shower of calcimine. If we had gone above to take a look, we would have been turned into artifacts characteristic of fire storms: seeming pieces of charred firewood two or three feet long—ridiculously small human beings, or jumbo fried grasshoppers, if you will.
>
> The malt syrup factory was gone. Everything was gone

but the cellars where 135,000 Hansels and Gretels had been baked like gingerbread men. So we were put to work as corpse miners, breaking into shelters, bringing bodies out. And I got to see many German types of all ages as death had found them, usually with valuables in their laps. Sometimes relatives would come to watch us dig. They were interesting, too.

So much for the Nazis and me (pp. vi–vii).

This is the same slaughterhouse Vonnegut revisits in 1969, in the pages of what he calls his last novel. The first chapter tells us how this is the book he has been trying to write all along, his "Dresden book." Even a cursory examination of the six novels, from *Player Piano* through *Slaughterhouse-Five,* reveals his preoccupation with the Dresden fire-bombing. Vonnegut, obviously haunted by this abrupt and violent initiation into contemporary reality, attempted throughout his career as a novelist to arrest this experience artistically, and he finally succeeded in *Slaughterhouse-Five.*

As John Somer concludes in Chapter Fourteen, the novels from 1952 to 1969 are not only of interest in their own right, but also dramatize the growth of Vonnegut's powerful and tormented imagination, his maturing grasp of the Dresden experience, and his technical innovations necessary for its artistic manifestation. Topically, each novel is complete in itself, but in general the matter of Dresden furnished the world picture for *Player Piano,* the psychological barrier for *The Sirens of Titan,* the backdrop for *Mother Night,* the informing principle for *Cat's Cradle,* the climax for *God Bless You, Mr. Rosewater,* and finally the essence for *Slaughterhouse-Five.* With the complete manifestation of his Dresden experience it is now possible to read and evaluate, from a mature perspective, his work to this point.

NOTES TO CHAPTER 2

1. Lawrence Mahoney, "Poison Their Minds with Humanity," *Tropic: The Miami Herald Sunday Magazine*, January 24, 1971, p. 44.
2. Kurt Vonnegut, Jr., "Physicist, Purge Thyself," *Chicago Tribune Magazine*, June 22, 1969, p. 44.
3. "Carol Troy Interviews Kurt Vonnegut," *Rags* (March, 1971), pp. 24–25.
4. Transcript. "60 Minutes," CBS News, September 15, 1970, p. 14.
5. Kurt Vonnegut, Jr., "Up Is Better Than Down," *Vogue*, August 1, 1970, p. 144.
6. Loretta McCabe, "An Exclusive Interview with Kurt Vonnegut," *Writers' Yearbook, 1970*, p. 105.
7. Carol Kramer, "Kurt's College Cult Adopts Him as Literary Guru at 48," *Chicago Tribune*, November 15, 1970, Section 5, p. 1.
8. Howard M. Harper, Jr., "Trends in Recent American Fiction," *Contemporary Literature*, 12 (Spring, 1971), 208.
9. "Up Is Better Than Down," p. 144.

Chapter 3

WHY
THEY READ
VONNEGUT

JEROME KLINKOWITZ

IN SPRING OF 1970 Kurt Vonnegut, Jr., studied the campus popularity of *Steppenwolf* and *Siddhartha* in an essay, "Why They Read Hesse." His answer: "America teemed with people who were homesick in bittersweet ways, and . . . *Steppenwolf* was the most profound book about homesickness ever written." Of the basic sort as "I miss my Mommy and Daddy,"[1] this homesickness ascribed to Hesse may be the clue to Vonnegut's own popularity with the young. I will not offer a lengthy analysis of his in-

18

dividual novels; that, more incisively than for J. D. Salinger a decade ago, has already been done, and the third section of this book presents a careful synthesis of Vonnegut's literary achievement. But there are many answers to be found in Vonnegut's career as a writer, a career now in its twenty-first year. During it Vonnegut did much "to finance the writing of the novels," as he tells us in the preface to *Welcome to the Monkey House* (p. xiv), and just what he did, within and without fiction, gives sounder basis to an understanding of his appeal.

For one thing, he became a paperback writer. "And I need a job, so I want to be a paperback writer," the Beatles sang a few years ago; in 1949 Vonnegut quit as a General Electric p.r. man to be a writer, the very Sherwood Anderson-like act which, like Anderson, he continued to celebrate in much of his fiction thereafter. American publishers must have thought that this material wouldn't sell in hard covers, because they marketed Vonnegut in unreviewed pulp editions. Yet Vonnegut reached a large if uncritical public: the greater majority of Americans buy less than one hardbound book a year, but drugstores remain crowded with racks of paperbacks—among them, the works of Kurt Vonnegut, Jr.

Popular magazines accepted Vonnegut's work, and he favored middle-class America with dozens of stories appearing in both sides of the competition, including *Redbook* and *Cosmopolitan, Esquire* and *Playboy, The Ladies' Home Journal* and *McCall's,* and at one time in the same weekly issues of *Collier's* and *The Saturday Evening Post.* His appeal was broad: several stories pleaded for pacifism and deplored military uses of science, while one, "Harrison Bergeron," was reprinted in the hawkish *National Review.*[2] Because the subject of his first novel, *Player Piano,* was in part technology, Vonnegut earned the reputation of a science-fiction writer. But *Player Piano* and the science-oriented stories he published in *Collier's* and the *Post* in fact considered the effect of innovation on contemporary culture, and even the four stories Vonnegut did write for science-fiction journals emphasized the workings of science and technology among very conventional, middle-class American lives. "I supposed," he has said, "that I was writing a novel about life, about things I could not avoid seeing and hearing in Schenectady, a very real town, awkwardly set in the gruesome now."[3] Some magazine stories, such as "Report on the Barnhouse Effect,"[4] consider questions—military misuse of science, peacetime harnessing of atomic energy—that were debated on other pages of the same issue. Most are focused, despite their futurism, on present habits of existence. Narcoticlike radio waves from outer space are marketed on earth like color TVs or frozen pizzas;[5] cranky oldsters, treated to a preservative fountain of youth, simply persevere in their crankiness;[6] and future citizens, who are blessed with the ability to live ideal lives apart from their imperfect bodies, nevertheless retain all their human foibles.[7] For better or for worse, Vonnegut's science-fiction stories read at times like television situation comedies. The hallmark of these stories is that although technology changes, sociology remains the same. Familiar people encountering a new life have nevertheless familiar problems. Vonnegut's most radical departure from the *status quo* comes when Eliot Rosewater forecasts the eventual obsolescence of all workers, when the problem will become "How to love people who have no use" (p. 210). His solution is to relocate the Rosewater Foundation in a shabby walk-up office over a lunchroom and liquor store, serving the public like any small businessman.

By far the greater majority of Vonnegut's stories feature no science or technology at all, and are simple, sometimes sentimental tales of middle-class America. Again, some have the flavor of contemporary magazines, especially "All the King's Horses,"[8] which suggests Korean War topicality with its brave American P.O.W.s facing a sinister Oriental guerrilla and a dispassionate Russian officer. "Long Walk to Forever," presented as "a sickeningly slick love story from *The Ladies' Home Journal*," was drawn from Vonnegut's own life. "Shame, shame," he reflects, "to have lived scenes from a woman's magazine."[9] Conventional life, as depicted by such magazines, is at the center of such stories (which may, as Leslie Fiedler suggests, "fit formulas which are often genuine myths").[10] Some deal with small, frivolous incidents and ironies (interior-decorating schemes, summer vacations), while others are telling critiques of morals and manners. Most are written from a very stable point of view, that of an average citizen, often "a salesman of storm windows and doors, and here and there a bathtub enclosure."[11] Vonnegut's salesman leads a generally mundane life, but on one occasion sells a tub enclosure to a movie star, and on another, a full set of his top-line windows to a neighbor of the Kennedys at Hyannis Port. His experience conforms to that of other Vonnegut narrators in similar positions—real-estate salesmen, contact men for investment-counseling firms—who learn that people rich and famous sorely lack the blessings of simple, middle-class life. One story, "The Foster Portfolio,"[12] treats this theme with a touch of irony. Herbert Foster, who has inherited a large fortune, insists on remaining in his "jerry-built postwar colonial with expansion attic," with his discount-store furniture, and even with his worries about payments on his second-hand car—all so that he has the excuse to moonlight weekends as a honky-tonk pianist. But most of Vonnegut's stories are more honestly homely. "Custom-Made Bride"[13] features a designer who has crafted for himself a showpiece wife, but who misses the girl's former simple qualities. In many stories wealth is compared with middle-class frugality; the latter always wins. In "Bagombo Snuff Box"[14] a showoff tries to embarrass his ex-wife in her "small, ordinary home," but ends up profoundly humiliated himself. "The Package"[15] shows a retired businessman trying to impress an old friend with his luxury house; he is, of course, shamed by the other's life of poverty and self-sacrifice. "Hal Irwin's Magic Lamp"[16] tells of a poor man who makes half a million on the stock market, cleverly revealing the bounty to his wife by means of a "magic lamp." The wife, however, wishes for their simple life; her wish is answered by the Great Depression, and they are happy again. In "Poor Little Rich Town"[17] Vonnegut sets several forces at work: a quiet upstate town is chosen as the site for a new electronics complex; high-salaried technocrats will be moving in, real-estate values will soar; and the plant's efficiency expert himself has already arrived, habitually setting about improving all aspects of town life. For a time the townspeople carry on a flirtation with the new life, but in the end they soundly reject it, to the detriment of their pocketbooks but not of their souls.

Whether Vonnegut's magazine pieces of the 1950's are great fictional art, and whether they conform to myths indicative of our deepest cultural feelings, need not be debated here. What I have hoped to establish is that Vonnegut wrote these stories, dozens of them, from a consistently middle-class point of view. This point of view is often their best asset, offering Vonnegut some of his strongest plots, clearest themes, and funniest lines. The middle-class slant is not simply a requirement of the form; if we look at Vonnegut's nonfictional work, we will see that it is an integral part of his expression. His review of *The Random House Dictionary*,[18] for instance, is written as a middle-class appreciation: "Prescriptive, as nearly as I could tell, was like an honest cop, and descriptive was like a boozed-up war buddy from Mobile, Ala." He often uses the same standards when called to appear on television talk shows and documentaries. For the WBBM-TV (Chicago) report on the generation gap, "Nothing Like Us Ever Was" (January 27, 1971), Vonnegut made a simple comparison. "This is an alcoholic nation," he said. "Much big business is done by people four sheets to the wind." When we learn to deal so well with the other part of the population high on pot, he concluded, the generation gap will be bridged. The American middle class is a constant point of reference in Vonnegut's commentary on life. His review of Len Deighton's *Bomber* leads him to generalize on "War as a Series of Collisions."[19] "During the Great Depression in Indianapolis," he remembers, "collisions between steam locomotives were arranged at the Indiana State Fairgrounds—to cheer up the folks. The folks enjoyed the suspense and then the crunch and the steam. They marveled at the wreckage, picked up pieces of steel which had been bent like taffy, saying reverently, 'My God—looky there.'" "Looky there," like "So it goes" in *Slaughterhouse-Five*, is his refrain to a series of grisly quotes from Deighton's book, suggesting the ultimately prosaic nature of modern, mechanized warfare. In another essay, after he is surprised to learn so many of his high-school classmates died in the war, "I read those casualty lists again . . . made old friends and enemies stop mowing lawns and barbecuing steaks in my imagination, made them climb back into their graves." But he was also amazed to find that among his living classmates was Mrs. Melvin Laird, wife of the Secretary of Defense. "When you get to be our age, you all of a sudden realize that you are being ruled by people you went to high school with. You all of a sudden catch on that life is nothing *but* high school."[20] Daily life as a measure of judgment pervades Vonnegut's work. High school, big and small business, are frequent standards: so is family life. His playlet, "The Very First Christmas Morning,"[21] characterizes children at the inn as selfish, middle-class kids—who are blessed in becoming selfless. Even heaven, as depicted in *Happy Birthday, Wanda June,* is a middle-class vision: " 'In heaven, shuffle-board is everything. It was almost worth the trip to find out that Jesus Christ in heaven is just another guy who plays shuffleboard. He wears a blue and gold warmup jacket.' "

When Vonnegut criticizes middle-class American life, he does not do it from a position of superiority. In *God Bless You, Mr. Rosewater* Eliot's sophisticated wife is herself criticized because "She had never seen Rosewater County, had no idea what a night-crawler was, did not know that land anywhere could be so deathly flat, that people anywhere could be so deathly dull." Vonnegut knows it well, and, like Asa Leventhal in Bellow's *The Victim,* is frequently mindful of that part of humanity which "did not get away with it," in this case those who have not escaped the Middle West. Returning for a writers' conference at Western Illinois University, he describes the institution's reputation as "such a jerkwater school," the town's as "such a hell-hole." He admits that things weren't that bad, but feels sorry for everyone as they sit at a party at the TraveLodge Motel, listening to "the Muzak and the

sounds of drag races out on Route 136."[22] Like Thoreau,
Vonnegut sees people living lives of "quiet desperation."[23]
But instead of retreating to a Cape Cod Walden, Vonnegut
keeps near these sources in his fiction; like Eliot Rosewater,
he confides that " 'I'm going to love these discarded Americans, even though they're useless and unattractive. *That* is
going to be my work of art.' "

The most conclusive proofs for Vonnegut as a spokesman
of the middle class are that he does not view himself as an
intellectual writer, and that in fact much of his material
is grossly anti-intellectual. In *Player Piano* he expressed
the same aversion to rule by "experts" that Richard Hofstadter says anchors anti-intellectualism in middle-class
American life. Vonnegut complains that he was for years
dismissed as a science fictionist because "The feeling persists that no one can simultaneously be a respectable writer
and understand how a refrigerator works."[24] And although
he attends writers' conferences, he regards them as finally
irrelevant: "You can't teach people to write well. Writing
well is something God lets you do or declines to let you
do."[25] That comment drew a bitter attack from John Ciardi,
who pilloried Vonnegut's argument and even the prose it
was written in, preferring instead the writer who is "a
member of a group." "That group," said Ciardi, "might
have met in a Greek agora, in a Roman bath, in a Parisian
café, or at an English university, but it met, argued, agreed,
conspired, hated, and loved."[26] Vonnegut is no such writer.
"I am self-taught," he says. "I have no theories about writing that might help others."[27] When he did teach at the
University of Iowa Writers Workshop, his major goal was
to instill, not critical axioms, but a simple "sense of
wonder."[28] He sees himself as neither intellectual nor
prophet, but rather as "an old fart with his memories and

his Pall Malls."[29] Of his writing career: "It seems like a perfectly straightforward business story."[30]

" 'You can safely ignore the arts and sciences,' " advised Eliot Rosewater. " 'They never helped anybody. Be a sincere, attentive friend of the poor.' " Art fails several Vonnegut heroes—Rosewater, Howard Campbell, and Billy Pilgrim—and in "Physicist, Purge Thyself," an address delivered before the American Association of Physics Teachers, Vonnegut criticized both art and science. "I sometimes wondered what the use of any of the arts was with the possible exception of interior decoration," he admitted.[31] On the other hand, "a virtuous physicist is a humanistic physicist. . . . He wouldn't knowingly hurt people. He wouldn't knowingly let politicians or soldiers hurt people. If he comes across a technique that would obviously hurt people, he keeps it to himself."[32] When Vonnegut traveled to Biafra during its last days, he found the occasion to again consider the role of the intellectual. He was amazed to find out that the dot on the map that was Biafra contained "700 lawyers, 500 physicians, 300 engineers, eight million poets, two novelists of the first rank, and God only knows what else—about one third of all the black intellectuals in Africa. Some dot." He recounts how "Biafrans got the best jobs in industry and the civil service and the hospitals and the schools, because they were so well educated," and that "They were hated for that—perfectly naturally."[33] But he wonders "if there was a chance that one thing that had killed so many Biafrans was the arrogance of Biafra's intellectuals."[34] Vonnegut forever speaks from the point of view of that middle-class citizen who, according to Hofstadter, suspects "experts working in any area outside his control."[35] Such thinking is easily categorized as McCarthyism of the 1950's, and Vonnegut's work written at the center of the 1950's experience at times responds with an eerie echo. But Vonnegut was unknown in the 1950's, and is famous only in the 1970's. The appeal of his statements may be a new style of anti-intellectualism, a protest against what a *Time* reviewer described as "a persistent attempt to adjust, smoothly and rationally, to the unthinkable, to the unbearable."[36] In the cold-war years Americans were taught to live under the bomb, in an eroding ecology, in deteriorating cities; against all of this, as an increasingly public personality, Vonnegut protests.

Yet there is a continuity to Vonnegut's works, stretching, he himself claims, back to the 1930's. His "youth-minded notions" which have made him so popular derive, he claimed in a *Life* interview, "from my parents. I thought about it and decided they were right."[37] In "Times Change" he wrote, "I've wanted to record somewhere, for a long time, something easily forgotten: my generation was raised to be pacifistic, but it fought well in a war it felt was just. This is surely true of the pacifists in the present high-school generation: they aren't cowards, either."[38] Vonnegut's appeal has been compared to the popularity of Senator Eugene McCarthy in 1968; each, as Wilfrid Sheed has indicated, "operated out of a venerable Midwestern culture that came as complete news to most Americans."[39] Maybe it is surprising that a youth hero should be able to say of himself, "Look at me . . . I have kids, a car, and I pay my bills on time."[40] Yet Vonnegut's views are after all not revolutionary; he represents in fact a counterrevolution to the real direction of "progress," ever the path of advancing technology and of science for its own sake.

I shall conclude with references to one of Vonnegut's most obscure stories, and then to his most famous speech.

In "Runaways,"[41] published in *The Saturday Evening Post* in 1961, he pictured a teen-age couple who at length find themselves "not too young to be in love," but in fact "Just too young for about everything else that goes with love." The story gently mocks youthful rebellion, counseling that there are some responsibilities that kids, for a while, should simply not have to bear. In his commencement address at Bennington College in May 1970, only a few weeks after the killings at Kent State, Vonnegut gave the same advice. In the intervening years a youth culture had been born, and all generations had been willing to accede young people the responsibility for changing, and indeed saving, the world. That is "a great swindle," Vonnegut complained. In all seriousness he advised the graduates that for at least part of the time after they received their diplomas "they should go swimming and sailing and walking, and just fool around."[42] Young people, Vonnegut insisted, cannot themselves change the world: they don't have the money or the power. Moreover, it is an impossible responsibility to bear. I will argue in Chapter Eleven that Vonnegut's major novels speak against man's position as romantic center of the universe, a posture which makes him responsible for all evil and hence hopelessly alienated from himself. When Vonnegut applies the same distinctions to youth he is clearly repeating statements characteristic of his writing for middle-class magazines. He is a pacifist; he distrusts the unbridled intellect; he argues for simple, humane values. All are elements of a fundamental American decency, dating to his childhood in the 1930's and sustained in his writing of the 1950's, which perhaps in the last decade has been submerged under new forces and ideas against which youth rightly protests. When Vonnegut so accurately reflects that protest, it should be no surprise that he is forty-eight years old, has kids, a car, and pays his bills on time. He is simply speaking for its ultimate origins.

NOTES TO CHAPTER 3

1. Kurt Vonnegut, Jr., "Why They Read Hesse," *Horizon,* 12 (Spring, 1970), 30.
2. 17 (November 16, 1965), 1020–1021.
3. "Science Fiction," *Page 2,* ed. Francis Brown (New York: Holt, Rinehart and Winston, 1969), p. 117.
4. *Collier's,* 125 (February 11, 1950), 18–19 ff.
5. "The Euphio Question," *Collier's,* 127 (May 12, 1951), 22–23 ff.
6. "Tomorrow and Tomorrow and Tomorrow" [orig.: "The Big Trip Up Yonder"], *Galaxy Science Fiction,* 7 (January, 1954), 100–110.
7. "Unready to Wear," *Galaxy Science Fiction,* 6 (April, 1953), 98–111.
8. *Collier's,* 127 (February 10, 1951), 14–15 ff.
9. *Welcome to the Monkey House,* p. xv.
10. "The Divine Stupidity of Kurt Vonnegut," *Esquire,* 74 (September, 1970), 196.
11. "Who Am I This Time" [orig.: "My Name Is Everyone"], *Saturday Evening Post,* 234 (December 16, 1961), 20.
12. *Collier's,* 128 (September 8, 1951), 18–19 ff.
13. *Saturday Evening Post,* 226 (March 27, 1954), 30 ff.
14. *Cosmopolitan,* 137 (October, 1954), 34–39.
15. *Collier's* 130 (July 26, 1952), 48–53.
16. *Cosmopolitan,* 142 (June, 1957), 92–95.
17. *Collier's,* 130 (October 25, 1952), 90–95.
18. "The Latest Word," *New York Times Book Review,* October 30, 1966, p. 56.
19. *Life,* 69 (October 2, 1970), 10.

20. "Times Change," *Esquire*, 74 (February, 1970), 60.
21. *Better Homes and Gardens*, 40 (December, 1962), 44 ff.
22. "Teaching the Unteachable," *New York Times Book Review*, August 6, 1967, pp. 1, 20.
23. *Welcome to the Monkey House*, p. 55.
24. "Science Fiction," pp. 117–118.
25. "Teaching the Unteachable," p. 1.
26. "Manner of Speaking," *Saturday Review*, 50 (September 30, 1967), 18.
27. *Welcome to the Monkey House*, p. ix.
28. Franklin Dunlap, "God and Kurt Vonnegut, Jr., at Iowa City," *Chicago Tribune Magazine*, May 7, 1967, p. 84.
29. Kurt Vonnegut, Jr., *Slaughterhouse-Five*, p. 2.
30. "The High Cost of Fame," *Playboy*, 18 (January, 1971), 124.
31. *Chicago Tribune Magazine*, June 22, 1969, p. 44.
32. *Ibid.*, p. 48.
33. "Biafra," *McCall's*, 97 (April, 1970), 135.
34. *Ibid.*, p. 138.
35. *Anti-Intellectualism in American Life* (New York: Vintage, 1963), p. 12.
36. "The Price of Survival," *Time* (April 11, 1969), p. 108.
37. Wilfrid Sheed, "The Now Generation Knew Him When," *Life*, 67 (September 12, 1969), 66.
38. "Times Change," p. 60.
39. Sheed, p. 66.
40. Rollene W. Saal, "Pick of the Paperbacks," *Saturday Review*, 53 (March 28, 1970), 34.
41. *Saturday Evening Post*, 234 (April 15, 1961), 27–28.
42. "Up Is Better Than Down," *Vogue* (August 1, 1970), pp. 54, 144–145.

Chapter 4

TEACHING
KURT VONNEGUT
ON THE
FIRING LINE

———————•·•———————

● JESS RITTER

IF YOU TEACH modern literature at San Francisco State
College, you have to keep on your toes. For one thing,
President S. I. Hayakawa, internationally renowned expert
on modern thought and politics, insists that liberal-arts
teachers—and literature professors in particular—are
largely responsible for student unrest.

"Liberal-arts professors teach alienation, because it's
fashionable," the noted semanticist claimed.

Another problem is that when you teach courses like

"Blues, Rock, and Black Humor"; "The New Grotesque"; and "Social Surrealism: The Literature of Radical Juxtaposition," academic and school deans keep asking for book lists and course descriptions.

And then, if you're identified as the mod-lit prof who knows Heller, Hesse, and Vonnegut, your office hours take on the atmosphere of a Fillmore West Extension Center.

SCENE ONE, TAKE ONE

The door opens and Victor glides in—no knock. I know it's Victor because of the springy blond afro, shirtless torso, bare feet, and tattered cut-off Levi's. Victor sells his handmade leather belts and handbags from a blanket spread on the lawn down in front of the Commons.

"Hey, man." Victor has already taken a chair. "Space Daisy tells me you dig Vonnegut, man, you really read all his books? Fahr out!"

"Space Daisy?" I had been reading literary criticism for an evening class.

"Yeah, my old woman. She's in your whatchacallit, 'Language of the 70's' class? Freakin' title for a freshman English class, man, I been reading the booklist, all that Heller and Southern and Vonnegut and Barthelme. How come you don't have Hesse in there? You gotta get into Hesse's head trips. You ever read *The Sirens of Titan* on acid, man? Wow!"

"Space Daisy?" A mod-lit man at San Francisco State has to be versatile, all right, but I'm still buying time.

"You know, Debbie King. Tiny chick, long red hair? We live in this commune up the hill from the Haight. It's got real good *karass*, you know what I mean? Except for a few dudes shootin' crystal and snorting coke. This summer we're splitting for a commune in the mountains up near Ukiah. Get away from the dope and bad city vibes."

Victor rambles familiarly, as if we'd shared the same pad for months. I place Space Daisy, alias Debbie King— long hair, granny glasses, and fiercely braless trembling twin fawns nuzzling at the opaque white peasant blouse. (Every girl born in southern California in the 1950's was named Debbie, or Patti, or Joni, or Toni.) Daisy, her head buzzing with Women's Lib, Third World, alternative education, her face too tight for her age when we talk in my office, unable yet to accept or reject the guilt of her spoiled Hollywood Hills childhood. Debbie read everything on the class list and asked for more. Read *Catch-22* and then *Good Soldier Schweik* behind it; read *Cat's Cradle* and *Slaughterhouse-Five*, then everything else by Vonnegut.

(I hear from the Midwest and East Coast that literature people worry: "The young don't read." I don't know what "young" they're talking about. The young I know read— maybe not freshman anthologies or *Silas Marner* or *Harper's*, but Heller, Vonnegut, Hesse, R. Crumb and *Snatch Comix*, McLuhan, Pynchon, Kesey, *The Whole Earth Catalog*, Brautigan, and *Rolling Stone*. In fact, they read *too much* for their Peace of Mind.)

VONNEGUT IN THE TRENCHES

Governor Reagan administers the salary paid me by the taxpayers of California. The governor thinks my job is to keep the house in good order. *I* think my job is to brood a lot about modern literature and about the consciousness of the kids who are inheriting our sorry world and then about how to put the two together.

My office mate and I have consistently included Kurt

33

Vonnegut's novels in our courses on the modern novel over the past four years. We use different course titles, but we're getting at the same thing: how literature helps shape and reflects the consciousness of our age. We daily experience how wildly popular Vonnegut's novels are with readers from sharply diverse backgrounds—chicano, Wasp, street hippie, black militant, and occasional Bokononist.

So whatever limited explication of Vonnegut's novels I try here is aimed at getting into reader consciousness, at understanding what it is about Kurt Vonnegut's writing that so mesmerizes and yet energizes this generation.

The great psychic migration of American youth since World War II can be charted by the novels they read and the novelists whose reputations they created: Jack Kerouac and the Beats for getting out of plastic suburbia and On the Road. Beginning a search for authenticity and soul, for poetry not spindled on the printed page and dissected by Footnote Kings but hurled from a lectern by a reeling Dylan Thomas, chanted at jazz and poetry concerts, wailed out of jukeboxes by Hank Williams, Lightnin' Hopkins, Creedence Clearwater, and Bob Dylan. Kerouac and the Beats represent the psychic revolt of the 1950's; J. D. Salinger represents the inner flight from McCarthyism, from the Corporation, from the Other-Directed self: the lacerating self-consciousness of Holden Caulfield and the Glass family.

Then Golding and *Lord of the Flies* for the early 1960's, with a vision of human limitation and capacity for evil that matched the 1950's generation's sense of helplessness before the rapidly escalating cold war and certain bomb at the end of it all. We also dug Golding because of the classy symbolism, so neat and easy to figure out: see, we can be New Critics too.

Then somewhere in the late 1960's Kurt Vonnegut, Ken Kesey, and Joseph Heller took a generation's consciousness on a sharp left turn down the crooked road to the absurd. Yet it was a recognition of the absurd that was not a surrender to meaninglessness but a wholehearted, raucous Bronx cheer for the false pieties and Aesopean language of rampant technology and the cold war.

Victor's friend Army, a draft counselor, put it this way last spring, shouting over the head-piercing wail of the East Bay Flash playing the noontime Commons rock concert: "Holden Caulfield was a *kid*, you know? Yossarian and Eliot Rosewater had to scuffle with the draft, and Vietnam, and the system."

VONNEGUT ON THE OBSTACLE COURSE

The structural discontinuities (which are really a new continuity) and radical juxtapositions of space fantasy and homely everyday existence in Vonnegut's novels catch the imagination of a generation born and bred to the TV montage reality of contemporary life. Moving from his early formula short stories through his novels, Vonnegut has perfected his version of what I call social surrealism, a fictional technique utilizing the radical juxtapositions, non-spatial time sense (i.e., the world of dreams), and radical irony for purposes of social satire. The social surrealist sensibility flickers like heat lightning in the films of Godard and Fellini; the novels of Thomas Pynchon, Jakov Lind, Friedrich Dürrenmatt, Günter Grass, and Joseph Heller; in the music of Country Joe MacDonald, Bob Dylan, and Frank Zappa; in the incredible put-on *Esquire* reportage and novels of Terry Southern and Dan Wakefield.

A few years back, Susan Sontag defined a distinct surrealist sensibility suffusing post-World War I art:

> . . . in the theatre, in painting, in poetry, in the cinema, in music, and in the novel. . . . The Surrealist tradition in all these arts is united by the idea of destroying conventional meanings, and creating new meanings or counter-meanings through radical juxtaposition (the "collage-principle"). . . . One may also see a kind of involuntary collage-principle in many of the artifacts of the modern city: the brutal disharmony of buildings in size and style, the wild juxtaposition of store signs, the clamorous layouts of the modern newspaper, etc.[1]

Vonnegut's fictional method of radical juxtaposition is a product of his richly comic sense of the absurd.[2] "There is something comic in modern experience as such, a demonic, not a divine comedy, precisely to the extent that modern experience is characterized by meaningless mechanized situations of disrelation," comments Sontag.[3] To Vonnegut and his audience, the noble, isolated grandeur of classic tragedy is no longer possible in an age of concentration camps and mass death by bombing. Tragicomedy is the style of the age, a style that establishes the juxtapositions of *God Bless You, Mr. Rosewater, Slaughterhouse-Five, Dr. Strangelove, Bonnie and Clyde, Little Big Man,* Lenny Bruce's Masked Man, and Country Joe and the Fish's "Fixin' to Die Rag."

Our consciousness of the absurd in everyday affairs—of a world ruled by the "Utterly Indifferent God," leads to two fictional—and personal—responses: nihilistic despair or a stubborn counterassertion of man-created meaning (or the leap into faith, which Camus terms "philosophical suicide"). Camus's Sisyphus wipes his brow and starts his absurd boulder once again up the mountainside, satisfied that *recognition* of the absurd is a sufficient point of departure. Heller's Yossarian rages against the cosmic indifference of Catch-22 and refuses to serve a system which perpetrates this indifference; Vonnegut's battered heroes either refuse to contribute to human suffering or mitigate it by a lame but heartfelt compassion. "I found me a place where I can do good without doing any harm, and I can see I'm doing good," says Boaz in *The Sirens of Titan*. Eliot Rosewater offers advice to Mary Moody's new twins: "Hello, babies. Welcome to Earth. It's hot in the summer and cold in the winter. It's round and wet and crowded. At the outside, babies, you've got about a hundred years here. There's only one rule that I know, babies—'God damn it, you've got to be kind.' "

Basically, a comic recognition of the absurd is a counter-strategy, giving the absurd meaning. Vonnegut's ordinary-language echoes of this recognition *place* the absurd, fit it into the everyday affairs of his characters. From *Mother Night* to *Slaughterhouse-Five,* the absurd is ordered around by "Hi Ho," "So be it," "Busy, busy, busy," "So it goes." Vonnegut's uneasy canonization by the Yippies, for example, makes perfect sense; both Abbie Hoffman and Vonnegut use the put-on, radical irony, as an analytical tool for stripping away the masks of the absurd. Paul Krassner, founder of the archetypal underground magazine *The Realist,* seems to be writing most newspaper headlines.

VONNEGUT AND HIS PET CANARY

The legion of Vonnegut readers I know devour all his novels and hunt around for the short stories. A great Vonnegut-swapping goes on; students share especially their hard-to-get copies of *Canary in a Cathouse*. The key principle here is that students talk about Vonnegut's world, his *mythos*. They react to him as a myth-maker and fabulist rather than as a dramatic and narrative novelist. Vonnegut hangs ideas on his fables, making them easily accessible to young readers. In this sense, he is no science-fiction writer; science fiction as such is part of his store of fables. Vonnegut uses Kilgore Trout, his invented science-fiction writer, as one of many *voices*, voices speaking multidimensional fables.

We can detect the origins of Vonnegut's fabulist method in his early slick short stories: into ordinary, everyday lives drops something unusual or other-worldly; the fable commentary arises from this confrontation. Thus the corporation-trapped deer in "Deer in the Works," an unexpected fortune in "The Foster Portfolio," gratified wishes in "Hal Irwin's Magic Lamp." We can also read a systematic maturation of technique and meaning between such early fables as the chess game in "All the King's Horses" and the latter cyclic use of, say, the Tralfamadore fables in *The Sirens of Titan, God Bless You, Mr. Rosewater,* and *Slaughterhouse-Five.* Much as William Faulkner created his mythical Yoknapatawpha County, so Kurt Vonnegut is creating a mythical modern universe. And like most myth-makers, from Edmund Spenser to Günter Grass, he draws on recurring imagistic correlatives to reality. The planet Tralfamadore suggests technology gone awry, time turned inside out; water images abound, water representing fertility and life (Ice-9, frozen water, *death-in-life*); pools and fountains (both flowing, and dry and barren) recur; Eliot Rose*water* and Kilgore *Trout* represent life-giving water forces; rivers (and canals) with "carp the size of atomic submarines" figure in *The Sirens of Titan, God Bless You, Mr. Rosewater,* and *Slaughterhouse-Five.*

There are always birds—canaries, Titanic bluebirds, thrushes, sounding the "Poo-tee-weet" of the artist. The point here is that Vonnegut's readers appreciate both the fascinating ideas established by the fables and the imaginative manner in which the ideas are fleshed out by the recurring imagery. Vonnegut's world becomes familiar to his readers; they are drawn in by the yarn-spinning of the "old fart with his memories and his Pall Malls." The fables and mythical imagery raise his novels beyond the dialectical crudities of the Ayn Rand style novel of ideas. The literature of aesthetic alienation and escape-into-art doesn't go down very well with a generation struggling for physical and ecological survival. Vonnegut's fables get a leg up on present dizzying reality, and that's what this generation of readers wants.

VONNEGUT AT THE LECTERN

And yet I get disquieting evidence that many of Vonnegut's younger readers appreciate him for not quite the right reasons. While his techniques may be hip, his morality is strictly sober middle class. In this respect, he greatly resembles George Orwell, the Orwell who returned to a solid assertion of basic middle-class values in *Keep the Aspidistra Flying.* Certainly Vonnegut's recurring fictional themes hit at the central concerns of his readers—runaway technology, the enormity of evil, a detestation of the rich and their indifference to human need and want. But listen to Jack, a twenty-two-year-old communard-cum-SDSer, speaking for many in my last avant-garde novel class: "Vonnegut knows where it's at, you know? Look at those

Rosewater bastards and their class on Cape Cod. He knows we gotta smash the system."

And then Susan, wan Susan, in her Mickey Mouse and red-letter "Cocaine" T-shirts, who offered to rip off a copy of Wilhelm Reich's *The Mass Psychology of Fascism* for me: *"Cat's Cradle* says screw it, man, go do your own thing. There's nothing left to do but 'boku-maru,' rub up, get with it."

Trying to establish Vonnegut's middle ground between nihilism and instant revolution, I mumble something about Manicheanism, pointing out such passages as, "It was the belief of Bokonon that good societies could be built only by pitting good against evil, and by keeping the tension between the two high at all times."

But notions of revolution or dropping out bring fantasies of gratification to many, impatient with the annealing power of art, or freely given human love, or the artist serving as the coal-mine canary, giving warning of disaster. So I suggest to them, then, that we might consider wearing Vonnegut's books like Roland Weary, the all-American violence freak in *Slaughterhouse-Five,* wears the small, bulletproof Bible over the heart, as protection against German bullets.

Above all, however, Vonnegut's readers appreciate his act of bringing fiction out into the streets, making it easily available in cheap paperbacks full of inventive, teasing fables and metaphysical tomfoolery. He's not afraid of sentimentality, salting it down, though, with acerbic absurdist humor—a tonality of irony that matches perfectly the watchful, wary irony of a generation choking in corporate solemnity. Like Eliot Rosewater and his foundation, Kurt Vonnegut has relocated art and the novel in a dingy office over a lunchroom and liquor store, overlooking the main street of Rosewater, Indiana, or the East Village, or Berkeley.

SCENE TWO, TAKE FIVE

At noontime there's a soft knock on the office door. Victor and Space Daisy again. After an hour and a half of trying to demonstrate Stendhal's "relevance," I'm sliding into contemplation of a rich, greasy cheeseburger. I shuffle papers around on the desk and say something about needing lunch.

"We brought lunch for you, if you'd have some time to talk," says Victor. He has a great crop of goose pimples on the arms and shoulders not covered by a purple tie-dyed undershirt.

"It's organic," explains Space Daisy, hefting a large Baggie onto my desk.

I see a dozen carrots and what looks like Sunkist orange bread.

"Cream-cheese-and-chopped-nut sandwiches on home-made pumpkin bread. I made the bread." Daisy smiles modestly.

I weigh the lonely cheeseburger against pumpkin bread.

"You see," says Daisy, "Victor also makes puppets, and his friend Street Eddie shoots Super-8 movies. Now, what we want to do is make a puppet movie about *Slaughter-house-Five*, showing Billy Pilgrim and Montana Wildhack on Tralfamadore instead of my writing this term paper on Vonnegut. . . ."

I reach for a cream-cheese-and-chopped-nut sandwich on pumpkin bread, settling back, locked on the vision of Montana Wildhack's locket dangling between those Earthling breasts. "Okay, now what you *need* to include is that incredible Tralfamadorian fable about the war and time running backwards . . ."

NOTES TO CHAPTER 4

1. *Against Interpretation* (New York: Farrar, Straus & Giroux, 1966), pp. 269–270.
2. In an operational sense, "absurd" here simply refers to ridiculous or irrational human behavior; the "absurd" in this study is that condition defined by Albert Camus as "this confrontation between the human need and the unreasonable silence of the world . . . the Absurd is not in man (if such a metaphor could have a meaning) nor in the world, but in their presence together." (*The Myth of Sisyphus*, trans. Justin O'Brien [New York: Vintage, 1959], pp. 16, 23.)
3. *Against Interpretation*, p. 270.

THE
LITERARY
FIGURE

Chapter 5

CHASING
A LONE EAGLE:
VONNEGUT'S
COLLEGE WRITING

ROBERT SCHOLES

KURT VONNEGUT IS a vulgar sentimentalist—a quality he
shares with Dickens, for instance. He is also a crude humorist—a quality he shares with Mark Twain. Like other
writers who have reached a broad spectrum of the popu-
lace, he is a difficult case for elitist criticism to confront.
Thus he has had the honor of an attack in *The New York
Review of Books,* which is radical in its politics but reac-
tionary in its aesthetics. Vonnegut is a literary maverick,
who runs with no pack and must have been surprised to

find himself the darling of the hippie kids while all the time he was just trying to shake some sense into Middle America. He has written short sentences, small paragraphs, tiny chapters, and little books in an attempt to reach busy, unliterary folk with his criticism of life and his help in making it bearable. He is himself, of course, the lovely false prophet Bokonon, the foolish philanthropist Rosewater, and above all the kindly, untrustworthy, honest, quadruple turncoat Howard Campbell of *Mother Night*.

How he got that way is an interesting question, with some of its answers buried in the mysteries of identity but others more accessible, to be found in libraries and other such places. There are some important clues, for instance, in a series of pieces he wrote as an undergraduate for the *Cornell Sun*, in the spring and fall of 1941. They show us a Vonnegut nearly fully formed but still in the process of formation, and they reveal some of the forces that helped to shape him.

Vonnegut began to write pieces under his own byline for the *Sun* in the spring of his freshman year at Cornell. He started by taking over a column called "Innocents Abroad," which specialized in college humor, reprinting jokes from other magazines and papers, which in turn reprinted from others, so that the same body of material kept busily circulating with virtually no infusion of new blood. College humor, in its great days, had spawned a school of excellent American writers, and there is a sad but interesting story in the partial failure of such writers as Thurber, White, Benchley, Parker, and Perelman to move far from that trivial genre which they exploited so thoroughly. But in the spring of 1941, with World War II looming over the horizon, the task of the college humorist posed special problems, which Vonnegut acknowledged in his first piece:

> With the hilarious nature of this golden age we live in, with Adolph Hitler, labor riots, and the Cornell Widow, one cannot help but see the screamingly funny side to everything—or such is the hope of one dope who spends his time clipping witticisms from exchange papers and having the gall to demand a by-line for it.

Vonnegut then began his career with this gem, under the heading "Quip Clipped by Drip":

> Little ear of corn: "Where did I come from?" Big ear of corn: "The stalk brought you."　　　—*Northeastern News*

His next column was introduced with another personal paragraph:

> Whether anyone else gives a hang or not about keeping out of World War II, we do, and from now on, readers may rest assured that material appearing in this column has been carefully edited so as to exclude anything smacking in the slightest of propaganda.

In these, two of his first published paragraphs, Vonnegut revealed both his budding talents as an ironist and some of the fundamental attitudes that have shaped his work. There was no need, in a joke column, to publicly disclaim propaganda. In fact, the disclaimer itself was a kind of propaganda: Vonnegut making his own pacifistic views known. But what he meant by propaganda was talk in favor of entering the war, not talk against it. Still, "Innocents Abroad" was not an ideal forum for Vonnegut's serious concerns, however it may have appealed to his love of jokes. Thus he must have been pleased to get a chance at the wholly original column "Well All Right," which also appeared regularly on the *Sun*'s editorial page. On April 22 he wrote the following "Well All Right" column, under the subhead "Bayonet Drill at the Rate of Seven in 20 Seconds, or, Oh for a Couple of Nazis":

A military potentate has recently returned from an extensive tour of the United States armed forces with the happy news that the general morale is high and admirable. We recently got a cross-section of military morale of our own—we were the only civilian on a bus ride from Hartford, Connecticut, to Ithaca.

We sat next to one of the nation's happy warriors, an enlisted man of eighteen, whose attitude filled us with confidence in the face of the dictatorships.

He described with boyish enthusiasm bayonet drill, which seems to be a hilarious sport. Seven life-like dummies are set up in a realistic trench, and each soldier starts from a given point at a full run, dives into the trench, and maims each of his seven passive enemies as quickly as he can with his bayonet—all timed by stopwatch. Our talkative source of information (these may be military secrets) said that a good man could do the job in twenty seconds, and that there were a number of good books written on bayonet technique if we were really interested.

We thanked him, and recalled a delightfully interesting pamphlet we had seen which covered the subject—translated from the French into English and issued by the War Department in 1917.

He went on to recite a series of actions which he repeats to himself when going into mock action, something like this: "Parry, stab, withdraw, smash (with the rifle butt), etc.," and it's supposed to go faster than the eye can follow.

We asked him what he thought his chances would be if he were pitted against a Nazi soldier who had been practicing with a bayonet for five years. His eyes glistened, and he said that he just wished he had the chance. He hates Germans—all of 'em.

We were going to ask him what he had against Bee-thoven but decided that we probably wouldn't get a very good answer.

At this time, of course, Vonnegut was having an experience rare for white Protestant Americans. He was a member of a minority group which was feeling the active antagonism of others. Before and during World War II anti-German feeling in the United States was not as virulent as it had been at the time of World War I, but it was there, and the German-American Vonnegut was very sensitive to it. And of course, all the time that great joker History was holding a reservation for this young man in Slaughterhouse-Five, Dresden, from which he would be privileged to emerge after the British-American bombing of that open city—an unscathed prisoner of war surveying a smoking ruin that had once been a center of German civilization. How can art hope to compete in irony with a life which arranges such intricate absurdities? But back in Ithaca, New York, in the spring of 1941, young Vonnegut continued clipping jokes for "Innocents Abroad," but never getting far from thoughts of the war. On May 9 he began with some words addressed "To the Cornell Military Department . . .":

> We, along with the chemical engineers and those boys in advanced drill, are smug about the important and lucra-tive part we will play when war comes. Uncle Sam needs zoologists and plenty of them—that's us.
> Up in the front lines our commanding officer will say, "Vontegal" (that's the way Bool's Flowerdale addresses its bills to us—should we pay them?), "what the hell kind of a butterfly is that," and we'll be the only man in the trench that can tell him. That's the sort of thing that wins wars!
> It's a waste of our time and yours, boys, trying to teach

us how to blow things up. We don't know a fuse-setter from Lieutenant Wilcox and never will. We're cut out for bigger things. And we're not just being a sorehead because we didn't get a blue and gold medal like the rest of the fellows.

As the spring semester came to its end, Vontegal kept up the jokes, but he also got a few opportunities at "Well All Right." He devoted one of these to that perennially pressing problem, fraternity financing. But even on this subject he found his own way of propagandizing, for the financial problems of fraternities in his view were caused partly by "defense taxation" which was likely to increase "as the war fever heightens." After a chillingly detailed forecast of the growth of financial difficulties, he opened his last paragraph this way:

> It's a nasty picture no matter how you look at it. From an abstract point of view it will be interesting to watch, just like bombing.

Another "Well All Right" column he devoted to a lengthy and serious study of the way newspapers slant events. His examples were drawn mainly from the current invasion of Crete, which he felt was being reported from a strictly pro-British point of view. His sober last advice was, "We must know the shortcomings of the British—and of ourselves—as well as of the Germans if we would create any kind of lasting remedy when the dangers of the moment are averted." Vonnegut regained his comic touch with his last "Well All Right" piece of that semester, subheaded, "We Impress Life Magazine with Our Efficient Role in National Defense":

> LIFE Magazine was at drill to take our pictures Tuesday afternoon, and we were sorry that we didn't have a

more impressive and less scratchy uniform. We were delighted to show them what we were doing for national defense which was the object of the photographer's mission.

Lieutenant Wilcox and Colonel Metcalf were pretty upset and excited by the visit. Lieutenant Wilcox's voice cracked twice while trying to calm us down over the public address system. It was a terrific strain, with the marvelous showing that Harvard made three weeks ago hanging over our heads.

We had never considered that we were doing anything for national defense before. As a matter of fact, one of the officers had told us that we were a detriment to that cause and that we'd better have a necktie next time. Everybody was trying to look like they were keyed up to the national emergency. Some looked blood-thirsty, some pensive—we looked square into the lens of the camera and grinned. The cheerful optimism of a soldier, we figured, will do wonders for American morale when it beams out on LIFE's millions.

After spoiling a couple of plates, the cameraman told us to look natural which we did in spite of the good name of Cornell. They made us pose in what they thought were typical attitudes. We all leaped forward in the bleachers, gazing at a French 75 as if it was the most wonderful little gadget ever designed. Lieutenant Wilcox conducted a mock class for the sake of the photographs, asking us to identify several parts of a breech-block which were laid out on a table. To impress the visitors we yelled out such phoney technical terms as "flathatcher" and "biffle-block," which had its desired effect and seemed to sound OK to the officers, too.

They had us read maps. With shutters clicking over our shoulders we would plot mysterious curves over charts. Some fellows got pretty bitter about Lieutenant Wilcox being in all the pictures, but nobody said anything to his face.

We predict that LIFE's circulation will jump by 7,000 for the Cornell issue, and that America will rip into national defense with redoubled enthusiasm when they see what a deadly bunch of artillerymen from Ithaca are working hand in hand with them.

The following autumn, as a mature sophomore, Vonnegut regularly wrote "Well All Right." He managed to keep the war and all that out of his column most of the time, except for one splendid outburst in defense of a fellow German-American, subheaded, "We Chase a Lone Eagle and End Up on the Wrong Side of the Fence":

> Charles A. Lindbergh is one helluva swell egg, and we're willing to fight for him in our own quaint way. Several sterling folk, Sun members not excluded, have been taking journalistic potshots at the Lone Eagle, effectively, too. The great work is spreading. Give the stout, redblooded American—the average mental age is fourteen, we're told —a person to hate, tell him to do so often, and he and his cousin Moe will do a damned fine job of it, providing there are plenty of others doing the same.
>
> The mud slingers are good. They'd have to be good to get people hating a loyal and sincere patriot. On second thought, Lindbergh is no patriot—to hell with the word, it lost its meaning after the Revolutionary War.
>
> What a guy! Look at the beating he takes. Why on God's green earth (we think He's sub-let it) would anyone lay himself open for such defamation if he wasn't entirely convinced that he must give the message to his country at any cost? To offer an obstacle to the premeditated Roosevelt foreign policy is certainly to ask for a kick in the face.
>
> There was another bum who stood in the way of America's divine destiny during the shambles of 1917.

Hughes, that's the guy, former Chief Justice Charles Evans Hughes. That's the sort of louse that makes trouble.

Crusades, not that they're not worth twice the cost, cost about five million men these days. It's America's purpose to defend its way of life, to bankrupt itself rather than let Hitler take our South American trade—a farce which ends in red ink every time—and to send the best crop of young technicians the country has ever known, who could make this fabulously wealthy nation self-sufficient within itself, into battle.

Charles A. Lindbergh has had the courage at least to present the conservative side of a titanic problem, grant him that. The United States is a democracy, that's what they say we'll be fighting for. What a prize monument to that ideal is a cry to smother Lindy. Weighing such in-consequential items as economic failure and simultaneous collapse of the American Standard of Living (looks good capitalized—it'll be fine for chuckles in a decade), and outrageous bloodshed of his countrymen, the young ones, is virtual treason to the Stars and Stripes—long may it wave.

Lindy, you're a rat. We read that somewhere, so it must be so. They say you should be deported. In that event leave room in that boat for us, our room-mate, Jane, mother, that barber with the mustache in Willard Straight, and those two guys down the hall—you make sense to us.

Editor's Note: The opinions expressed above are those of the author and do not necessarily reflect the views of The Sun.

The Editor's Note was printed in heavy type. Obviously, the rest of the staff did not share Vonnegut's views. His connection with the *Sun* seems to have been severed at around that time, and Pearl Harbor put an end to most American protests against the war. But the unmistakable emotional intensity of that last editorial suggests how powerfully events were conspiring to crystallize the attitudes that have shaped Vonnegut's mature work. At the end of the year he left Cornell and joined the American Army. As it turned out, he had an appointment with the R.A.F. in Dresden on February 13, 1945, for the completion of his education in pacificism.

Chapter 6

IN
VONNEGUT'S
KARASS

DAN WAKEFIELD

THE FIRST TIME I read anything by Kurt Vonnegut, I was
sitting in a barbershop in Indianapolis, leafing through a
dog-eared copy of *The Saturday Evening Post* while waiting to have my favorite barber give me one of those kind
of haircuts that prompted jocular fellows to quip, "Hey, I
see you got your ears set out!" Har, har, har. (People said
"Har, har, har" then to let you know something was funny;
it was one of those doldrum years like 1953 when people
seemed especially self-conscious and wanted to be what
was called "One of the boys.")

To return to Vonnegut's story: I hardly remember it, but vaguely recall that it was about a little boy who played a large musical instrument, a tuba I think. It was not so much the story itself that impressed me as the fact that it was written by Kurt Vonnegut, Jr. The impressive thing about *that* was that Vonnegut, like me, was born and raised in Indianapolis, and also like me had gone to Short-ridge High School and written for the Shortridge *Daily Echo,* the first high-school daily paper in the entire United States of America!

Vonnegut had graduated from Shortridge ten years be-fore me, but his name was known to all of us aspiring writers who worked on the *Echo.* He, like us, had first been published in those pages, no doubt starting out like all other neophytes by covering meetings of the Stamp Club or freshman wrestling matches or the appointment of new officers of the ROTC. And, from such humble beginnings, he had gone on to be a professional writer, a writer whose stories were published in the Big Magazines, meccas of literary success like *Collier's* and *The Saturday Evening Post!* And if *he* could do it, maybe it meant—well, there was just the hope that perhaps we too could aspire to such glory. (As a matter of fact, glorious or no, a remarkable number of former writers for the Shortridge *Daily Echo* have gone on to make a career as authors of some sort or other, including Vonnegut, me, the novelist Jeremy Larner, the sportswriter Bill Libby, *Newsweek* correspondent and political author Richard T. Stout, *Life* staff writer Wally Terry, former *Life* staff writer and now editor-publisher of *Earth* magazine, Jim Goode, journalist John Bartlow Mar-tin; and I'm sure there are others.)

If, as a young man in Indianapolis, you were so bold and reckless as to let anyone know that you hoped to become a writer when you grew up, it was usually regarded with the same seriousness as a little kid's expressed desire for a career in the Fire Department. Of course, there *had* been writers who came from Indianapolis, Famous Men like James Whitcomb Riley and Booth Tarkington. But they were dead. Sometimes, though, if you spoke of the dream of authordom, a knowing citizen would stroke his chin and say, "Well, I understand the Vonnegut boy does some writing. Even gets paid for it sometimes."

It was not known, however—to me or my Indianapolis informants, anyway—whether he got paid enough to live on. I heard somewhere that he worked for one of those big corporations, like Western Electric or General Electric, one of those corporations that everyone seemed to work for in the fifties. It was said that he worked in their public-relations department, and wrote his stories and things for magazines at night. It was said that he was married and had a lot of children to support. At odd moments, looking out of train windows, or drinking a beer, or studying for a test in my cubicle at Columbia in New York City, I would think of this guy Kurt Vonnegut, Jr., and wonder how he was making out. I was rooting for him, in my own mind, mostly from selfish motives; in some superstitious way it seemed to me that if *one* guy who came from Indianapolis and had gone to Shortridge High School could make a living as a writer, then another guy could too (the other guy being me).

Sometime during that hazy period—I think we are still in the early fifties—I heard he had published a novel, and somehow I got ahold of it. The novel was called *Player Piano,* and was set in the future. It was about this fictional town of Ilium, New York, where the corporation owned everything, and people were divided along very stratified lines of work and leisure, all of which was planned out by the corporation. It expressed the way a lot of people felt in the fifties about the way things were going; about the kind of life we were all going to end up with, a sort of American version of 1984, with the corporation as Big Brother. None of us could foresee then that though the corporations would remain powerful, a time would come when great masses of young people would refuse to go to work for them anymore, would simply pretend that they didn't exist, and would invent other styles of life that they found more suitable. In this sense, *Player Piano* is the only one of Vonnegut's books that I think seems a little "dated" when read in the seventies; it was so accurately and spiritually a vision borne of the frustration of the fifties. But it was, and is, a good book—it was believable and sad and also very funny.

I was cheered not only because I liked the book but because this Indianapolis guy had written and published it. I thought that meant he had it made. Like many people, I assumed if you got a book published that meant you were an established writer and you lived off your royalties. Little did I know that in the vast majority of cases the publication of a book meant that you got a couple of reviews here and there and a thousand-dollar advance. (I didn't learn that till 1959, when I had my own first book published.)

It was difficult then to "follow Vonnegut's career," because nobody in the literary world mentioned him. Your best bet was to get a lot of haircuts and see if you could find any new stories he had written in the copies of *Collier's* and *The Saturday Evening Post* that were lying around the barbershops.

The next word I got about Vonnegut's career came from

my mother. My mother had met his mother-in-law. There must be a special bond between mothers of writers, as well as mothers of girls who are married to writers. These mothers are long-suffering ladies whom fate has dealt an unkind blow. The mother just wants her child to be happy, and have a nice life, a good income, and be in good health. It is possible for a writer to turn out that way, but not likely. Their incomes are unsteady, at best. They tend to drink more than other people, which is bound to affect their health. (A psychologist's recent study showed that of the seven Americans who won the Nobel prize for literature, five were alcoholics and one "drank heavily"; the other was Pearl Buck.) My mother accepted her (or my) fate with courage and a spirit of helpfulness. She was always managing to meet the relatives of writers, to find out whatever tips they might have for me (and her). During my years in college, my mother managed to meet Kurt Vonnegut's mother-in-law, journalist John Bartlow Martin's mother, and Ralph McGill's sister.

But the news from Vonnegut's mother-in-law was dire. According to what Vonnegut's mother-in-law told my mother, who told me, Vonnegut might decide to give up writing altogether. His stories at that time weren't selling, and he was very discouraged, according to this third-hand account.

Sometime later, when I was living the wine-and-spaghetti life in Greenwich Village and managing to eke out an existence writing pieces for *The Nation* magazine, I heard from someone that Vonnegut had become a "science-fiction writer." That seemed dire to me also, science fiction then being a category that was very unfashionable, and smacked of "commercialism," whatever that might mean in terms of writing.

In 1963 I escaped New York for a period in Boston and New Hampshire, and around those environs I heard that Vonnegut was living on Cape Cod and teaching English at a grammar school. I don't know if that is true, as I never asked him, but that was "the word" then on Vonnegut. There was also a more cheering word, in the form of a novel he had written called *Cat's Cradle,* that a lot of people were talking about. They said it was quite wonderful. I read it, and agreed. In the book, Vonnegut invented a new religion (he is always inventing new religions) called Bokononism, with a prophet named Bokonon. One of the concepts Bokonon gave the world was the *karass,* which Vonnegut explained like this:

> Humanity is organized into teams, teams that do God's Will without ever discovering what they are doing. Such a team is called a *karass* by Bokonon. . . . "If you find your life tangled up with somebody else's life for no very logical reasons," writes Bokonon, "that person may be a member of your *karass.*"

Not long after reading about that, I met Kurt Vonnegut, Jr., for the first time in my life. It was at a very nice dinner at the home of some friends in Cambridge, Massachusetts, in 1964. There were eight people at the dinner, and I didn't get to say much to Vonnegut, nor he to me, as everyone there had a lot of things to say to everyone else. There were only two things I remember him saying. One was that during the treacherous period when he quit his corporation job and devoted full time to writing, there came a particular year that seemed to him like a "magic year" when all his stories sold and his writing went very well and he figured he could really do it. The other thing was private, and I won't tell you that, but I liked both things I remember him saying, and I liked *him*. He laughed a lot, and was kind to everyone.

The following year I finished writing a book called *Between the Lines,* and I asked the publisher to send a set of galleys to Vonnegut in case he would be so kind as to want to make a comment about it. The book was essentially a collection of magazine articles and essays, but I added a personal, autobiographical narrative to it that explained something of what was happening to me when I was writing those things. The introductory part was all about how I grew up in Indianapolis, and how my dreams of athletic stardom were smashed when I found that I could not break the seven-minute mile. I got back a wonderful letter from Vonnegut about the book. He confessed that he, too, had been unable to break the seven-minute mile, and that we had had so many of the same teachers and same experiences as I described that, as he put it, "I almost feel that there shouldn't be two of us."

I was grateful for his nice letter, and elated by it. I began to feel guilty that I had not read all of his works, so I set about trying to find the ones I had missed, which were the ones in between *Player Piano* and *Cat's Cradle.* It wasn't easy, in those days, to just walk into a bookstore and get any book you wanted by Kurt Vonnegut. *Cat's Cradle* was a growing "underground" success, "underground" meaning that the publisher never told the public much about it, but that a lot of people who read it urged it upon their friends as an experience not to be missed. I was able to get *Mother Night* in a paperback edition, but *The Sirens of Titan* was out of print, and I finally was able to borrow a private copy of one from an editor of the house that had published it.

I liked these very different books very much. Now, you

may think this was due to dumb prejudice because Vonnegut had liked *my* book, but I assure you that I am perfectly capable of not liking books written by the dearest of friends, or books by reviewers who have said nice things about books of mine. If I don't like a book written by a friend, I don't lie and pretend I like it; I just don't say anything at all. And, in turn, I have friends who do the same for me. Silence, in this area, is indeed golden. If you know a friend has read your book, and he hasn't commented to you about it, just don't ask. Stay friends.

Vonnegut is the sort of writer whom you either like a lot or dislike a lot; if you like one of his books, you are likely to enjoy the others. If you read one or two and don't like them, you might as well stop and accept the fact he's not for you. But even if you like them all, you have favorites. One of my favorites turned out to be *The Sirens of Titan,* and that surprised me, because it was supposed to be the most "science-fiction" type of all his books, and I don't like science fiction. By that I mean I don't like books that have green monsters with five arms, and lost tribes that are ruled by electronic lizards.

But Vonnegut's "science fiction" wasn't like that at all. It was about people, doing things that people might do if things had just turned out a little differently; or maybe if we *knew* more of what was really going on. One of my favorite lines is in *The Sirens of Titan.* (I have quoted it to explain many things that have little or nothing to do with science or fiction.) In this book, as in others, Vonnegut has invented another religion; in it, a man is supposed to fall from space and say a particular holy piece of scripture that will mark him as the long-awaited prophet. Well, this man falls out of the sky, and the believers gather around, and he knows he is expected to say something of great import, but he doesn't know what it is, so he just says the truth: "I was a victim of a series of accidents, as are we all." The believers cheer; that is indeed the exact thing he was supposed to say. So I wrote Vonnegut telling him of my pleasure in these books of his, and another just out called *God Bless You, Mr. Rosewater.* A lot of that one takes place in Indianapolis. In all of Vonnegut's books there is at least one person who is from Indianapolis; it is like Alfred Hitchcock always making a walk-on appearance in each of his movies.

I heard in a year or so that Vonnegut had gone out to Iowa to teach at the Iowa Writers Workshop. Then I heard he was back at Cape Cod. We kept in touch by means of our books, which we sent to each other, and wrote friendly letters about. In 1968 I went out to California to try to write a novel I had been trying to write for most of my adult life. That winter, maybe over into 1969, his novel *Slaughterhouse-Five* came out. He didn't send me a copy, probably because he didn't know where I was, but I eagerly bought one, and thought it a marvel of a book. I wrote him about it, saying that in some strange way that had nothing to do with the subject matter, it reminded me of *Walden;* that it was the first book I had read since I read *Walden* while living in New Hampshire in 1964 that gave me the feeling of "lights coming on" in my head as I read it. He wrote back saying he thought I had overestimated the book, but thanked me anyway. He mentioned he had gone to Indianapolis for an autographing party at the bookstore of the L. S. Ayres department store. "I was there for three hours," he reported, "and sold eleven copies. All of them to relatives, I swear to God."

By that time Vonnegut was a hero on most college campuses in America, his book was a best seller, he was being written up in every magazine under the eye of God, he was asked to give graduation addresses, launch ships, and bless babies, but in good old Indianapolis, his home-town, his personal appearance drew only a handful of relatives. A third-string astronaut's wife from Hackensack, New Jersey, would have been a bigger draw. I guess it figures. The old "prophet-in-his-own-country" routine. So it goes.

But I see I have gotten ahead of the story, have jumped an important part of the plot. Which is, when Vonnegut left the Iowa Writers Workshop, and went back to Cape Cod to work on *Slaughterhouse,* the book that finally "hit" for him, how did he support himself? Vonnegut himself tells us, in *Slaughterhouse:*

> And somewhere in there a nice man named Seymour Lawrence gave me a three-book contract, and I said, "O.K., the first of the three will be my famous book about Dres-den."

The way I heard it—not from Vonnegut himself or from Sam Lawrence, but the way writers hear these things about other writers and publishers' advances and so on—I heard that when Sam Lawrence first met Vonnegut he said to him, "How much money do you need to live on for the time it will take you to write your book?" And Vonnegut figured out the sum, and told Sam, and Sam gave him the sum, in advance of royalties. Which is something like a gamble or an act of faith, or both, on the part of Sam as the publisher. It turned out to be a good gamble and an intelli-gent act of faith.

I *do* know how Sam Lawrence happened to meet Von-negut, because Sam told me the story himself. It was like this. Sam, who had been the director of the Atlantic Monthly Press and published *Ship of Fools* and the first

J. P. Donleavy books and many other distinguished writers, had set up his own company in Boston, in conjunction with Dell Publishing, in New York. Sam was of course looking for authors. One day he read a review in *The New York Times* of the new Random House dictionary by Kurt Vonnegut. It was an astute and humorous review about dictionaries, and Sam liked it a lot and wrote to Vonnegut saying he liked it and if Vonnegut were ever in Boston, why didn't he drop in to Sam's office. And one day, without previous plan or announcement, Vonnegut dropped in. And it all began, the very nice relationship of Vonnegut as author and Sam as his publisher.

When I finally finished my own lifetime-in-progress novel, I had my agent submit it to ten publishers, one of whom was Sam Lawrence. I was living in Boston at the time, and I was nervous as hell wondering who, if anyone, would like my novel. Early reports came in: some people loved it and some people hated it. I heard early on from Sam that he was reading it and liking it. One night, pacing my fabulous book-lined study on Beacon Hill and trying not to jump out of my skin with nervous dread and anticipation, I did the very unbusinesslike thing of calling up Sam at his home and asking if he would send a copy of the novel to Vonnegut and see what *he* thought of it. The novel was set in Indianapolis, and Vonnegut is a native of that place and he probably could give a good estimate of whether the novel was any good or full of crap. Sam said O.K., he'd do that if I got him an extra copy to send to Vonnegut on the Cape, and I found an extra and had another shot of bourbon and ran down the hill to deliver the damn thing to Sam, by hand. I honestly didn't know what in the world Vonnegut would think about my novel. I had, as you know now, met him once in my life and exchanged nice letters with him. He had liked my journalistic books, but a novel is of course a different and more delicate kettle of fish.

The next thing was I got a telegram from Vonnegut that congratulated me on "your very important novel." Then Sam showed me a letter Vonnegut sent him, saying of my very own book that it was "the truest and funniest sex novel any American will ever write."

Wow. As it turned out, happily, Sam published my novel, and Vonnegut let him use that terrific quote on the jacket, and I couldn't have been more pleased. Also, before publication, Sam asked Vonnegut if he would make any editorial suggestions or criticisms of the book, and Vonnegut wrote a very intelligent two-page letter about it, making about seven suggestions of minor changes or possible additions, and I think I did about four of them.

Sam also asked Vonnegut if he could help us think up a good title for the book. My working title had been *Sons and Mothers*, and Sam pointed out that this was too confusing, there being so many other books that sounded like that, such as *Sons and Lovers*, *Mothers and Sons*, just plain *Sons*, and so on. So we all tried to think of titles, and Vonnegut sent in a long list of potential titles. His own favorite was: *Getting Laid in Indianapolis*.

I thought that was a little too blatant, but I appreciated the suggestion. We finally ended up with *Going All the Way*, which I felt was faithful to the fifties tone and spirit of the book. Titles are very hard.

A month or so after all that, Vonnegut said he was coming up to Boston for the day and perhaps we could have lunch. I looked forward to that, because I had never really had a chance to sit down and talk to Vonnegut alone. We met at Jake Wirth's, which is Vonnegut's favorite restaurant in Boston. It is an old authentic German place, very plain, with lots of wurst and potato salad and thick honest sandwiches and steins of beer. The lunch was very pleasant, and like Vonnegut himself, low-keyed and kind of ironically amusing. The only thing I really remember him saying was, when he first saw me as I came in: "That's quite a head of hair you've got."

I had let my hair get long, all right, down over my ears. His comment didn't seem critical, just observational. I think we talked some about Indianapolis, and some people we knew in common there. Writers rarely, if ever, talk about writing. Maybe we did just a little, concerning some of his suggestions about my novel.

Later that spring I heard that *Life* magazine asked Vonnegut if he would like to review my novel. He said he would, but insisted on saying in the review that he was a friend of mine. This was a revolutionary thing to do—I mean, to *say* that. Most reviews are written either by friends of the author or enemies of the author, but they never admit it in the review, they pretend they just came upon this book out of the clear blue sky and are making a wholly objective judgment on it. But Vonnegut wouldn't make that pretense. He started his review by saying: "Dan Wakefield is a friend of mine. We both went to Shortridge High School in Indianapolis. . . . His publisher is my publisher. He has boomed my books. So I would praise his first novel, even if it were putrid. But I wouldn't give my Word of Honor that it was good." He went on to give his Word of Honor that it really was good.

So then everyone knew I was a friend of Vonnegut, which was fine with me, I am proud to be so counted; the only trouble was a lot of people started asking me for his address or his phone number or an introduction to him and all I would say was I knew he lived on Cape Cod, which was public knowledge from various articles about him. I knew he was being bombarded with requests and letters and queries about his life and work, and people just showing up on his doorstep, and wanting him to go ZAP or something and tell them the secret of the universe.

What was happening, especially with his adoption by the youth cult, reminded me of a story I had heard in New York about another writer who in my day was popular with children. That was the marvelous sports writer John R. Tunis, who wrote terrific sports books for boys, like *The Iron Duke, The Duke Decides,* and *A City for Lincoln.* Anyway, this friend in New York told about a kid from his hometown who, around the age of twelve, ran away from home. And where did he go? He went to the home of John R. Tunis, hoping to live there. Mr. Tunis of course had to call the boy's parents and send him back home.

Today the same kid probably wouldn't be reading sports books, and if he were precocious, he might have read Vonnegut and run away from home in hopes of living at *his* house. Anyway, a lot of kids showed up at his house, till it got to the point where he said publicly something to the effect that he really didn't *like* kids. It was similar in a way to the plight of Eugene McCarthy; Vonnegut didn't go looking for the kids, they adopted *him.*

I was especially uneasy when some very nice young friends of mine who lived on communes in Vermont and Massachusetts told me they wanted to go visit Vonnegut. I liked them, and I figured Vonnegut would like them too, but I said they would have to do whatever they wanted on their own, as I just didn't feel I could aid in what he might well construe as an invasion of his privacy.

They went ahead anyway, and it turned out O.K. One of them, Steve Diamond, gave me an account of what happened. There was Steve, a young writer, and his writer buddy Ray Mungo, and their friend Verandah Porche, "Queen of the Bay State Poets for Peace," and a few others. They went to Vonnegut's house, and he came to the door and said, "What can I do for you people?" Steve said they didn't want him to "do anything" for them, and they feared he thought they wanted some favor. Anyway, Vonnegut suggested they take a walk, and he led them out to a very beautiful spot near his house, and they all sat down on the ground. They talked, with some uneasiness, and then Steve suddenly said to Vonnegut, "Actually, there is a real reason we have come here. We are forming an organization called 'The Old Farts.' To belong, you have to smoke a lot of Pall Malls, and you have to have a porch to sit on. We would like you to be President."

All that was an allusion to Vonnegut's self-description in *Slaughterhouse-Five,* and he laughed and they laughed, and everything was O.K. They invited him, Sam Lawrence, and me to come to the May Day Festival that they and their neighboring communes were holding in 1970. We all went up, and it was a pleasant but rather restrained day, less festive than I had expected.

The main thing I remember was Vonnegut talking to Ray Mungo, who had founded the commune where the event was being held. Ray was explaining their future plans, and said that they had lived on that farm for three years now, had learned how to survive on it, and they felt they should pass it on to some of the throngs of younger kids who were coming up that way in escape from the cities; and they, as pioneers, should go farther north, where it would be more difficult, and they would learn how to survive under more primitive conditions.

"You see," Ray explained, "we would like to be the last people on Earth."

Vonnegut pondered that for a moment and then asked, "Isn't that kind of a stuck-up thing to want to be?"

I don't think I had heard the term "stuck-up" since high

school, but it seemed to apply quite nicely to the situation. Ray is no phony—he is in fact a remarkable young man and a very gifted writer—but he does have a real "prophetic" streak in him. Vonnegut does not, though some people assume it from his work.

Some friends of mine out here in Los Angeles, where I am living at the moment, were a little surprised about that very thing when they had dinner with Vonnegut on a trip he made out here in the spring of 1971. Both of them are writers, and mutual friends got them together for this dinner with Vonnegut. The next day my friends called me up and said how terrific Vonnegut was, and how frankly they had been afraid they wouldn't like him and were so glad they did.

"Why," I asked, "were you afraid you wouldn't like him?"

There was a silence, and then my friend said, "We were afraid he would be—'prophetic.' "

"But he's not," I said.

"Not at all," said my friend. "He's really a listener—he listened very closely to what everyone else was saying, and every once in a while he would make some wry, very funny, and pertinent comment."

No, he is not the prophetic type, and it is just another one of the ironies he finds in our weird existence that he should have been adopted as a kind of prophet by so many people, in so many places.

Excepting, of course, Indianapolis.

Chapter 7

KURT VONNEGUT FOR PRESIDENT: THE MAKING OF AN ACADEMIC REPUTATION

JOE DAVID BELLAMY

IOWA CITY. The spacious faculty lounge in the new ultra-modern English-Philosophy Building (EPB) at the University of Iowa. We are waiting in this glittering room for the appearance of Kurt Vonnegut, Jr., who taught here a few years back, before he won a Guggenheim and signed a three-book contract with Seymour Lawrence and became famous. From my spot in this sea of legs and Arrid Extra-Dry and sprawling book bags, I have a terrific view of the big chartreuse chair where Vonnegut will be sitting down. Perfect.

Some people in the back are still milling around by the coffee urn. That bearded man there, just raising the cup to his lips, is Robert Scholes, the critic. The door swings open, and in walks Vance Bourjaily and someone, and with them is, yes, there he is—unmistakable—there's Vonnegut.

The audience rolls back like the Red Sea before Moses, and Vonnegut meanders purposively to the chair with his bow-legged, unpretentious gait. It is the sort of "diffident bloodhound lope"[1] that could allow a man to stumble gracefully or even fall down flat, then get up and walk away as if nothing had happened. He makes it. He sits, facing us. He is a huge, slouching, loose-jointed man with a really impressive mustache. Seated here, he resembles exactly—as C. D. B. Bryan, also present, will later write in the *New York Times Book Review*—"a corduroy covered bat-wing chair that has been dropped 2,000 feet from a passing airplane."[2]

"I know you'll ask it."

"Are you a black humorist?" someone quips.

"You asked it," Vonnegut booms.

He talks easily, this great wounded bear of a man; and when he laughs, he booms. He has a presence, like a politician, without being portly. He fills a room. He is moody, truculent one instant, laughing contagiously the next. The audience follows on cue.

He begins to talk about his latest book: "I was present in the greatest massacre in European history, which was the destruction of Dresden by fire-bombing. . . . We got through it, the American prisoners there, because we were quartered in the stockyards where it was wide and open and there was a meat locker three stories beneath the surface, the only decent shelter in the city. So we went down into the meat locker, and when we came up again, the city was gone and everybody was dead—a terrible thing for the son of an architect to see. . . ." Vonnegut's eyes avert—those eyes have seen God in a burning bush. He has come down from the mountain with eyes like Charlton Heston's in *The Ten Commandments* by Cecil B. De Mille. His beard would be white now if he had one. This man should be president, someone is thinking. Now it is time for a joke.

This is the first time I have ever seen Kurt Vonnegut, Jr., in person, in action.

I JOIN THE KARASS

The first time I ever *read* Kurt Vonnegut was two years before, when I heard he was going to be one of my instructors that fall at the Iowa Writers Workshop. I bought *Cat's Cradle* and put it on a shelf in my abysmal, gray apartment, and one day when I was trying to write and the Hamm's (Land of Skyblue Waters) wasn't working and my eyes were straying around the room, I lit on *Cat's Cradle* again and picked it out and started to read. "Call me Jonah," I read. . . . I turned off my study light and spent the afternoon reading.

Shortly after that well-spent afternoon, I found out that Vonnegut had just won a Guggenheim and wasn't going to be one of my instructors that fall after all. So it goes. So it didn't go. Later that year Robert Scholes's *The Fabulators* came out in Iowa City, and seeing that it was a critical consideration of Kurt Vonnegut (and some other writers I liked), I actually laid down my five bucks and carried home a copy. Though it seemed perfectly clear to me that Vonnegut's growing critical and academic respectability

73

had wrenched him right out of his *karass* with me, I had almost no inkling at that time that through another series of accidents I would end up writing about it here.

THE FUTURE CLOSE UP

The extent of the pilgrimage he was to make (not to mention the no doubt quixotic adventures he would be having along the way) could hardly have been guessed then by anyone, especially those hardened realists around Iowa City who know better than most that writers don't usually get what they deserve. But, in fact, as we have now seen, Vonnegut was to move from his Guggenheim to the publication of his "big book," and then on to Harvard and Broadway. He was to parley his move from the revolving drugstore bookracks into the college bookstores—which began with the republication of his books in 1966—into faculty offices, and with increasing momentum, into classrooms, anthologies, movie contracts, TV appearances, and even critical respectability. Following a lengthy retrospective review by C. D. B. Bryan in *The New Republic,* Scholes's assessment in *The Fabulators,* and the appearance of *Slaughterhouse-Five* (with its attendant reviews), Vonnegut was to be treated seriously and in rapid succession by other such venerable tastemakers as Wilfrid Sheed, Leslie Fiedler, and Benjamin DeMott—and, surprisingly enough, *in* the mass circulation magazines, though a few scholarly journals were sizing him up as well, and others are not far behind. Just now Vonnegut seems poised on the verge of becoming the subject of a cover story for *Time* and a simultaneous deluge of dissertations. And yet, perhaps the most astonishing element of all in this Vonnegut's odyssey is why the all-encompassing cultural embrace has taken so long to develop in the first place.

YOU'RE HOTTER 'N A TWO-DOLLAR PISTOL, POP

Like Professor Barnhouse, a protagonist in one of Vonnegut's earliest published stories who becomes "the most powerful weapon on earth" by cultivating his psychic powers after accidentally throwing ten sevens in a row in a crap game,[3] Vonnegut is "self-taught."[4] In a sense, of course, most writers are self-taught, but one gathers that Vonnegut, a chemistry major with a spotty education and an unusual apprenticeship, is more self-taught than most. This factor, along with the possibly related accidents of publication and classification, are the most obvious explanations for the slow emergence of Vonnegut's serious reputation.

"You are writing for strangers," he used to scrawl on the blackboard at the beginning of each writing class at Iowa. "Face the audience of strangers." What he meant by this seemed to be, according to some of his ex-students: Don't expect to be automatically understood or loved or even appreciated. A writer must be a "skilled seducer . . . to persuade people to share his dreams."[5] Surely this lesson was the fruit of his bitter professional experience as a freelancer, when as a junior public-relations hack for a good company he gave up his job and his future and staked his life on the silly notion that an unpublished, unknown writer from Indianapolis, who wasn't even an English major, should be able to support his family and himself in the United States of America by writing fiction for a living. "It was damned unpleasant for a number of years," he said later, an "hysterical effort."[6]

Not only was the dewy-eyed amateur prematurely pigeonholed as a "sci-fi" writer, but a second-rate one at that, as his first novel, *Player Piano*, was written off by many as crudely written and largely derivative, a rehashing of Orwell and Huxley. The volume of hack work he *did do* in the fifties, to keep himself afloat, tended to confirm this judgment; and even if all of these early stories were not science-fiction stories, many were, at best, skillful, and at worst, slick, gimmicky, and "popular," just a notch or two above the pulps.

Some, such as "Miss Temptation" or "Long Walk to Forever," treated straightforward boy-meets-girl, boy-gets-girl themes. There were tear-jerkers written for the women's magazines ("D.P.") and others ("The Foster Portfolio," "More Stately Mansions," "The Kid Nobody Could Handle") from the most-unforgettable-character-I've-ever-met genre with period decorations, settings, and costuming, and heart-warming surprise endings where characters either get what they want to get or get what's good for them. By and large these stories do make interesting enough reading—even in those days Vonnegut knew how to tell a good story—but it is hardly any wonder that the stories frequently made use of stock themes, were stylistically run-of-the-mill, and failed therefore to generate lavish praise.

A writer-critic I know, in fact, who shall remain unnamed, turned down an invitation to review the most recently published story collection, *Welcome to the Monkey House* (which repeated much of the early work), for the *New York Review of Books* because it seemed to him, he said, "just old-fashioned slick stories." He "didn't intend it seriously, I didn't think; he seemed to be doing it for the money, which he says himself in the preface; so I just thought I would take him at his word."

This frank toleration for Vonnegut's economic motivations seems to have been fairly rare, however. Typically,

Vonnegut's toil in the lists, seen by himself as one reasonably honorable way to turn an honest buck in the fifties, has been given short shrift by those writers and critics more at home in a university setting, who are more apt to take the cultivation of a reputation as a serious matter and to have the leisure and economic security to do so.

Following *Player Piano* and the years of story writing, the publication in paperback of *The Sirens of Titan* and *Mother Night* (headier stuff) and *Canary in a Cathouse* did little to revitalize Vonnegut's reputation. The books went without benefit of reviews, and the latter, of course, was simply the best of his hack work, dressed up between two covers, interesting enough now to buffs but far from vintage Vonnegut.

Why the eventual hardcover publication of *Cat's Cradle* and *God Bless You, Mr. Rosewater* went relatively unheralded is a tougher mystery to unravel. If, like *Catch-22*, the books had to depend on a snowballing word-of-mouth reputation, it may very likely have been the result of a lag in sensibility. Vonnegut's "mistake" here was in being out-of-joint with the times or, in this case, slightly ahead of the times—for exactly as long as it took the increasingly socially aware reading public, its conscience grated by the atrocities of Vietnam, to catch on to the game of shattered time sequences and the applicability of Vonnegut's brand of gallows humor to their experience of the present.

The black-humor label, which Vonnegut credits Bruce Jay Friedman with affixing to him (in Friedman's foreword to his *Black Humor* anthology, edited for Bantam Books in 1965), became part of this process of recognition and indicated the beginning of a more hospitable attitude toward Vonnegut's work. But even here Vonnegut was thrown in with a decidedly mixed bag of writers, which tended to obscure rather than to clarify his unique vision of things. Critics tended to reject the black-humor label because of its lack of precision, and a number of the writers classified as black humorists (including Vonnegut and Barth, among others) jumped at the chance to disassociate themselves, either because they didn't like the company or feared being associated with yet another ephemeral "school" as it quietly disappeared into oblivion. "The label is useless except for the merchandisers," Vonnegut was saying at Iowa. "I don't think anybody is very happy about the category or depressed about being excluded from it—Vance Bourjaily was, and took it very well, I thought."[7]

While it is true, to a great extent, that the times have finally caught up with Vonnegut, part of his emergence as a major figure, as should now be clear, must be credited simply to his growth and improvement as a writer. Though heresy to admit, it is nonetheless accurate, I think, to observe that the benign neglect of Vonnegut's first decade as a writer was partially justified. Here was a marvelously original but erratic writer. He was a "skilled seducer" in the making, but a long way from fulfilling his potential, tempering steadily in the hard-nosed slick and exploding mass-circulation-paperback trade, a uniquely modern professional initiation. *Welcome to the Monkey House* gives perhaps the clearest perspective on this growth, for in almost *every* case the more recent stories are the all-around better stories; the title story, the best in the collection, is the most recent of all.

During his faculty-lounge performance in Iowa City, Vonnegut himself admitted frankly that much of the early work had been either crude or pot-boiling stuff, though one suspects he may only have appreciated this retrospectively. Half-seriously, he credited his success as a writer to the fact that he was not trained in the humanities—so that he never "learned to dislike" anything he wrote. "I loved every word I wrote," he said, "which is important for a writer—I mean, even though a lot of it was miserable crap."

How *could* a writer who had just written "Tom Edison's Shaggy Dog" write *The Sirens of Titan,* or a writer who had just written "Long Walk to Forever"—"a sickeningly slick love story" (p. xv)—write *Cat's Cradle?* Possibly the same way another self-taught writer who had just written *Soldier's Pay* and *Mosquitoes* could write *The Sound and the Fury* and *As I Lay Dying*—and in both cases, editorial resurrection was necessary through republication. Vonnegut's republication is a factor that should by no means be underestimated in an assessment of his emergence as a dominant figure by the early seventies.

VONNEGUT'S RISE TO RESPECTABILITY

A number of other factors important to Vonnegut's rise are, I think, worth pondering. In the first place, Vonnegut himself was smart enough to figure out that his categorization as a "science-fiction" writer was not working to his advantage; and he took an active part in sloughing off the stigma of the sci-fi label and, as part of the same process, in suggesting that some so-called science-fiction writing was in fact worthy of serious consideration. His essay on "Science Fiction" for the *New York Times Book Review* in 1965 is the most readily accessible and most public example of this. In the essay Vonnegut says that after publishing *Player Piano* he "learned from the reviewers" that he was a science-fiction writer. "I supposed," he went on,

> that I was writing a novel about life, about things I could not avoid seeing and hearing in Schenectady, a very real

town, awkwardly set in the gruesome now. I have been a sore-headed occupant of a file drawer labeled "science-fiction" ever since, and I would like out, particularly since so many serious critics regularly mistake the drawer for a tall white fixture in a comfort station.[8]

In the most direct way possible Vonnegut was indicating that he wanted to be taken seriously, and by "serious critics." And surely, by that time, with five of his novels behind him, such attention was overdue, as he accurately perceived. Similarly, he was ready to admit that his earliest work had been, as he would later call it disparagingly in his preface to *Welcome to the Monkey House*, "the fruits of Free Enterprise" (p. xiv).

Vonnegut was saying this sort of thing to everyone he met, no doubt. He was saying it on the college lecture circuit—"I speak a lot at universities now"[9]—and at writers' conferences, which, like conventions for the science-fiction crowd, he seems to have become cynical—if knowledgeable—about through attending too many.[10] He was still saying it, in fact, in the EPB faculty lounge that day in Iowa City.

A related sort of minor strategy, which Vonnegut confided to us budding writers in the lounge that day, has been the accomplishment of his aspirations as a virtuoso blurb-writer. Write a lot of original blurbs for books you like, he recommended, and then you get to be in great demand as a blurb-writer and your name will be plastered all over other people's book jackets and advertising copy, and this doesn't cost you a cent and is great for public relations. This approach would be especially recommended for a writer, he said, who might have a real zinger of a name in any way resembling a name like, say, Vonnegut.

But the maturing of Vonnegut's comic-satiric vision, his

feeling for, or just plain synchrony with, the Zeitgeist, and his improving technical finesse must be considered as dominant factors in the upswing of his fortunes. At a time when critics such as Susan Sontag and Richard Poirier were learning to appreciate the Beatles and the Supremes *as well as* Bach, and comic strips as well as Shakespeare— without shame—and were providing sophisticated justifications for such tastes, Vonnegut could begin to assume something of a position merely as a "pop" writer. The age of "pop" was at hand. But Vonnegut was more than just a pop writer; he was the thinking man's pop writer. He was an American writer who was actually writing about ideas and incorporating contemporary experiences in his work; and his basic assumptions, his attitudes and prejudices, were, as Benjamin DeMott has pointed out, "perfectly tuned to the mind of the emergent generation."[11] To the surging youth culture, the proper conduct of life, man's inhumanity to man, and the possibility of the end of the world, were and are viable issues. And Vonnegut as fatalistic moralist, cynical pacifist, holy atheist, anti-intellectual philosopher, apocalyptic futurist, and grim humorist complexly encompassed all the right paradoxes.

And not only that: but, more important, I think, than anyone has yet to emphasize, Vonnegut had latched on to a truly original contemporary idiom, as American as TV or napalm or napalm-abhorrers, as fragmented and discontinuous as contemporary experience. A consideration of Vonnegut's idiom, I would say, should take into account everything from his great ear, his sense of the way Americans talk, his sense of timing (as active and keen as Paul McCartney's—a compliment one does not bestow lightly), to his formal idiosyncrasies, beginning with *Mother Night* in 1961: the short chapter form; the sharp image; the short, quick scene; the fragmented time sequence; the speed of narration generated by these formal character-istics. If one were to play Marshall McLuhan here, one might point out that Vonnegut's fiction is a clever formal approximation of, or at least shares many elements of the experience of, watching television. This might offer an-other explanation for Vonnegut's appeal to the TV genera-tion, those who have *always* had television, not to mention those of us, more or less aged, who, according to McLuhan, have also had our sense ratios hopelessly rearranged by it.

TASTE THAT BEATS THE OTHERS COLD

One might just as well go on to hypothesize simply enough that, aside from other factors such as his discovery of a style and a pace attuned to the TV age, Vonnegut may owe his rise to his achievement, to his art. Is such a thing pos-sible?

Starting in 1966, Vonnegut finally began to receive the sort of critical attention from "serious critics" that he had been asking for previously. Robert Scholes's "Mithridates, He Died Old: Black Humor and Kurt Vonnegut, Jr." in *The Hollins Critic* (later included in Scholes's seminal book, *The Fabulators*, in substantially the same form) and "Kurt Vonnegut on Target" by C. D. B. Bryan in *The New Republic* were the essential groundbreaking efforts. Both pieces mentioned pertinent biographical details, the fact that Vonnegut had "not received the acceptance due him from the reading public,"[12] and went on to treat several of the novels and to place Vonnegut in historical perspective by assigning him a pedigreed niche (Scholes, at *length*) in a distinguished tradition (Voltaire and Swift, according to Scholes, seemed appropriate antecedents). Vonnegut's recognition "as an important American writer is all but accomplished already," Scholes rhapsodized, predicting "a literary success of the best sort."[13] For Bryan, Vonnegut was "the most readable and amusing of the new humorists."[14] Clearly, Vonnegut's reputation was winging beyond the drugstore and barbershop stage, from which it was about to soar.

This same duo of Scholes and Bryan attended the 1969 labor and delivery of *Slaughterhouse-Five* to the reading public in the *New York Times Book Review;* and if any skeptics were looking for more proof of Vonnegut's legitimacy, they now had it, both in the form of a splendid novel and an enthusiastic reception of it. In his front-page review, Scholes called Vonnegut "a true artist" and placed him "among the best writers of his generation." Bryan's piece, combining an interview and a summary of the career to that date, mentioned a star-studded list of Vonnegut's "earliest fans" and "the fact that Vonnegut's novels are now being taught at universities" and were accruing a "cultish attention . . . [among] the under-30's."[15]

Later that year Wilfrid Sheed did an appealing personality piece on Vonnegut for *Life. Writer's Yearbook, 1970* carried a lengthy interview, and by the fall of 1970 Vonnegut was being treated by that honorable and honorific bell cow of American letters himself, Leslie Fiedler, and in the pages of *Esquire,* long since past its days as an aspiring tit magazine and coming on strong with some heavy critical-intellectual fare.

"Understandably enough," Fiedler said:

> many survivors of the old critical regime find it difficult to persuade themselves that if, recently, they have come to esteem Vonnegut, it is not because they have been converted to the side of Pop, but because—though they did

not at first realize it—he has all along belonged to the other side of High Art.

But this "other side" of High Art, Fiedler maintained, is in fact not High Art but "the mainstream of myth and entertainment: a stream which was forced to flow underground over the past several 'decades' because of the influence of critics such as T. S. Eliot and Cleanth Brooks." And it is to *this* mainstream of myth and entertainment, "to what we know again to be the mainstream of fiction,"[16] that Vonnegut *does* belong. In his way, then, Fiedler paid Vonnegut the ultimate compliment in his frame of reference by promoting him beyond High Art, which he sees as part of a dead tradition as far as the novel is concerned, and into his special category of mythic and still-vital alternatives, the *real* mainstream of fictional art.

In a more traditionalist vein, Benjamin DeMott—in his cover story for *Saturday Review* in May, 1971—saw Vonnegut's best work as transcending dogma and sermonizing and simplicity of theme that the youth cult grooves to. But here Vonnegut is seen as a tried-and-true classicist. Vonnegut's highest comedy is produced, according to DeMott, "when the subject in view is that of classical satire, namely self-delusion." In this context, Vonnegut is a "potent satirist," DeMott believes, "and an undeservedly good break for the age." This is because, DeMott sums up, with an obvious reference to Scholes's formulations, as "a *fabulist* [italics mine] in love with images of goodness, generosity, [and] hope" he has still managed to articulate "the blackest suspicions of a skeptical, cynical generation without running on into orgies of hate or ironical partisanship of evil."[17]

It is easy enough to see, I think, one might even say *aside* from its merits, why Vonnegut's work has finally be-

come so attractive to the critics. Though the spadework
has started, much more presumably will be necessary; for
the texture of Vonnegut's work invites, if not literally *cries
out* for, critical analysis and interpretation. The jolting connections, the recurrent imagery, the extractable meat of
seductive thematic material, the elusive simplicity of
technical virtuosity, the cross-references from book to book
(and within each book), are intriguing to even the casual
reader. As Jerome Klinkowitz has aptly pointed out, Vonnegut "teases us" with a whole "Mod Yoknapatawpha
County."[18]

A case in point, which leads nicely into the last major
point I wish to make about Vonnegut's rise, is that matter
of "Call me Jonah" at the beginning of *Cat's Cradle*. Those
were the first three words of Vonnegut's I ever read, and
with those three words Vonnegut hit me with an avalanche
of implications that I have *yet* to get out from under. Even
if "Call me Jonah" is nothing more than a "gratuitous
though delightful"[19] parody of the opening of *Moby Dick*
together with an invocation of the biblical story of Jonah
and *his* whale, it succeeds, as Robert Scholes has mentioned, in "preparing us for a story on the Job theme" with
its "anti-Joblike conclusion." Yet it does more than that. It
leaves you with the suspicion, doesn't it, that *Cat's Cradle*
may very likely be *full* of hidden whale imagery or other
references to *Moby Dick* or Jonah? One of these days I'm
going to take the time to find out—if somebody doesn't do
a dissertation on it first.

KURT VONNEGUT FOR PRESIDENT

The further implication for me of Vonnegut's metaphor in
the first three words of *Cat's Cradle,* suggesting a number
of stories wherein heroes are put through trials and labors

to test their virtues, etc., is that the author himself is just such a figure. In a way, he is Job, Jonah, Ahab, Christ, and Lot's wife all rolled into one. Prominent in nearly every published critical evaluation or review of his work, every glib summary or interview or portrait, especially since the appearance of *Slaughterhouse-Five,* has been the reiteration of the details of Vonnegut's now famous trial-by-fire in Dresden and comment, always highly sympathetic, about Vonnegut's burden, about how the magnitude of the event devastated his psyche and nearly struck him dumb, and how he has spent the last twenty-five years of his life struggling to come to terms with this single overwhelming event. This biographical detail has captured the imaginations of the public and the publishing world, of the youth culture and the critics, as few others have since the days of Ernest Hemingway. What's more, Vonnegut looks the part and acts the part. He is perfectly cast.

The photograph which accompanied Robert Scholes's laudatory front-page review of *Slaughterhouse-Five* in the *New York Times Book Review,* for example, consciously or unconsciously, was a stroke of public-relations genius. Vonnegut is pictured before the bust of a very white lady atop a pillar, presumably Lot's wife, and facing us, he has a perfectly remarkable expression on his face, the look of a man who has seen the end of the world and come back to tell the story. His eyes are closed. He is suffering cryptically. And he is suffering, we readily imagine, not merely from what he has *seen* but from his labors, from his years of service to an ideal of artistry, stifled so long not merely because of the difficulty of the artistic task he had set for himself but because of the uncooperativeness of the world, the demands it made of him to prostitute himself for its ignoble commercial purposes. Clearly, this man pictured before us has *earned* whatever small reward the world may be able to offer him.

In short, I believe that one explanation for Vonnegut's rise to fame is his role as a throwback to the good old days when life may or may not have made sense, but when artists, at least, *suffered.* Artists don't suffer much anymore, but Vonnegut is one who does. Artists aren't eyewitnesses to anything anymore, but Vonnegut was. He was there; he suffered. And significantly, I think, while he has managed to evade the "boring norms of realism"[20] in his work, he has done this without forfeiting the historically connected mystique of the existential hero-author.

Back in Iowa City Vonnegut is telling a cocktail-party joke. "So I wrote my first book, *Player Piano,* about Schenectady, and it was published. But I would run into people who would down-grade me. I ran into Jason Epstein, a terribly powerful cultural commissar, at a cocktail party. When we were introduced, he thought a minute, then said, 'Science fiction,' turned, and walked off. He just had to place me, that's all." Vonnegut laughs. He is creating an atmosphere of tremendous sympathy for himself. This is one thing he is very good at.

"But I continued to include machinery in my books and, may I say in *confidence,* in my life. . . . Machinery is important. We must write about it. . . . But I don't care if you don't; I'm not urging you, am I? To hell with machinery." Tremendous. A living legend. Kurt Vonnegut for president!

Is it an accident, I wonder in looking back, that Robert Scholes, C. D. B. Bryan, and, later, Leslie Fiedler (not then present in Iowa City but a participant with Vonnegut during a symposium at Brown in 1969) had all met Vonnegut and knew him personally, were subject then to this

tremendous personal appeal at about the time or just before each of them became interested enough in him to
commit themselves to print on the subject of his work?
Fortunate for Vonnegut and for us, I think, and suspicious
possibly in a lesser writer, but in this case simply good luck
for all concerned.

After Iowa City, the next time I saw Kurt Vonnegut he
was sitting around with some CBS newsmen on TV, giving
his advice on a moon landing. And after that I saw him
again on "60 Minutes," being interviewed in the orchestra
pit of a darkened theater by Harry Reasoner. The media
had undoubtedly caught on to his animal magnetism and
sheer physical potential. He had passed his screen test. He
filled the screen, as he filled a room, with the right kind of
cool-image electricity, the right sense of subdued violence
and heroic promise. Yes, indeed. As I watched those brooding eyes on my screen, the "eyes of a sacrificial altar-bound
virgin,"[21] Vonnegut seemed to me at that moment, as he
must have for many others, a highly credible embodiment
of the possibly fallacious idea that suffering ennobles.

NOTES TO CHAPTER 7

1. Wilfrid Sheed, "The Now Generation Knew Him When,"
   Life, September 12, 1969, p. 66.
2. C. D. B. Bryan, "Kurt Vonnegut, Head Bokononist," *New
   York Times Book Review,* April 6, 1969, p. 2.
3. "Report on the Barnhouse Effect," *Collier's,* 125 (February
   11, 1950), 18–19 ff.
4. *Welcome to the Monkey House,* p. xiii.
5. Roger Henke, "Wrestling (American Style) with Proteus:
   Symposium Highlights," *Novel,* 3 (Spring, 1970), 205.
6. Loretta McCabe, "An Exclusive Interview with Kurt Vonnegut," *Writer's Yearbook '70,* No. 41, 1970, p. 100.

7. See John Casey's partial tape transcript-interview of Vonnegut's Iowa City appearance: *Confluence,* II (Spring, 1969), 4–5, or as reprinted in *Apocalypse: Dominant Contemporary Forms,* Joe David Bellamy, ed., (Philadelphia, New York, Toronto: J. B. Lippincott, 1972).

8. Kurt Vonnegut, Jr., "Science Fiction," *New York Times Book Review,* September 5, 1965, p. 2.

9. C. D. B. Bryan, "Kurt Vonnegut, Head Bokononist," *New York Times Book Review,* April 6, 1969, p. 2.

10. Kurt Vonnegut, Jr., "Teaching the Unteachable," *New York Times Book Review,* August 6, 1967, pp. 1, 20.

11. Benjamin DeMott, "Vonnegut's Otherworldly Laughter," *Saturday Review,* May 1, 1971, p. 30.

12. C. D. B. Bryan, "Vonnegut on Target," *The New Republic,* October 8, 1966, p. 21.

13. Robert Scholes, "Mithridates, He Died Old: Black Humor and Kurt Vonnegut, Jr.," *The Hollins Critic,* III (October, 1966), 8.

14. C. D. B. Bryan, "Kurt Vonnegut on Target," *The New Republic,* October 8, 1966, p. 21.

15. C. D. B. Bryan, "Kurt Vonnegut, Head Bokononist," *New York Times Book Review,* April 6, 1969, p. 2.

16. Leslie Fiedler, "The Divine Stupidity of Kurt Vonnegut," *Esquire,* September, 1970, p. 196.

17. Benjamin DeMott, "Vonnegut's Otherworldly Laughter," *Saturday Review,* May 1, 1971, p. 38.

18. Jerome Klinkowitz, "Kurt Vonnegut, Jr., and the Crime of His Times," *Critique,* XII (#3, 1971), 38.

19. Robert Scholes, "Fabulation and Satire," *The Fabulators* (New York: Oxford University Press, 1967), p. 51.

20. Benjamin DeMott, "Vonnegut's Otherworldly Laughter," *Saturday Review,* May 1, 1971, p. 30.

21. C. D. B. Bryan, "Kurt Vonnegut, Head Bokononist," *New York Times Book Review,* April 6, 1969, p. 2.

Chapter 8

A TALK WITH
KURT VONNEGUT, JR.

—————————•—•—•—————————

ROBERT SCHOLES

I
[EDITOR'S NOTE:]
HE FOLLOWING CONVERSATION between Robert Scholes
and Kurt Vonnegut, Jr., took place in October of 1966,
while Vonnegut was teaching at the University of Iowa
Writers Workshop. The full transcript is offered herewith.
Catching Vonnegut at the turning point of his career,
when his earlier works were coming back into print and
being widely reviewed, and while he was working on
Slaughterhouse-Five, it presents not only a candid view of

the artist, but also an encapsulation of ideas in the making, including such phrases and concepts as "poisoning minds with humanity" which were to appear in subsequent interviews and commentaries. Nothing has been omitted. Vonnegut talks about a "forthcoming" Broadway production of *Cat's Cradle;* although it never materialized, the conversation here offers valuable insights into Vonnegut's notions of theater and its potentiality. Neither, in the spirit of spontaneity, have any colloquialisms been refined or faux pas been removed, nor have any "names been changed to protect the innocent"—since, as Vonnegut professes in the disclaimer to *The Sirens of Titan,* "God Almighty protects the innocent as a matter of Heavenly routine."—J.K.

SCHOLES: Kurt, to begin with, I am curious myself about how you got involved in this business of writing. Did you always mean to be a writer?

VONNEGUT: No, well, I think it was the only out for me. I had a very disagreeable job at General Electric, and this was an out.

SCHOLES: Are there agreeable jobs at General Electric?

VONNEGUT: Oh yes, I think there are. I think president of General Electric is a very agreeable job, and also chairman of the board.

SCHOLES: And the rest of them, though, are more or less disagreeable.

VONNEGUT: Well, I was quite low on the rungs of advancement there, and I was selling stories to *Collier's* and *The Saturday Evening Post* and was very happy to leave rather than to get to the top the hard way.

SCHOLES: Yeah, I suppose, then, you were not the product of a creative writing school or program yourself.

VONNEGUT: I didn't know they existed at that time. I went

to an excellent high school which encouraged creative writing, which was Shortridge High School in Indianapolis.

SCHOLES: You grew up in Indianapolis.

VONNEGUT: Yes.

SCHOLES: And what happened in between high school and (I don't want to say General Motors . . . but . . .)

VONNEGUT: Same thing. Makes no difference.

SCHOLES: I get all the corporations mixed up.

VONNEGUT: No, it's . . . Father suggested that I become a scientist. My father himself was an architect and quite demoralized about the arts, as he hadn't made any money for ten years because of the Depression. So he told me to be a chemist, and since it was his money, I went and started to become a chemist at Cornell University. And the war came along, thank God, in the middle of my junior year, and I left most gratefully for the infantry. This is actually a career of a quitter. I have quit and quit and quit.

SCHOLES: I am afraid a lot of careers take that same pattern, but fortunately we're interviewing you here today. You started out to be a chemical engineer. Does that account, do you think, for the interest in technology that seems to run through your work?

VONNEGUT: Well, it accounts for my familiarity with technology somewhat, and through what seemed misfortunes to me at the time I have learned something about physics, chemistry, and math and the sorts of people that are successful in those areas, so I have been able to take off on them with a fair amount of expertness. After the war I went to the University of Chicago and studied anthropology for three years, and then went to work for General Electric as a public-relations man, and because of all this background in science that I had had, they made me a flak, a publicity man for the research laboratory there, which is an excellent industrial research laboratory.

SCHOLES: I see.

VONNEGUT: So I saw these people at work and knew them quite well and went to their parties and so forth and proceeded to hurt their feelings in my first book which was . . .

SCHOLES: *Player Piano*.

VONNEGUT: Yes.

SCHOLES: Yes, I've wondered about *Player Piano*. In particular one of the things that interested me was this great summer festival that the technicians hold somewhere up in the North Woods. I wonder if there's a real background to that.

VONNEGUT: Yes, there is. There was a . . . called Association Island and it was owned by the (let's see, what was it) . . . there was some association of electric-light manufacturers in the early days of the electrical industry and they were friendly competitors and they met to discuss business on this island once a year and this became sort of a Boy Scout festival.

SCHOLES: Uh-huh.

VONNEGUT: What the competitors did not know for quite a while was that they were all owned by General Electric.

SCHOLES: Ha ha ha ha . . .

VONNEGUT: And that no matter what happened to the competition, General Electric won.

SCHOLES: Marvelous.

VONNEGUT: But this became in later years a morale-building operation for General Electric, and deserving young men were sent up there for a week and played golf and there were archery contests and baseball contests and swimming contests and plenty of free liquor, and so forth.

SCHOLES: So the bizarre events in *Player Piano* are pretty realistic after all, are they?

VONNEGUT: Well, *Player Piano* when it came out was not a widely read book except in Schenectady, New York. The island was shut down after the book came out.

SCHOLES: No kidding.

VONNEGUT: It no longer exists.

SCHOLES: I'll tell you something I read last summer that may interest you. I was talking to someone going out to the West Coast who had just been at a session out in the northern part of California which reminded me very much of the episode in *Player Piano*. Apparently some large organization out there invites up-and-coming young men in all professions, and old men, too, so that you find admirals and generals and businessmen and whatnot, and they seem to go through a ritual quite like the ritual described in *Player Piano*.

VONNEGUT: Yes, it's fun to work. It's a cheesy little religion which is satisfactory for a week or so, and . . .

SCHOLES: Some last long and some last a little while.

VONNEGUT: Yes. As most husbands coming back from one of these things won't tell their wives what happened there, and, you know, because it's so silly.

SCHOLES: Yeah. Not because there's anything really wrong.

VONNEGUT: No! Oh, no! It's a very clean operation.

SCHOLES: Yeah, the Boy Scout atmosphere sounds very strong.

VONNEGUT: I think the book would have sold a great deal better if I had intimated that there were party girls flown in and so forth, but there are not.

SCHOLES: Yeah, you may not be realistic, but you have your standards, I suppose.

VONNEGUT: Yes.

SCHOLES: This brings me to another point. I'm very interested in how you came to write the kind of stories that you started writing, and still write, which have some connections with science fiction and generally seem more fantastic in some ways than the orthodox kind of writing. How did it happen that you wrote that sort of stuff?

VONNEGUT: I suppose I admired H. G. Wells a lot and Mark Twain and so forth, and somehow got those wires crossed, and at Cornell when I was studying chemistry what I was really doing most of the time was writing for the *Cornell Daily Sun*, which you know.

SCHOLES: Uh-huh.

VONNEGUT: And I became managing editor of the *Sun* and I wrote about, oh, three columns a week, and they were impudent editorializing, as college-humor sort of stuff.

SCHOLES: Yeah.

VONNEGUT: And I continued to editorialize. That was congenial, and so I've always had to have an ax to grind in order to write.

SCHOLES: Was the *Sun* then a commercial enterprise as it is now?

VONNEGUT: Yes, well, it was always independent of the university. It was a separate corporation, and the prospect was in my day that the managing editor and the editor-in-chief and the advertising director would all split some sort of financial melon at the end of the year, and in my day that came to about a thousand dollars, but World War II destroyed our melon.

SCHOLES: Uh-huh.

VONNEGUT: And the *Sun* slowly died for lack of staff.

SCHOLES: Well, it was going strong when I was back at Cornell in the late fifties, and there was a melon again to be split, I think.

VONNEGUT: Yes. How much, do you know?

SCHOLES: I haven't any idea.

VONNEGUT: Yeah, it's probably about three or four thousand now.

SCHOLES: I would think so, but probably not worth any more than the one thousand of back then.

VONNEGUT: Yeah.

SCHOLES: But it says something about free enterprise, I think. That the newspaper should be good because there's a melon to be split.

VONNEGUT: Yes. Well, every so often a professor at Cornell would threaten to have an editor of the *Sun* fired for some piece of . . .

SCHOLES: Impudence?

VONNEGUT: Impudence. And he would discover that the *Sun* had no connection with the university and that the man he was threatening to fire was in fact the chief executive of a separate corporation.

SCHOLES: Which is a lovely thing, to be encouraged in other places, I think. Well, one of the labels that gets pasted on your work a lot is this term black humor, which seems to get applied to nearly everybody who writes nowadays, at one moment or another. I wonder whether someone like yourself objects to it or whether you more or less accept it as a description of what you do.

VONNEGUT: Well, I find it mystifying. What it seems to be is a sales-promotion label. It's as though someone took a great bell jar and caught a certain number of crickets under it and gave a name to all those crickets, and this is, what, Bruce Jay Friedman . . .

SCHOLES: That book of his was the first place I saw the term.

VONNEGUT: Yes. Called *Black Humor,* and in it with Terry Southern, Barth, who else?

SCHOLES: Uh. Céline, I think. Albee is even in that book.

VONNEGUT: Yes.

SCHOLES: Donleavy.

VONNEGUT: Yes. Well, Friedman—in a way—Friedman as a very young man became sort of the grandfather of all the black humorists by being editor-in-chief of a book called *Black Humor.*

SCHOLES: I know. I looked him up the other day someplace. He's about thirty-four-years old, I think, or thirty-three.

VONNEGUT: Yeah.

SCHOLES: He's very young.

VONNEGUT: No. But anything that gets people interested in books is good for all authors, so I can't really complain about this if people are talking about books; and if they want to talk about black humor as the latest thing, that's fine.

SCHOLES: As long as it isn't maybe just a fashion which will . . .

VONNEGUT: Yes . . .

SCHOLES: . . . change in another year or two and all those old crickets will have to be swept out and new ones caught.

VONNEGUT: Well, the expert we ought to have here is David Hayman, I think, who is, what, *the* resident expert on humor, I think, isn't he?

SCHOLES: He's working now on a book on the clown in European literature, which will be very interesting, I think, when he gets it done.

VONNEGUT: Yes, but as a specialist, why, he becomes very outraged about black humor because he feels that this is

97

a continuous development going back I don't know how many years. He's probably pushed it back six or seven hundred years by now.

SCHOLES: Well, I think it probably goes back to Aristophanes, who seems to have a lot of the same instincts that you do.

VONNEGUT: Yeah.

SCHOLES: Though he never worked for General Mills, or General Electric, or whatever.

VONNEGUT: Well, I read Aristophanes when I was fourteen.

SCHOLES: Oh.

VONNEGUT: And liked it very much, and of course read it, as fourteen-year-olds do, because I was told it was dirty.

SCHOLES: Uh-huh.

VONNEGUT: And it certainly was. It was great. I won twice, you know; it was not only dirty, it was good.

SCHOLES: Right. Well, the marvelous thing about Aristophanes is that he is funny and he's *still* funny. The jokes still work, somehow. They may be dirty jokes, some of them, but they are jokes, whereas some of the current dirty literature isn't even funny.

VONNEGUT: No. Not comical in the least . . . the corners of your mouth pulled down as you're reading it. There are not carefully rigged gags in there as there are in Aristophanes.

SCHOLES: Aristophanes reminds me of this thing that I just saw this afternoon . . . the long, really very long, essay on your work in *The New Republic* in which the essayist, after praising you for any number of things, complains a little bit at the end that you aren't bitter enough . . . not enough of a satirist. I wonder how you feel about that yourself. Are you trying to write satire and failing?

VONNEGUT: Well, he says I am, and he would be a better judge of that than I would. An outsider would be, you know, as my wife is a better judge of what I am doing than I am, and this man in the, what, Bryan, in *The New Republic,* feels I should be more savage and he offers as an example the fact that I was a prisoner of war and saw the bombing of Dresden, which was a man-made disaster of the very first order in European history. It was the largest massacre in European history, and he feels I should be enraged by this and that the rage should show. You mentioned Aristophanes. He's surely not an angry satirist.

SCHOLES: No, he isn't, and this is what one likes about him, I think. When you think of the really angry satirists, though, you think of Swift, I suppose, and one of the prices Swift pays for his anger is his insanity, I guess.

VONNEGUT: Yes.

SCHOLES: And that in a way detracts from the quality of the work, I think. It provides for the bite, but it also makes you back off a little bit from Swift and say somehow it isn't that bad.

VONNEGUT: Yes.

SCHOLES: You know, it's plenty bad, but it isn't *that* bad.

VONNEGUT: Yes, well, I find Ambrose Bierce is another example of a man who spills over into actual hatred for mankind.

SCHOLES: I think Twain does, too, at the end.

VONNEGUT: As an old man, yes. Yes, he does. And I find Norman Mailer frightening that way, too. Of course, he never means to be comical, or I suppose he does mean to be comical but ever so often this really almost Gestapo hatred for mankind shows through.

SCHOLES: Right.

VONNEGUT: The murderousness, in which case the reader is right to draw back.

SCHOLES: Well, I'm sure that the reviewer in *The New Republic* didn't really want to prefer Twain's late works to the early works that most of us common and uncommon readers seem to admire.

VONNEGUT: Well, of the very late works is, what, *Captain Sormfield's Visit to Heaven* and . . .

SCHOLES: Right, and *Pudd'nhead Wilson* I guess is fairly late.

VONNEGUT: Yeah, well it gets . . . actually he's closer to the frontier toward the end, it seems to me. It's a very primitive sort of humor in the frontier, when he's an old man than he was as a young man.

SCHOLES: I guess when he was out West he looked toward Hartford, and when he got to Hartford he turned around and looked back.

VONNEGUT: Yes. Has someone said that?

SCHOLES: I don't know. Now they have.

VONNEGUT: Yeah. Well, I remember one of these, he started this fragmentary book on etiquette and I guess it was . . . one of the articles was how to behave at a funeral; and the very last line is "Do not bring your dog."

SCHOLES: Ha ha ha ha . . .

VONNEGUT: Ha ha ha ha . . .

SCHOLES: Well, that's charming, it's not angry at all.

VONNEGUT: No.

SCHOLES: No.

VONNEGUT: Well, it's mordant, I think. Isn't "mordant" the right word?

SCHOLES: Yeah. Black humor I suppose is what we . . .

VONNEGUT: Yeah. That's plenty black.

SCHOLES: . . . come around to. But also humorous. It seems to me that if this term "black humor" has any validity, it must be pointing at something a little different from . . . satire.

VONNEGUT: Well, something that's bothered me about the current black humor, some of it, is that the author seems to regard it as shameful that human beings excrete and have sex lives, you know . . .

SCHOLES: Uh-huh.

VONNEGUT: . . . is mock people for their bodily functions.

SCHOLES: I think Swift had a strong streak of that in him, too.

VONNEGUT: Yes . . . But that's a sad place to begin. That we can do nothing about.

SCHOLES: Right. Right. Except brood, I suppose. And Swift did his share of brooding. There are writers who seem to find it very amusing that human beings have all the plumbing equipment they have, but don't seem disturbed by it. I should think Rabelais would be of that kind, and maybe Aristophanes himself would find it amusing that we have at the same time high ideals and all this plumbing.

VONNEGUT: Yes, and most of our money spent on getting rid of unsightly waste.

SCHOLES: Right, right, yes.

VONNEGUT: And body odors. No, it would be very nice to have Aristophanes or Rabelais around—two humane men with some sort of Utopia in mind. Each of them had a Utopia.

SCHOLES: Right.

VONNEGUT: Swift, of course, wanted the horses to take over.

SCHOLES: Ha ha ha . . .

VONNEGUT: And Clarence Day wanted the cats to take over.

SCHOLES: I didn't realize that.

VONNEGUT: Yes. Clarence Day wrote a thing called "This Simian World."

SCHOLES: I heard the title.

VONNEGUT: Yeah.

SCHOLES: I know him, of course, as the *Life with Father* . . .

VONNEGUT: Yeah. Well Clarence Day, incidentally, is, I think Thurber talks about him—Thurber talks about the tragic roots of humor, and Thurber I think somewhere says that a comedian is from a sad home and that a humorist is from a tragic home, and Clarence Day's father evidently was a truly savage man who scared little Clarence to death, and out of this came this very funny play about a childhood that was not in the least funny.

SCHOLES: So that the play was not a reflection—not a direct reflection—of the home life but a kind of defense against . . .

VONNEGUT: Yes.

SCHOLES: . . . the actual home, I suppose. Gosh. Let me ask you another question. We said a while back that you got interested in science because of your early training you had in it. What about science fiction as a way of doing literature, as opposed to black humor? You've been called both things, I suppose—a science-fiction writer and a black humorist. Are you a science-fiction writer?

VONNEGUT: Well, I wrote a thing in *The New York Times* last year about this, objecting finally because I thought it was costing me a lot of money in reputation . . .

SCHOLES: Uh-huh.

VONNEGUT: . . . because most people regard science-fiction writers as interchangeable with comic-book writers, as they frequently are.

SCHOLES: They frequently are, but there have been some pretty astonishing things . . .

VONNEGUT: Oh, extraordinary, extraordinary work, yes, and all writers are going to have to learn more about science, because it's such an interesting part of their environment. It's something that worries me about some of our students in the workshop, as they know nothing about machinery, about the scientific method, and so forth, and to reflect our times accurately, to respond to them— to their times reasonably—they have to understand that part of their environment.

SCHOLES: You begin to sound like C. P. Snow on the two cultures.

VONNEGUT: Yes, well . . .

SCHOLES: Do you agree with him?

VONNEGUT: Well, C. P. Snow and I are both very smug on the subject of two cultures, because we both have two cultures, you see.

SCHOLES: You know some science and you write some literature.

VONNEGUT: Yes. Yes.

SCHOLES: Yeah, well, H. G. Wells I guess was the granddaddy of you and C. P. Snow in a way. I assume Snow admired Wells and read him fairly early in the game.

VONNEGUT: Well, I'm sure every Englishman did, and Wells is much admired in England still, I believe. Very good stories that Wells wrote. And he started out as a chemist, I believe, very briefly, and gave it up and . . . as did H. L. Mencken, incidentally. He started out as a chemist.

SCHOLES: Now, that's one I didn't know.

VONNEGUT: Yes.

SCHOLES: He really went to the other extreme, didn't he?

VONNEGUT: Yes.

SCHOLES: Yeah, I read a little bit of Wells recently, some old short stories, things that came out in the *Yellow Book*, of all places.

VONNEGUT: Oh.

SCHOLES: You think of the *Yellow Book* as full of *esprit* and Aubrey Beardsley, but Wells appeared in it also with a little science story about some science students, and he had a real gift for writing, even on a casual piece like that, I think.

VONNEGUT: Yes. Well, he wasn't a bad prophet, either, and it's helpful to have prophets. It would be helpful to have politicans who would listen to them.

SCHOLES: Ha ha ha . . .

VONNEGUT: Ha ha ha . . .

SCHOLES: Well then, you wouldn't write *Cat's Cradle,* would you, if the prophets and the politicians listened to one another?

VONNEGUT: No. I'm giving a seminar. I'm not quite sure what it is, as every week we discuss something new, and one subject I want to discuss is what books do politicians read, so that all these would-be writers can find out that nobody of any importance is ever going to pay any attention to them.

SCHOLES: It would be a good thing, 'cause it seems to me a lot of writers—a lot of American writers right now— are trying in one way or another to get closer to politics than maybe a writer can or should get to it. I think Mailer has tried this . . . Mark Harris seems to be fluttering around . . .

VONNEGUT: Yes.

SCHOLES: . . . politics considerably, also, with that . . . did you read that Nixon book of his?

VONNEGUT: No.

SCHOLES: *Mark the Glove Boy* was the name of it, and most of it was a fantasy about assassinating Richard Nixon. Curious thing for a writer to be doing. Which reminds me that a number of these people who get called black humorists seem mainly to be fantasists, to be imagining things that they either fear or like, and just writing down what they imagine. Terry Southern seems to me as a kind of pure wish-fulfillment writer very often, or fear-fulfillment writer.

VONNEGUT: Yes, I think maybe wish-fulfillment. On *Candy*, of course, he was paid to do it as pornography.

SCHOLES: I always think of *The Magic Christian*. Have you read that?

VONNEGUT: Yeah. No. I read part of *The Magic Christian* that appeared in *Esquire*, I think.

SCHOLES: This is one sequence after another of a very rich man embarrassing and humiliating people—people usually who deserve it for one reason or another.

VONNEGUT: Yeah.

SCHOLES: This isn't satire either, and it isn't exactly the kind of comic thing that you do. It is sort of getting even in writing.

VONNEGUT: Yes, well, in this same issue of *The New Republic* here there's a review of Friedman's work by Kauffmann.

SCHOLES: Bruce Jay Friedman?

VONNEGUT: Yeah, Bruce Friedman. And, what, Stanley Kauffmann, huh?

SCHOLES: Right.

VONNEGUT: And in there he says exactly what you said—

Kauffmann does. That Friedman is using his creations as objects to keep his fear at bay and the reader's fear at bay.

SCHOLES: Does he write about, what, *Mother Night* and *Stern*, or are there new . . .

VONNEGUT: He writes . . . no . . . he writes . . .

SCHOLES: I mean . . . *Mother Night* . . . I mean . . .

VONNEGUT: No . . . Friedman . . . Friedman just brought out a collection of ten short stories, one of which is that "brazzaville teen-ager." Did you happen to see that in there?

SCHOLES: No.

VONNEGUT: Well, it's awfully hard to explain, but Friedman incidentally makes you laugh, which most of the black humorists do not.

SCHOLES: He certainly does—*A Mother's Kisses*—frightening as it is in its way is a very funny book, and though that mother seems a little bit too grand to be true, there's also a touch of many mothers in her, I think. I think there's a fair amount of laughter in a lot of writers that often get treated as if they were trying to be satirists, as if they were trying to reform the world when really they're not trying to do that at all but trying to make some sort of comic structure out of things which can be pretty bad.

VONNEGUT: Yes. Well, that's a rewarding thing to do—to make someone laugh—and I have tried to do it and felt that it was sort of an imperative that I . . . anything I wrote had to make someone laugh or it was a failure, and I think part of this comes from the fact that I was the youngest kid in my family by far.

SCHOLES: Aha!

VONNEGUT: And I think this is true of stand-up comedians

customarily, that they are the youngest child or among the youngest in a huge family, and it is a most satisfactory way to get attention. You don't get punished for it.

SCHOLES: You get turned into a fool or a clown.

VONNEGUT: Yes.

SCHOLES: Or something.

VONNEGUT: And you become better at it.

SCHOLES: Naturally.

VONNEGUT: And it's a thing that can be done very well.

SCHOLES: And I suppose fools are partly born and partly made.

VONNEGUT: Yes.

SCHOLES: And you can practice it. It seems to me to be a very good and real thing—laughter—and I haven't got much faith myself in satire ever reforming anybody or making them better or changing the world. Laughter doesn't pretend to do that. It just does a little immediate good, I suppose.

VONNEGUT: Well, I've worried some about, you know, why write books . . . why are we teaching people to write books when presidents and senators do not read them, and generals do not read them.

SCHOLES: Uh-huh.

VONNEGUT: And it's been the university experience that taught me that there is a very good reason, that you catch people before they become generals and presidents and so forth and you poison their minds with . . . humanity, and however you want to poison their minds, it's presumably to encourage them to make a better world.

SCHOLES: I'm delighted that you used that expression "poison their minds," because I spent part of the summer reading and rereading some of your books and writing an essay of my own about them, and as I was reading them and thinking about them and working on this essay, it came to me that one of the real services that your kind of writing does is very much like what A. E. Housman, who's a sort of black humorist in poetry, talks about in a poem of his called "Terence, This Is Stupid Stuff," and he cites the ancient king Mithridates who trained himself by taking poison in small doses to resist the stuff.

VONNEGUT: Uh-huh.

SCHOLES: And it really came at him. It seems to me that black humor, if it is anything, is small manageable doses of poison neatly packaged and the comedy making it palatable that helps us to get through the terrible things in the world.

VONNEGUT: Well, it would be nice if it worked. There was a friendly review of two of my books that was in *Harper's* last spring. It was by a guy named Richard Schickel who was a stranger, word of honor, at the time he wrote it, and I have since gotten to know him.

SCHOLES: Uh-huh.

VONNEGUT: But one of the things he said was that I'd found in laughter an analgesic for the temporary relief of existential pain.

SCHOLES: Ah.

VONNEGUT: And this may not be true. I wish it were. It's a very nice sentence.

SCHOLES: Well, I haven't seen Schickel's thing, but I was struck the same way by your things. In fact, I got to thinking about this existential business, and Camus and the *Myth of Sisyphus* and all of these things, and it seemed to me that the French go on and on so about bearing things but they never give you much in their works to make things more bearable.

VONNEGUT: No. No. I was thinking about the Depression. This was a great time for comedians . . .

SCHOLES: Uh-huh.

VONNEGUT: . . . the radio comedians. And a very bad time in the history of the country, far more unbearable than the First or Second World Wars, I think.

SCHOLES: Back in the home front, I should imagine.

VONNEGUT: Yes. The Depression did break people's spirits. And the comedians who—there was one each day, at least, as Fred Allen, Jack Benny, and so forth, you got your little dose of humor every day, and the people did cluster around radios to pick up an amount of encouragement, an amount of relief.

SCHOLES: Well, I was born in 1929 myself, but I can remember waiting for Sunday nights when you used to get Benny *and* Allen both.

VONNEGUT: Yes. Yes. And then finally Henry Morgan.

SCHOLES: Right.

VONNEGUT: It was Benny, Allen, and then Henry Morgan.

SCHOLES: It was quite an evening.

VONNEGUT: Yeah.

SCHOLES: It made you get through the week, all right.

VONNEGUT: Well, I got a letter from Morgan. I don't know him, but we did have a brief interchange of letters, and I told him I remembered a joke of his from, it must have been about 1936, which was that Morgan says, "You know that cat that inherited five million dollars last year? Well, he died. Left his money to another cat."

SCHOLES: Ha ha ha . . .

VONNEGUT: Ha ha ha . . . And that helped.

SCHOLES: Yeah.

VONNEGUT: Yeah. It got everybody through three more days of Depression.

SCHOLES: Yeah. It's so wonderful; it's so wonderful.

VONNEGUT: Yes.

SCHOLES: It takes what really happens—people leaving their money to cats—and pushes it . . .

VONNEGUT: Yeah. If somehow television isn't able to—well, they haven't done much funny stuff, I guess. Back in the days of radio, gags were treasured, as they were remembered and told the next day and for the next few days.

SCHOLES: I can remember things from Fibber McGee and Molly . . .

VONNEGUT: Yeah.

SCHOLES: . . . that still stay with me. They must be about that same vintage, also.

VONNEGUT: Yeah.

SCHOLES: I remember a great episode of Fibber McGee and Molly's, and it's sort of a real Depression episode. Fibber gets the idea that he's going to make money by cashing in on this soup company that has a deal where if you don't like their soup you get double your money back.

VONNEGUT: Uh-huh.

SCHOLES: And he buys an enormous number of boxes of cans of this soup and finally, being an honest man, he decides that he will taste it before he cashes in on all of the cans. He doesn't heat it or anything—he's not that honest—but he does decide he'll open a can and taste it, and I remember very well the moment. Molly was around watching him, and there was a bit of hush, and he tastes it and he says, "Why, it's delicious."

VONNEGUT: Yeah.

SCHOLES: And there he was.

VONNEGUT: Yeah. Of course, another way to play the Depression or any tragedy is to play it straight, for its beauty, is to find some beauty in the tragedy of it, and

Verlin Cassill has certainly done that in many of his short stories.

SCHOLES: A story like "The Father."

VONNEGUT: Yes. He's not going to laugh at it; he's going to look at it the way it really was, and it comes out a perfectly gorgeous thing in the hands of the right man. It did in Verlin's case.

SCHOLES: Right.

VONNEGUT: Most humorists don't dare do it.

SCHOLES: Now, in both cases, though, it's sort of finding the pattern, finding a shape and some sort of meaning in the business instead of just seeing it as aimless, I guess, isn't it?

VONNEGUT: Yes. Finishing one of Verlin's stories about the Depression is . . . you get your catharsis through a groan. I think you really have to groan, as when I read "The Father," I groaned, and it was the same relief as a laugh, I'm sure. The results are . . . I don't think the body cares which you do, really, but you must do one or the other.

SCHOLES: The muscles probably have the final answer in these things.

VONNEGUT: Yeah.

SCHOLES: Well, there's some news that we got this fall about your work that I think other people will be interested in. I remember hearing from you late in the summer that your novel *Cat's Cradle* is going to be made into a musical comedy, which startled me a bit. Did it startle you, or had you always expected this to happen?

VONNEGUT: No. I never expected anything good to happen. I had never expected the university to hire me. I thought I was going to starve to death. I didn't think *Cat's Cradle* could be made into a musical, because a musical is built around usually a very short period of time and one or two simple ideas.

SCHOLES: Uh-huh.

VONNEGUT: And *Cat's Cradle* ranges over many years and involves part of the industrial history of the United States, and it requires a certain amount of scientific sophistication to appreciate. There just seems to be too much information to process. And so when Hillard Elkins, who produced *Golden Boy* with Sammy Davis, Jr., asked me to turn it into a musical—he optioned the thing so I dutifully went on without consulting with him, condensed the thing, just cut it way down, and he came up to my home on Cape Cod and said, "No, no, no. Just do it straight. Put everything in it you want to put in it and don't worry about it. Let me worry about it."

SCHOLES: Um. You were trying to get the dramatic unities in the . . .

VONNEGUT: I was trying to save him money. I wanted this show to get on.

SCHOLES: Ha ha ha . . .

VONNEGUT: Because I get paid as people come through the turnstile, you see, it's pretty much speculation until the curtain actually goes up. But he had been thinking about it a great deal, and in order to process a heck of a lot of information in a hurry that provides quick windows into the past, we're going to use film along with actors and dancers, and so forth.

SCHOLES: Has this been tried much, do you know, on the stage?

VONNEGUT: Uh . . . Well, there've been all sorts of trick things done with projecting images on a scrim, you know, as rooftops, and there was one very fancy production of *Major Barbara* which had stunning visual effects as, you know, gardens that would go off into the distance, many miles, apparently. And there was one technique that they've experimented with which I think involves a beaded curtain and motion-picture cameras, where an actor can go up to the top of a real fire escape and disappear behind the beaded curtains as his image appears on the beaded curtains, projected, and . . .

SCHOLES: Wow!

VONNEGUT: . . . and he jumps off the fire escape . . .

SCHOLES: Wow!

VONNEGUT: . . . and crashes on the ground—that sort of thing, you know. But this is disturbing to audiences, I think. They think too much about technique, and I think we're going to probably use just lantern slides as people are used to lantern slides, you know, and WHAM we'll shoot a picture of a scene thirty years ago and leave it up there about two seconds and then get back to the actors.

SCHOLES: There'll be something going on at the stage . . .

VONNEGUT: Yeah.

SCHOLES: . . . all the time. Well, this sounds a little bit like happening technique . . .

VONNEGUT: Yes. Sure.

SCHOLES: . . . where you have different things . . .

VONNEGUT: Yes. It's very McLuhan. It's very in, and I'm sure it'll be terribly expensive.

SCHOLES: Yeah.

VONNEGUT: Elkins came up to see me on the Cape, and I have a son who sky-dives, he's sixteen years old.

SCHOLES: Parachutes, you mean?

VONNEGUT: Yes.

SCHOLES: Wow!

VONNEGUT:. . . and he's made five jumps. And so Elkins looks like a very tough guy. I asked Elkins, "Do you skydive, Hilly?" and he said, "No, I bring musicals to New York City for $750,000."

SCHOLES: Ha ha ha . . . Yeah. Sky-diving sounds easy by comparison. You know, I read somewhere that Tennessee Williams thought of having a movie sequence of *The Glass Menagerie*. It's in the first . . .

VONNEGUT: Oh, is it in the script? I didn't know about the movie part. I know that he projected lines on the wall. Where someone would say a particularly poignant line a lantern slide would WHAM shoot that line up on the wall, and it would hang there through the next few lines.

SCHOLES: That's not one that I heard. I heard that he had a sort of flashback movie thing planned for the look back into the past . . .

VONNEGUT: Yeah.

SCHOLES: . . . that you get in that play. That business of hanging lines up there reminds me of a thing you were doing in a manuscript you read from here last year where you were repeating the last words of paragraphs.

VONNEGUT: Yes.

SCHOLES: Are you still playing around with that?

VONNEGUT: Well, I'm still playing around with it. I got a little embarrassed with it, though—it's such a mannered thing—and if you do it for a whole book you get embarrassed.

SCHOLES: Yeah.

VONNEGUT: It's a terribly literary thing to do.

SCHOLES: But maybe a chapter or two you could get away with it on. I was thinking you must be interested in these technical effects, printing effects and other things. I notice *Mr. Rosewater* has a very unusual printing format in the margins.

VONNEGUT: Yes. Well, that was a typographer's plaything.

I explained to him that I wanted to be *avant garde* and that he should do something on the order of Bauhaus, you know.

SCHOLES: Uh-huh.

VONNEGUT: Which is, what, 1922.

SCHOLES: Uh-huh.

VONNEGUT: Is that *avant garde?*

SCHOLES: Yeah.

VONNEGUT: And, of course, typographers don't get to play much, and so he really had himself a time. And I've heard poets complain about it because they try to read it as poetry. What it is is playing with the margins.

SCHOLES: Right. And it's not your playing but the typographer's.

VONNEGUT: It's his, yes. He set that rhythm.

SCHOLES: Yeah. The book of yours that seems a little bit different from all the others, and I think perhaps my favorite of them all, is *Mother Night*. It seems a little darker than the others, a little less comic, but by no means a satire. Do you feel that it stands out among your other works as being different from them, or is that . . .

VONNEGUT: Yes, well, I think it does. It's more personally disturbing to me. It had meanings for me. Oh, because of the war and because of my German background, and that sort of thing.

SCHOLES: Uh-huh.

VONNEGUT: So, sure, I did tend to get somewhat involved with that. At that time I needed money, and this came out as a paperback. As a Gold Medal paperback. In those days if you had published something you could go to a paperback house and give them one chapter and an outline and they would give you money which would pay your grocery bill, anyway.

SCHOLES: Yeah.

VONNEGUT: That was always the end of it, but there were times when you had to take it or leave it. And in the midst of writing that I went to London and we joined a private theater group and saw one play, which was *The Caretaker*.

SCHOLES: Uh-huh.

VONNEGUT: It was the first Pinter play, or the first one to come to this country, and the first to make any appreciable impression on England, and, Lord, what a thing that was to see! Like no other play! And, gee, I didn't want to write a book anymore, you know, I wanted to be a playwright. I wanted to be Pinter. And so I was rather gloomy as I finished up the book.

SCHOLES: Is that how the hero got to be a playwright in the book?

VONNEGUT: No. He was a playwright before I went to London.

SCHOLES: Not the sort of playwright that Pinter was.

VONNEGUT: No. Gosh, I didn't know there could be a playwright like Pinter. That was so different.

SCHOLES: A lot of these new English playwrights are interesting. Arnold Wesker is a pretty interesting playwright, too . . .

VONNEGUT: Yes. Yes. When we were in London we got an introduction to the cultural attaché at the American embassy, who gave a party and invited C. P. Snow and his wife and Wesker.

SCHOLES: Wow!

VONNEGUT: And I was the American cultural counterbalance there, you see.

SCHOLES: Ha ha ha . . .

VONNEGUT: At the time I think I'd published one book, but Sir Charles was very nice. And Wesker was an elf

. . . came late and wore a sort of suede jerkin. He wore, you know, what the seven dwarfs in *Snow White* wore.

SCHOLES: I'll be darned.

VONNEGUT: Yeah.

SCHOLES: And I suppose he's been very Left since the beginning, a practicing communist or the next thing . . .

VONNEGUT: I suppose. He was complaining then about his fame, because no money came with it, and he kept saying, "When's the money going to come?"

SCHOLES: That doesn't sound like a communistic sort of thing . . .

VONNEGUT: Well, I think it does. In a capitalist society I think a communist wants everything he can get.

SCHOLES: That seems fair enough, really.

VONNEGUT: Interesting way of undermining a society, I think, is to take some of their money away.

SCHOLES: I was interested, as I think the man who wrote this piece in *The New Republic* was, in the little prefatory note that you added to the new hardbound version of *Mother Night* about your sitting through the bombing of Dresden as a prisoner of war. I would agree with this man that that is a pretty powerful piece of writing. Do you mean to do more with your own experiences in a literary way, or are you saving them . . .

VONNEGUT: Yes, I'm working on it now. It's what I've been working on for a long time, and it's extremely hard to think about. You know, you have these enormous concentration camps full of corpses, and then you have a city full of corpses, and, you know, is the city full of corpses right or wrong?

SCHOLES: Yeah. And you get into the mathematics of burying people.

VONNEGUT: Yes. I suppose that's what you have to do.

SCHOLES: Finally . . . there's so many different ways to do it—napalm, incendiary bombing, gas chambers—how do you tell the good guys from the bad guys in a situation like this?

VONNEGUT: Well, I think the only thing I have been able to think of doing as a result of seeing the destruction of that city there and knowing at the same time about the great crimes of Germany is to become the impossible thing, which is a pacifist, and I figure I'm under an obligation, having seen all this, you know, that that's the only possible conclusion I can come to, is that we must not fight under any conditions. And let someone else hit the happy middle ground, you know . . .

SCHOLES: It seems to me that the more one looks into these wars, the less they ever seem to prove or . . .

VONNEGUT: Ah, that World War II was a good one, though. That was . . .

SCHOLES: Well, that's the worst thing Hitler did, you know, was to make war creditable again.

VONNEGUT: Yes.

SCHOLES: To be a real bad guy.

VONNEGUT: Yes, and we came out as the authentic good guys, and then on into the reconstruction of Europe, too. And it's made us very smug and prone to make ghastly mistakes because we have been virtuous.

SCHOLES: Right, a little virtue is a dangerous thing, I guess.

VONNEGUT: Yes, I guess so.

SCHOLES: Well, I guess we're about out of time. Thank you very much for coming and talking, Kurt.

VONNEGUT: Well, thank you, Bob.

THE
LITERARY
ART

Chapter 9

TWO OR THREE THINGS I KNOW ABOUT KURT VONNEGUT'S IMAGINATION

TIM HILDEBRAND

1. *On the Edge with Kurt Vonnegut.* In *Player Piano,* the obvious "hero" is Ed Finnerty, a chronically malcontent boozer. When someone suggests he see a shrink, Ed lays it on the line:

> He'd pull me back into the center, and I want to stay as close to the edge as I can without going over. Out on the edge you see all kinds of things you can't see from the center . . . Big, undreamed-of things—the people on the edge see them first.

121

2. *Where Does Kurt Vonnegut Get His Ideas?* "If we have to start over again with another Adam and Eve, I want them to be Americans and I want them on this continent and not in Europe."—U.S. SENATOR RICHARD RUSSELL (Georgia)

3. *The Rational Kurt Vonnegut.* In his first novel, *Player Piano* (1952), Vonnegut is perfectly rational.

4. "Don't truth me and I won't truth you." (*The Sirens of Titan*)

5. Boaz, in *The Sirens of Titan,* Vonnegut's second book (1959): "I found me a place where I can do good without doing any harm, and I can *see* I'm doing good." He's speaking from the Caves of Mercury.

6. *Cosmic Meaninglessness of Existence Explained.* In *The Sirens of Titan* Vonnegut attempts to transcend meaninglessness by showing that it exists on a cosmic scale. Not only man is meaningless, but so is everything else in the universe. This seems to wipe out both pride and self-pity at the same time, not to mention God and the Devil. The messiah figure in *Player Piano* is a dropped-out technocrat who is totally manipulated throughout the book.

7. *Vonnegut Sees the Light at the End of the Tunnel.* In *Sirens of Titan* Vonnegut's religious figure is Winston Niles Rumfoord, founder of the Church of the Utterly Indifferent God. If God wanted us to be perfect, He'd have made us that way.

8. *Fatally Free.* "Everything that ever was always will be, and everything that ever will be always was."—WINSTON NILES RUMFOORD. There's a certain joy in that statement.

9. *Kurt Vonnegut's Fantasy. Mother Night,* Vonnegut's third novel (1961), is the first book of his to feature the short chapter form. There are 174 pages and 45 chapters.

Vonnegut once stated on educational TV that he wants his books to be read by those in power. Presidents, dictators, executives, etc., hopefully will find time in their busy schedules to read a few short chapters now and then.

10. In *Mother Night* Vonnegut also begins using his fatalistic cries: "So be it" and "Hi Ho."

11. Kurt Vonnegut Served in World War II. "My few furnishings were war surplus, like myself." (*Mother Night*)

12. Is This What Kurt Vonnegut Thinks? ". . . future civilizations—better civilizations than this one—are going to judge all men by the extent to which they've been artists. You and I . . . will be judged by the quality of our creations. Nothing else about us will matter."—"KRAFT" (the Russian spy in *Mother Night*)

13. In *Mother Night* Vonnegut turns for the first time to the past. The characters are all (somehow) survivors of World War II. The war has been over for sixteen years before Vonnegut writes about it. He probably did a lot of thinking.

14. Kurt Vonnegut Survived World War II. "And one thing she did to me was to make me deaf to all success stories. The people she saw as succeeding in a brave new world were, after all, being rewarded as specialists in slavery, destruction, and death. I don't consider people who work in those fields successful." (*Mother Night*)

15. Kurt Vonnegut's Place in History. A poem by Howard W. Campbell, Jr. From *Mother Night:*

> I saw a huge steam roller,
> It blotted out the sun.
> The people all lay down, lay down;
> They did not try to run.

My love and I, we looked amazed
Upon the gory mystery.
"Lie down, lie down!" the people cried,
"The great machine is history!"
My love and I, we ran away,
The engine did not find us.
We ran up to a mountain top,
Left history far behind us.
Perhaps we should have stayed and died,
But somehow we don't think so.
We went to see where history'd been,
And my, the dead did stink so.

16. *What Are World Wars For?*
"Any time anything of real dignity appears in this country, it's torn to shreds and thrown to the mob."

"You hate America, don't you?" she said.

"That would be as silly as loving it," I said. "It's impossible for me to get emotional about it, because real estate doesn't interest me. It's no doubt a great flaw in my personality, but I can't think in terms of boundaries. Those imaginary lines are as unreal to me as elves and pixies. I can't believe that they mark the end or the beginning of anything of real concern to a human soul. Virtues and vices, pleasures and pains cross boundaries at will."

"You've changed so," she said.

"People should be changed by world wars," I said, "else what are world wars for?" (*Mother Night*)

17. *A Plain Man Who Writes Simple Books.* "I admire things with a beginning, a middle, and end—and, whenever possible, a moral, too." (*Mother Night*)

18. *Vonnegut's Theory of Human Totalitarianism.*

I have never seen a more sublime demonstration of the totalitarian mind, a mind which might be likened unto a system of gears whose teeth have been filed off at random. Such a snaggle-toothed thought machine, driven by a standard or even by a substantial libido, whirls with the jerky, noisy, gaudy pointlessness of a cuckoo clock in Hell.

The boss G-man concluded wrongly that there were no teeth on the gears in the mind of Jones. "You're completely crazy," he said.

Jones wasn't completely crazy. The dismaying thing about the classic totalitarian mind is that any given gear, though mutilated, will have at its circumference unbroken sequences of teeth that are immaculately maintained, that are exquisitely machined.

Hence the cuckoo clock in Hell—keeping perfect time for eight minutes and twenty-three seconds, jumping ahead fourteen minutes . . . keeping perfect time for two hours and one second, then jumping ahead a year.

The missing teeth, of course, are simple, obvious truths, truths available and comprehensible even to ten-year-olds, in most cases.

The willful filing off of gear teeth, the willful doing without certain obvious pieces of information—

That was how a household as contradictory as one composed of Jones, Father Keeley, Vice-Bundesfuehrer Krapptauer, and the Black Fuehrer could exist in relative harmony—

That was how my father-in-law could contain in one mind an indifference toward slave women and love for a blue vase—

That was how Rudolph Hoess, Commandant of Auschwitz, could alternate over the loudspeakers of Auschwitz great music and calls for corpse-carriers—

That was how Nazi Germany could sense no important differences between civilization and hydrophobia—

That is the closest I can come to explaining the legions, the nations of lunatics I've seen in my lifetime. (*Mother Night*)

19. *Better Living Through Chemistry.* Chapter 41 of *Mother Night* is a conversation between Howard W. Campbell, Jr., and a policeman. The cop says:

> "The things I see—the things people say to me. Sometimes I get very discouraged."
> "Everybody does that from time to time," I said.
> "I guess it's partly chemistry," he said. . . .
> "Getting down in the dumps," he said. "Isn't that what they're finding out—that a lot of that's chemicals?"
> "I don't know," I said.
> "They can give a man certain chemicals, and he goes crazy," he said. "That's one of the things they're working with. Maybe it's all chemicals. . . .
> "Maybe it's different chemicals that different countries eat that makes people act in different ways at different times," he said.

And a few lines later the cop speculates:

> "Maybe, when they find out more about chemicals," he said, "there won't have to be policemen or wars or crazy houses or divorces or drunks or juvenile delinquents or women gone bad or anything anymore."

20. *Busy or Funny?* In Vonnegut's next book, *Cat's Cradle* (1963), he introduces Bokonon, who has a way with words: " 'Busy, busy, busy' is what we Bokononists whisper whenever we think of how complicated and unpredictable the machinery of life really is. But all I could say as a Christian then was, 'Life sure is funny sometimes.' "

21. *Don't Think Twice, It's All Right.* There are no heroes in Vonnegut's books. And no real villains, either. The irony in Vonnegut's characters often lies in the fact that their crimes are committed unconsciously. But in

Vonnegut's world, crime serves a useful purpose. "It was the belief of Bokonon that good societies could be built only by pitting good against evil, and by keeping the tension between the two high at all times." Vonnegut creates systems ("beliefs") that cannot fail because they are paradoxical and cannot *succeed* either. Vonnegut does not despair because evil exists; instead he concerns himself with the *tension* between good and evil.

22. "Now you folks come on and be happy, come on and be happy." That's a quote from a speech delivered by Lyndon Baines Johnson, in St. Louis, October 21, 1964. Bokonon's real name: Lionel Boyd Johnson.

23. *On the Role of The Righter.*

"I'm thinking of calling a general strike of all writers until mankind finally comes to its senses. Would you support it?"

"Do writers have a right to strike? That would be like the police or the firemen walking out."

"Or the college professors."

"Or the college professors," I agreed. I shook my head. "No, I don't think my conscience would let me support a strike like that. When a man becomes a writer, I think he takes on a sacred obligation to produce beauty and enlightenment and comfort at top speed."

"I just can't help thinking what a real shaking up it would give people if, all of a sudden, there were no new books, new plays, new histories, new poems . . ."

"And how proud would you be when people started dying like flies?" I demanded.

"They'd die more like mad dogs, I think—snarling and snapping at each other and biting their own tails."

I turned to Castle the elder. "Sire, how does a man die when he's deprived of literature?"

"In one of two ways," he said, "putrescence of the heart or atrophy of the nervous system."

"Neither one very pleasant, I expect," I suggested.

"No," said Castle the elder. "For the love of God, *both* of you, *please* keep writing!" (*Cat's Cradle*)

24. *Kurt Vonnegut's Fiction and Science Fiction. God Bless You, Mr. Rosewater* is Vonnegut's fifth novel (1965). Critics have often labeled him a science-fiction writer, but most science-fiction critics have felt uneasy about him. Vonnegut is more mainstream, they say. The difference between Vonnegut and science-fiction writers is that Vonnegut is essentially a preacher, a moralist, a man with a message. Most science-fiction writers concentrate on ideas, not people. Vonnegut's people orientation has led him to develop a supersense of irony that sets his consciousness apart from that of the typical science-fiction writer. But both Vonnegut and science-fiction writers are interested in how technology changes the world. From the book, here is Eliot Rosewater's speech to a group of science-fiction authors at a convention:

"I love all you sons of bitches," Eliot said in Milford. "You're all I read anymore. You're the only ones who'll talk about the *really* terrific changes going on, the only ones crazy enough to know that life is a space voyage, and not a short one, either, but one that'll last for billions of years. You're the only ones with guts enough to *really* care about the future, who *really* notice what machines do to us, what wars do to us, what cities do to us, what big, simple ideas do to us, what tremendous misunderstandings, mistakes, accidents and catastrophes do to us. You're the only ones zany enough to agonize over time and distances without limit, over mysteries that will never die, over the fact that we are right now determining whether the space voyage for the next billion years or so is going to be Heaven or Hell."

25. Kurt Vonnegut's Advice to the Newborn. In *God Bless You, Mr. Rosewater,* Eliot Rosewater tells us what he will say to Mary Moody's newborn twins: "Hello, babies. Welcome to Earth. It's hot in the summer and cold in the winter. It's round and wet and crowded. At the outside, babies, you've got about a hundred years here. There's only one rule that I know of, babies—'God damn it, you've got to be kind.'"

26. The Gospel According to Vonnegut. Vonnegut, raised an atheist, has always understood the function of religion in our society. Religion helps people accept the world as it is. And the world is the way it is because God, Government, and the Greedy want it that way. Where does that leave everyone else? Going to church, going to work, voting, mowing the lawn, washing the dishes, and hoping for heaven. Here's the way Vonnegut says it:

> "I do solemnly swear that I will respect the sacred private property of others, and that I will be content with whatever station in life God Almighty may assign me to. I will be grateful to those who employ me, and will never complain about wages and hours, but will ask myself instead, 'What more can I do for my employer, my republic, and my God?' I understand that I have not been placed on Earth to be happy. I am here to be tested. If I am to pass the test, I must be always unselfish, always sober, always truthful, always chaste in mind, body, and deed, and always respectful to those whom God has, in His wisdom, placed above me. If I pass the test, I will go to joy everlasting in Heaven when I die. If I fail, I shall roast in hell while the Devil laughs and Jesus weeps." (*God Bless You, Mr. Rosewater*)

27. Who Really Runs This Crazy Country?

"What gets me most about these people, Daddy, isn't how ignorant they are, or how much they drink. It's the way they have of thinking that everything nice in the world is a gift to the poor people from them or their ancestors. The first afternoon I was here, Mrs. Buntline made me come out on the back porch and look at the sunset. So I did, and I said I liked it very much, but she kept waiting for me to say something else. I couldn't think of what else I was supposed to say, so I said what seemed like a dumb thing. 'Thank you very much,' I said. That was exactly what she was waiting for. 'You're entirely welcome,' she said. I have since thanked her for the ocean, the moon, the stars in the sky, and for the United States Constitution . . ." (*God Bless You, Mr. Rosewater*)

Vonnegut has a knowledgeable sense of how people with power and money think. *God Bless You, Mr. Rosewater* tells the story of a rich man who wants to help people. Rosewater discovers that people are not helped by money, but by *people*. But the rich don't know this. Most of them don't even know why they're rich. They think they're rich not because of luck or talent, but because they *deserve* to be rich.

28.

Every night before I turn out the lights to sleep I ask myself this question: "Have I done everything that I can to unite this country? Have I done everything I can to help unite the world, to try to bring peace and hope to all the peoples of the world? Have I done enough?"
—LYNDON B. JOHNSON, *Baltimore, April 7, 1965*

29. *So It Goes: Slaughterhouse-Five.* Every time something dies, whether it be bedbugs, the novel, or the universe, Vonnegut mutters, "So it goes." In *Slaughterhouse-Five* there are exactly one hundred cases of "so it goes."

"The most important thing I learned on Tralfamadore was that when a person dies he only *appears* to die. He is still very much alive in the past, so it is very silly for people to cry at his funeral. All moments, past, present, and future, always have existed, always will exist. The Tralfamadorians can look at all the different moments just the way we can look at a stretch of the Rocky Mountains, for instance. They can see how permanent all the moments are, and they can look at any moment that interests them. It is just an illusion we have here on Earth that one moment follows another one, like beads on a string, and that once a moment is gone it is gone forever.

When a Tralfamadorian sees a corpse, all he thinks is that the dead person is just fine in plenty of other moments. Now, when I myself hear that somebody is dead, I simply shrug and say what the Tralfamadorians say about dead people, which is 'So it goes.'"

30. "Like so many Americans, she was trying to construct a life that made sense from things she found in gift shops." (*Slaughterhouse-Five*)

31. *The Failure of Literature in the Modern World, Chapter 37.* "Rosewater said an interesting thing to Billy one time about a book that wasn't science fiction. He said that everything there was to know about life was in *The Brothers Karamazov* by Feodor Dostoevsky. 'But that isn't *enough* anymore,' said Rosewater." (*Slaughterhouse-Five*)

32. *Through Time and Space with Kilgore Trout. Maniacs in the Fourth Dimension,* by Kilgore Trout: "It was about people whose mental diseases couldn't be treated because the causes of the diseases were all in the fourth dimension, and three-dimensional Earthling doctors couldn't see those causes at all, or even imagine them." (*Slaughterhouse-Five*)

33. *A Bit of Tralfamadorian Advice to Earthlings.* "Ignore the awful times, and concentrate on the good ones." (*Slaughterhouse-Five*)

34. Kurt Vonnegut Wins Epitaph Contest. "Everything Was Beautiful, and Nothing Hurt."

35. *Slaughterhouse-Five* is not like any of Vonnegut's other books. The others were straight novels; *Slaughterhouse-Five* is a *book*. It's more real than a novel, because you can hear Vonnegut the *person* shouting over the voice of Vonnegut the *writer*. The most "realized" character in the book is Vonnegut himself. "There are almost no characters in this story, and almost no dramatic confrontations, because most of the people in it are so sick and so much the listless playthings of enormous forces." (*Slaughterhouse-Five*)

36. *The Failure of Literature in the Modern World, Chapter 73.*

> Another one said that people couldn't read well enough anymore to turn print into exciting situations in their skulls, so that authors had to do what Norman Mailer did, which was to perform in public what he had written. The master of ceremonies asked people to say what they thought the function of the novel might be in modern society, and one critic said, "To describe blow-jobs artistically." Another one said, "To teach wives of junior executives what to buy next and how to act in a French restaurant." (*Slaughterhouse-Five*)

So it goes. . . .

Chapter 10

THE VONNEGUT
EFFECT:
SCIENCE FICTION
AND BEYOND

KAREN AND CHARLES WOOD

Even as he has exhibited the best qualities of the
Jamesian novelist of experience, Kurt Vonnegut, Jr., has,
since he came to critical prominence, carried the stigma
of being considered a science fictionist, and thus a Wellsian
novelist of ideas. The question raised is a simple one: in
order to be considered one of America's foremost contemporary writers, must Vonnegut be rescued from the
annals of science fictionists and placed firmly in the Jamesian, Joycean, or Faulknerian tradition of the fiction of ex-

perience? Or may he retain the aura of the novelist of idea, an aura which has made him what he is, and yet be considered one of America's best practicing writers?

It is time that the question of Kurt Vonnegut, Jr., as a science fictionist be dealt with. The question cannot be ignored; it is fundamental to the character of Vonnegut's writing and lies in the midst of all critical approaches to his work. Yet no full-scale examination of Vonnegut as a science fictionist has been made. Such an evaluation could, however, serve to clear much literary underbrush by answering two fundamental questions. The first—what is science fiction? The second—what is Kurt Vonnegut's relationship to the art or craft that is science fiction? In *The New York Times Book Review* of September 5, 1965, Vonnegut describes science fiction as a category designed for the ease of critics. Learning from the critics that he was a science-fiction writer, he responded, "I have been a sore-headed occupant of a file drawer labeled 'science fiction' ever since, and I would like out, particularly since so many serious critics regularly mistake the drawer for a tall white fixture in a comfort station." And yet, by almost any definition of science fiction, Kurt Vonnegut, Jr., is a science fictionist. He may be as unhappy about it as he likes, but the conclusion is inescapable. From this article and from Vonnegut's other comments upon the subject of being or not being a science-fiction writer, it seems clear that his dislike of the label arises not out of disrespect for science fiction or its practitioners, but rather from an understandable dislike of the general critical attitude toward science fiction. Vonnegut claims that science-fiction writers "love to stay up all night, arguing the question, 'What is science fiction?'" Noting that science-fiction writers constitute a lodge, he adds that "one might as usefully inquire, 'What are the Elks? And what is the Order of the Eastern Star?'" Yet if science-fiction writers themselves are unable to reach a consensus as to what their art is, it is not surprising that critics tend to take a confused and condescending view of the genre, and have trouble with Vonnegut's works. For, his own desires notwithstanding, science fiction and science-fiction writers exist, and Kurt Vonnegut belongs to the lodge. A working definition of science fiction must be possible, and is necessary if anyone is ever to understand just how Kurt Vonnegut operates as a writer without making an intuitive critical leap into Vonnegut's world.

The greatest barrier to getting at a definition of science fiction is in understanding that there are a number of things which science fiction is *not*. For a number of reasons these "nots" have generally been lumped into the field. In sorting out the real science fiction from its maverick cousins, one need not make value judgments, since some of the maverick forms are as good as or better than most real science fiction; but to gain an understanding of the genre, the distinctions must be made. First, science fiction is not really an ancient form of literature. Traditionally, science-fiction lovers, seeking a history for the genre, begin their tracing of the movement with Lucian of Samosota in the second century A.D. However, one only has to watch a brief segment of an Apollo moon mission to see that any similarities between Lucian's fanciful lunar voyage via a boat sucked up in a water spout and anything really scientific is purely coincidental. The necessary realization is that, as the label implies, science fiction is at least half science.

Secondly, science fiction is not space opera, which is generally defined as the converted horse opera, with the word "Mars" being substituted for the word "range," "space ship" for "horse," and so forth. Space opera is a breed of fiction that loosely uses the jargon of science fiction to put the standard adventure tale into a new format. It is, however, literature that is all but devoid of idea, with the plot of the story not at all being used for the communication of ideas. Adventure is the thing—the only thing —and much of the bad reputation of science fiction comes from the great quantity of bad space opera which is considered as science fiction.

Next, science fiction is not escape literature. Isaac Asimov has noted that science fiction dealt with "all the great, mind-cracking hopeless problems of today . . . twenty full years before anyone else did. How's *that* for escaping?"[1] Actually, science fiction is primarily social criticism, usually veiled in the remoteness of time and alien location. Good science fiction communicates most effectively by projecting current problems to their logical future conclusions. Nor is science fiction social parody (except when its parodies itself, as in Vonnegut's *Sirens of Titan*) because parody is normally an inversion or grotesque variation of things which exist now in the world. Science fiction, however, is an *extension* of current trends to logical and frequently horrible conclusions, and an understanding of science fiction's tendency to extend current social phenomena into the future is important, even critical, to a recognition of the nature of current science fiction.

Next, science fiction is not fantasy, a point which Kingsley Amis makes very strikingly in his *New Maps of Hell*. In distinguishing between fantasy and science fiction, one must demonstrate how the two types of writers establish their willing suspension of disbelief. The science-fiction writer does it by grounding his romance tales in credible science. The writer of fantasy has a far more difficult job of it: he must rely more upon artistic devices—tone, mood, setting, and such—to draw his reader into a state of mental belief. For this reason many writers of fantasy are artistically superior to most writers of science fiction.

Finally, science fiction is not meant to be realistic. It is, rather, a specialized version of romance. In romance literature, believability is not achieved through the supra-normal characters and unlikely actions. Credibility must be attained in other ways, and romances frequently obtain their credibility through realistic settings. True science fiction faces a similar problem, and solves that problem in a similar manner. Almost exclusively, science fiction relies upon its background of credible science to establish its believability. Thus it is much more closely akin to the romance than to realism. Consequently, all the ancient works, the space operas, the general escape literature, parody, and even fantasy are not simply different in degree from science fiction. They are markedly different in kind in this very important approach to gaining credibility. Science is the science-fiction writer's technique of gaining credibility.

Science fiction *is* literature of idea, as opposed to literature of experience. Mark R. Hillegas in his book *The Future as Nightmare: H. G. Wells and the Anti-Utopians* has made what is probably the fullest study of science fiction as literature of idea. H. G. Wells has been called the grandfather of science fiction. Certainly he did it all first and perhaps did it all best. He wrote several masterpieces of "scientific romance" and popularized the form, and he invented most of the themes of science fiction. A more subtle

influence on the genre has been his philosophy of literature, and some knowledge of that philosophy is necessary
for an understanding of the true nature of science fiction.
The dichotomy between Henry James and Wells can be
described as the debate over whether the novel should be,
as James insisted, "the only means of encompassing human
experience,"[2] or as Wells insisted, "it should subordinate
art to social message . . . and be engaged in the further-
ance of social welfare." Wells went so far as to say that he
had never been willing to accept the limitations placed
upon art by James or even to accept the novel as an art
form. To him, the message behind the novel was the important thing. Characterization, for Wells, became of mini-
mal importance in relation to the idea, and a "ventilation"
of the point at issue was what was wanted. Consequently,
Wells was not terribly concerned about the careful con-
struction of the novel, and even admitted that the bulk of
his own fiction was written lightly and in haste. Of far
more importance than characterization and careful con-
struction was the dialogue, so to speak, with the reader.
Wells envisioned himself as the persuader. The idea, then,
became the thing, and anything else was of at best
secondary importance. In short, none of the things that
Henry James claimed as the province of the novel as an
art form were terribly relevant to Wells. Human experience
for its own sake, precise and realistic characterization, and
truly credible action as experienced by real men and
women in today's world—all these things were either to be
avoided or were not very important. The value of the novel
for Wells was that it could deal with social problems, and
deal in the "tremendous work of human reconciliation."
Wells concludes, "We are going to write of wasted opportunities and latent beauties until a thousand new ways of
living open to men and women."

All this, then, is what is meant to define science fiction as a specialized form of literature of idea. But Vonnegut as a novelist of ideas is not the Utopianist that Wells sometimes was; he falls more clearly into the stream of what Mark R. Hillegas has called the anti-Utopians. Vonnegut does indeed write of wasted opportunities and latent beauties, but he would likely settle for just *one* new way of living which could be opened to men and women. But the importance of establishing Kurt Vonnegut as a novelist of idea *cum* experience lies in the fact that, once established as such, much of his message comes through more clearly. Speaking of *Player Piano*, Vonnegut says, "I supposed that I was writing a novel about life, about things I could not avoid seeing and hearing in Schenectady, a very real town, awkwardly set in the gruesome now." That novel, Vonnegut points out, was about people and machines. True enough—and so, if the critics are willing to be honest with themselves, is nearly every contemporary novel worth reading, in the sense that contemporary man has been altered by his relation to the machine, and even the writer who chooses not to deal directly with the machine must realize that he deals with a machine-influenced man and society. In simple terms, Wells lived in an age which could choose between the literature of idea and that of experience. Wells and James could carry on their lengthy feud over the nature of literature, differentiating the two modes, and all remained well. Vonnegut, however, writes in "the gruesome now." And the gruesome now is an age which has long passed beyond the stage when human experience could be said, by itself, to make the whole of the entity we have labeled "life," and have tried to capture on the printed page. Or, as Vonnegut puts it in *Slaughterhouse-Five*, when Eliot Rosewater is told that everything there was to know about life was stated in *The Brothers Kara-*

mazov: "but that isn't enough any more." Vonnegut writes in a world beyond alienation, a world so far removed from that of James and Joyce, and even of Faulkner and Hemingway, that any writer who hopes to penetrate its surface must, of necessity, approach it with a technique, even a craft, suited to this age and not the earlier one. Kurt Vonnegut is a vastly important literary figure because he does just that. The contention being made here is not that Vonnegut is "a science-fiction writer," but rather that Vonnegut is a writer who uses the techniques of that form to delineate human experience—a human experience of necessity broadened to include within its scope the technology which forms a goodly part of that experience. No longer can there be such a vast dichotomy between literature of idea and literature of experience.

The fact is that our world is now one in which "science" has so permeated our lives, machines have so impinged upon our existence, and the mysteries of the universe (best exemplified, perhaps, in our bland acceptance of color television coverage of men walking the surface of the moon) have so forced themselves upon us, that a literature which deals only with man's relationship to man is inadequate as an expression of "human experience." Literature of idea and literature of experience are no longer two different things; whether man likes it or not, he is now living in a world in which "idea" is the stuff of daily existence. No man who would experience the modern world fully can escape it. Kurt Vonnegut cannot escape it. But, because he has been filed and labeled as a science fictionist, he has seldom been fully understood. Science fiction has always been, after all, the orphan child of the literary world; the writer who wishes to be a genuine speaker of truth, it has been thought, can surely not be a science fictionist. And yet, in *God Bless You, Mr. Rosewater* we find Eliot Rosewater speaking of Kilgore Trout (Vonnegut's recurrent character who has written eighty-seven paperback science-fiction potboilers) in fervent terms. Trout, says Rosewater, will, in ten thousand years' time be the only hero of our age to be remembered. More important, however, Rosewater announces to a convention of science-fiction writers in a motel in Milford, Pennsylvania,

> "I love you sons of bitches. . . . You're all I read anymore. You're the only ones who'll talk about the *really* terrific changes going on, the only ones crazy enough to know that life is a space voyage, and not a short one, either, but one that'll last for billions of years. You're the only ones with guts enough to *really* care about the future, who *really* notice what machines do to us, what wars do to us, what cities do to us, what big, simple ideas do to us, what tremendous misunderstandings, mistakes, accidents and catastrophes do to us. You're the only ones zany enough to agonize over time and distances without limit, over mysteries that will never die, over the fact that we are right now determining whether the space voyage for the next billion years or so is going to be Heaven or Hell" (p. 27).

Again, a page or two later, in summarizing a short story supposedly written by Trout, Vonnegut has one of the characters say that the question he would most like to ask God would be simply, "What in hell are people *for?*" Here are ideas. Within three pages Vonnegut has brought up virtually all the issues being joined among those who take anything larger than a microscopic view of the world. His major theme, from one work to the next, remains the major issue of a world which lies beyond alienation and operates in terms of separation, with a barrier set up between and

141

among mankind which precludes not only communication in the truest sense, but also renders absurd and meaningless all communication on even the superficial level.

These are themes which are to be found again and again, not only in Vonnegut, but in much of western literature. But Vonnegut's rendering of these themes is such that it has been impossible for the critics to pass him off as just another writer "in touch with his own time." Because Vonnegut has instinctively turned to the techniques and methods of science fiction to render his vision, Kurt Vonnegut, Jr., has become the spokesman of his age. He is writing about "all the great, mind-cracking hopeless problems of today," as Asimov referred to them. While Mark Schorer wrote of "Technique as Discovery," Vonnegut, and all science-fiction writers, use discovery as technique; their method of approach to literature is to "discover" the universe and let the discovery provide their technique. But the question of whether or not Vonnegut is a science fictionist becomes relevant only if the answer clarifies some aspect of his literary artistry. The Vonnegut canon may be seen as the fusion of human experience and idea into a single entity. This entity operates only, as Vonnegut himself has pointed out so flawlessly, as machines, as wars, as cities, as big, simple ideas, as tremendous misunderstandings, mistakes, accidents and catastrophes permit it to. Thus, to term at least a portion of Vonnegut's work "science fiction" is not to degrade it, but to set it apart as a body of work which has managed an ultimate perception of an idea trying to get itself onto the printed page for centuries.

Vonnegut's first novel, *Player Piano*, is one of the best science-fiction novels ever written, and it rests uneasily in the science-fiction genre precisely because it is such a good novel—a novel, that is, in the Jamesian sense, a detailed examination of human experience. The devotee of science fiction comes away from *Player Piano* with the uneasy feeling that somehow this isn't science fiction at all, that there is something wrong here. What is wrong here is that someone finally wrote a science-fiction novel that puts the emphasis on characters—upon human experience and actions. It is not that these characters merely happen to be living in a grotesque future world, for that would be to say that Vonnegut is merely attempting to stick "real" fiction into a science-fiction framework, probably the most common misconception of his work and the approach that makes any real understanding of his accomplishment all but impossible. What Vonnegut has done in *Player Piano* is to turn conventional science fiction inside out. Science fiction traditionally, as literature of idea, works from the premise that in the beginning was the idea. Unfortunately, many science-fiction writers would seem to feel, there must be a plastic plot and some cardboard characters to illuminate the ideas and to progress them from point A to point Z, the end of the idea's development. At its worst, science fiction can become little more than an "essay" with the condescension of characters present because characters are supposed to be present in fiction. At its normal best, the characters still manage somehow either to get in the way of the ideas being developed or to get all but ignored in the rush to develop those ideas. Vonnegut's inversion is simply to have realized that people are the most important things in both the real and the fictional universe. He begins, not with the idea, but with Paul Proteus, possibly the most solidly realized character in all of science fiction, and while the secondary characters of the novel, such as Lasher, Finnerty, Kroner, and Anita, are less acutely delineated, some of these are drawn with such a fine, deft touch that they all but leap off the page. There are, in addition, such minor characters as Edgar and Wanda Hagstrohm, Luke Lubbock, Doctor Halyard, the Shah, Miasma, and dozens of others, to illustrate abundantly Vonnegut's constant concern with people, with the living, breathing mass that is humanity. Throughout the novel the emphasis remains on the frailties, the failings, the small heroisms, the tiny joys and gigantic sorrows which make up the experience of all the characters of the book, from Dr. Paul Proteus and his wife, Anita, right down to the small boy who sails paper boats when the fire hydrants are flushed down in Homestead. Science provides the conflict, but Vonnegut resolves his novel with people being basically the same, with universal elements being put up against the test—in this case a very contemporary one.

Because of this very theme, *Player Piano* falls neatly and more conventionally than anything else Vonnegut has written into the anti-Utopian strain of science-fiction literature, as originated by H. G. Wells. The "idea" is there, and it is not even a new one. Vonnegut has done what many other science-fiction writers have done. He has extended the current trends of society, as he saw them in 1952, to their logical, if extreme and horrible, end, and the result is a description of the nightmare world that he envisioned. Says Vonnegut of this novel, "I was working in Schenectady for General Electric, completely surrounded by machines and ideas for machines, so I wrote a novel about people and machines, and machines frequently got the best of it, as machines will." Vonnegut points out the existence of what he calls the science-fiction "drawer" and notes that "the way a person gets into this drawer, apparently, is to notice technology. The feeling persists that no one can simultaneously be a respectable writer and understand how a refrigerator works." It is, however, through this very "noticing" of technology that Vonnegut manages to get across much of what he has to say. The *idea* paramount in *Player Piano* is simply what Vonnegut has stated it to be—that machines frequently get the best of it. Vonnegut has been criticized for not abandoning or outgrowing the need for the device of science fiction as he matured as a writer. Despite his own dismay at being so labeled, Vonnegut hit in his very first novel upon the realization that our contemporary society is so technology-dominated that man simply has to notice technology: that is, know something of how a refrigerator works, or at least comprehend the importance of the refrigerator in his life. Conventional writers may choose to ignore the technological infringement upon our lives and grope faint-heartedly for the cause of the dismay in the lives of their characters. Vonnegut knows the cause, and for him the communication of the idea of *Player Piano*, and of nearly all his works, has been to admit that science exists and has become vastly important to our lives. The communication of such an idea would not be easy to accomplish without the techniques of science fiction. Therefore Vonnegut both philosophizes and characterizes, and when a statement is made, it draws as much importance from who says it, and how, as from the idea itself. Context is as important as content.

"He knew with all his heart that the human situation was a frightful botch, but it was such a logical, intelligently arrived at botch that he couldn't see how history could possibly have led anywhere else." The botch that, according to Paul Proteus, comprises the world of *Player*

Piano is delineated in Vonnegut's later works, refined until it seems almost to have its own existence in *Slaughter-house-Five*. Vonnegut has been defining the flaws of that world over and over again, turning his universe about like a many-faceted jewel and working here with this facet and there with that. The same ideas which are treated in the novels appear as well in his science-fiction short stories. Such pieces as "Report on the Barnhouse Effect," "Harrison Bergeron," "Welcome to the Monkey House," "The Euphio Question," "The Manned Missiles," "Epicac," and "Tomorrow and Tomorrow and Tomorrow"—all concern themselves repeatedly with technological problems only as those problems express and explicate character—the character of the human race. Vonnegut proves repeatedly, in brief and pointed form, that men and women remain fundamentally the same, no matter what technology surrounds them. The perfect example of this might be found in "Unready to Wear," in which the shucking off of the physical bodies of men has not changed their basic identities, but only freed them to become *more*, not less, human. The themes, however, which are treated of necessity in piecemeal manner in the short stories, are pulled together in the novels into a world which becomes more complete and whole as one reads on toward *Slaughterhouse-Five*. The absurd, alienated nature of the universe is dealt with in each novel, always with some new depth of perception, some new slant; characters from the short stories and the earlier novels find their way into the later works. The same city, Ilium, in upstate New York, remains a central symbol of the twisted future of mankind.

Ilium serves as the setting for *Player Piano* and is mentioned in several of the short stories; it serves also as a starting point for *Cat's Cradle*, Vonnegut's novel which deals with the end of the universe as the result of a long and complicated train of events. The Vonnegut world in this novel is one not so very different from our own. He is dealing with one of the constant themes of traditional science fiction, the cataclysmic ending of the existence of the universe through the action of man. But the universe that is destroyed is one which corresponds with considerable sociological, religious, and logical precision to the universe which exists in reality for most of mankind. It is this sense of immediate reality which makes *Cat's Cradle* the terrifying, if amusing, book that it is. Vonnegut uses here an objective correlative, a scientific world familiar to his readers, to communicate the genuine but unfamiliar absurdity of the universe. At the same time, he touches again upon themes which have concerned literary artists for centuries, but which have been largely ignored, or at best underdeveloped, in science fiction. Vonnegut uses his correlative to communicate the extension of a current trend in society to its logical end. Yet fused with this fiction of idea we find as well tones and techniques which have belonged to the literature of experience. And throughout the novel, we are aware that Vonnegut's concern is centered upon humanity, upon its nature, upon the events and the ideas which arise out of the human condition. The idea presented in this novel, an idea that has been dealt with repeatedly in both literature of idea and literature of experience, is that of alienation. Here the idea is presented through the establishment of a universe which is destroyed by man's fumbling efforts to break down the walls between himself and the world around him. The faith of Bokononism, man-created, acts as the agent through which individuals are brought together—but the technological sophistication of the universe proves to be too much, even for Bokonon. The existence of ice nine, also man-created, is responsible for the destruction of the same universe, which is, at last, in an absurd fashion, making some attempt to break down the very isolation which has led to the creation of ice nine itself. The action of the book turns in upon itself; in black-humorist fashion, Vonnegut presents a terrifyingly real world. He then tears it to pieces, and its destruction comes about strictly in the manner of science fiction. But because he has begun with the absurdity of human character and moved from there to the absurdity of a technologically centered universe *created by man, Cat's Cradle* is not only science fiction. It is also the next step beyond, the fusion of character and technology which has already taken place in reality and so must now take place in literature if that literature is to maintain any value to mankind.

When we turn back from *Cat's Cradle* to an earlier work, *The Sirens of Titan,* we find a book which is perhaps the purest science-fiction novel Vonnegut has produced. It is at the same time a spoof on science fiction, and a blackly humoristic treatment of most of the themes and motifs which recur in the genre. Here we find time travel, space travel, alien life forms, and the theme of anti-Utopia. There is, in the incomprehensible chronosynclastic infundibula, a fully conscious parodying of pseudo-science. But when all the parody and humor of the novel have been noted, there is more to be said. *The Sirens of Titan* deals with an idea, the ultimate destiny of the human race. One of the favored themes of science fiction, it is really only a science-fictionist version of the question more simply expressed in "Welcome to the Monkey House," as "What in hell are people for?" And surely the literature of experience has concerned itself also with this question. Hamlet's "To be or not to be, that is the question," is not all that different in its concern from Kilgore Trout's *2BRO2B*, as it is described in *God Bless You, Mr. Rosewater*. The past, however, has tended to provide positive answers. *The Sirens of Titan* asks the question as thoroughly as possible, and provides only an absurd, meaningless answer: the universe, insofar as we are able to determine at the end of the novel, exists for one purpose, and one alone—that of delivering a message from the planet Tralfamadore to another planet out at the edge of the galaxy. And that message is simply "Greetings." The importance of *The Sirens of Titan* to this examination of Vonnegut as a science fictionist lies in the fact that it allows us to see him using the themes and motifs of science fiction to produce a new answer to the old question. This is a necessary function of modern literature. We *must* wipe out the irrelevant answers, and at this point, we have no new ones. The school of the absurd, the styles of black humor and pop art, and even the existence of our empty technocratic society, all combine to demonstrate abundantly that on a real plane, man at this point on his way toward his ultimate destiny doesn't know what that destiny is. Herein lies the *idea* of *The Sirens of Titan*—and herein lies seed of Kurt Vonnegut's importance in modern literature. For a relativistic world, he sees no need for absolute answers. Irresolution needs no resolution, but should rather be appreciated as the ultimate reality. This penetration of man's bewilderment adds a dimension to Vonnegut's work which is missing in most of our previous literature.

Thus, one can look at *The Sirens of Titan* in three different ways. It is a fine piece of science fiction, simply because it is self-consciously science fiction and determined not to make a fool of itself by taking that fact too seriously. It is serious science fiction, in a sense, because it amalgamates within itself themes which "more properly" belong to the mainstream of literature and not to the pathetic little offshoot labeled "science fiction," yet insists that it can deal with those themes strictly on its own terms. And finally, it accomplishes to some degree the same fusion of literature of idea and experience found in *Player Piano* and *Cat's Cradle*.

When we compare *The Sirens of Titan* to other works of science fiction, we become aware of the curled lip of the author in the background, and are instantly convinced of his desire to parody science fiction. But because Vonnegut begins the novel with some commentary upon the phenomenon of man looking outside himself in a search for meaning, we are also instantly aware that Vonnegut is parodying *genuine* science fiction. In other words, he is parodying social commentary, that trendist brand of science fiction which deals with all the bitterest, most back-breaking problems concerning man. The parodic elements of the novel—Kazak, Titan itself, its huge bluebirds, the rocket ships, the infundibula—all combine themselves into something of an inversion of the objective correlative. These elements have neither temporal nor spatial existence, yet they exist for Vonnegut's readers and they create for their author a universe apart from everyday reality. That universe, which might be called a subjective correlative, serves to define and delineate the absurdity of man on his way to his destiny, whatever that destiny may be. Vonnegut, using the hackneyed themes of science fiction, seems to say that man has been teased "out of thought" long enough. It is time that he was teased back again—back to thought, to life, back to the path of his destiny, even though he is no longer arrogant enough to believe that he knows what that destiny is. Whether man belongs in Winston Niles Rumfoord's totally disconnected and meaningless universe is debatable; yet he is certainly not at home in the old, equally meaningless "reality" of the Jamesian world. Rather, Vonnegut presents a prototype universe. Hence *The Sirens of Titan,* when seen in the context of the entirety of Vonnegut's available work, is part of an organic, systematized world which is creating itself as Vonnegut writes. Whatever he has to say will be said in terms of his own world, one within which he does not have to justify his world view constantly, but can simply write, as writers once wrote in the context of the real world. Vonnegut must turn to his own world, create his own reality, because the cohesiveness of reality which has been the goal of writers for centuries has not materialized—or rather, has evaporated under the heat and pressure of a world dominated by science and technology. Yet even as *Cat's Cradle* has shown us an objective universe, much like our own breaking apart, *The Sirens of Titan* reveals the same absurdity in Vonnegut's subjective world, and shows the destruction of that world with as little compunction as is shown in the destruction of the old order in *Cat's Cradle.* Vonnegut's creations are "fictions," possessing at the same time the relative expendability and ultimate worth of Wallace Stevens' "supreme fictions."

Even in Vonnegut's more traditional novels and short stories one finds science's influence on the social order. *God Bless You, Mr. Rosewater* relies little on the modes of science fiction, yet as a novel it stresses the need for a new social philosophy, and, interestingly enough, it is Kilgore Trout, the recurring, pathetic, unappreciated science-fiction writer, who articulates one set of the ideas that Vonnegut is exploring. Trout, who is Eliot Rosewater's idol, tries to demonstrate Eliot's sanity by saying,

> "Americans have long been taught to hate all people who will not or cannot work, to hate even themselves for

that. We can thank the vanished frontier for that piece of common sense cruelty. The time is coming, if it isn't here now, when it will no longer be common sense. It will simply be cruel." (p. 210)

And when Eliot's father insists that a poor man with ambition can still pull himself up by his bootstraps, and that such will continue to be true in the future, Trout adds:

"Poverty is a relatively mild disease for even a very flimsy American soul, but uselessness will kill strong and weak souls alike, and kill every time.
"We must find a cure" (pp. 210–11).

And so, here again is Vonnegut, who would not be a science-fiction writer, dealing with ideas. The fact that *God Bless You, Mr. Rosewater* is not a science-fiction novel per se does not negate Vonnegut's accomplishment as a novelist who is able successfully to combine two widely differentiated trends from the past and in so doing to produce a literature which is relevant to the present age as neither of those two past trends can be by itself. *Rosewater*, on the contrary, shows Vonnegut's versatility; it shows him working with ideas and successfully fusing those ideas with a character-centered base. Yet the ideas behind the novel come through loud and clear. Perhaps they are most clearly expressed when Kilgore Trout explains that Eliot Rosewater's obsession with volunteer fire departments is not the mark of insanity:

"Your devotion to volunteer fire departments is very sane, too, Eliot, for they are, when the alarm goes off, almost the only examples of enthusiastic unselfishness to be seen in this land. They rush to the rescue of any human being, and count not the cost. The most contemptible man in town, should his contemptible house catch fire, will see his enemies put the fire out. And, as he pokes through the ashes for remains of his contemptible possessions, he will be comforted and pitied by no less than the Fire Chief."

Trout spread his hands. "There we have people treasuring people as people. It's extremely rare. So from this we must learn" (p. 211).

Similarly, Vonnegut deals with ideas in *Cat's Cradle*. The difference is of degree, and not of kind. Always, the awareness of humankind at the center of the dilemma makes itself felt in Vonnegut's novels. The idea behind *Cat's Cradle* is stated succinctly by Jerome Klinkowitz as:

> . . . a recognition of the finite for what it is: an external repository of certain elements, some of which may be evil but none of which are egocentrically identified with Man. Wylie Sypher, whose discussion of the loss of the self coincides with the theme of *Mother Night,* makes a plea for a new fiction which is answered in *Cat's Cradle*. Sypher speaks of "our need for unheroic heroism" or "anonymous humanism" which will relieve man of his untenable position as center of the universe, a position which the terrible amounts of evil wrought in the twentieth century have caused man to become alienated from his very self.[3]

Vonnegut has successfully used the techniques of literature of idea, again fusing them with those of the fiction of experience, in order to answer the plea for a "new fiction." But it is in *Slaughterhouse-Five,* Vonnegut's latest and most mature work, that one finds the best fusion of the trends of the past. *Slaughterhouse-Five* is structured in terms of Billy Pilgrim's ability to travel in time. The time-travel theme extends back into science fiction to H. G. Wells's *The Time Machine,* but Vonnegut's manipulation of the theme for his own ends, here and in *The Sirens of Titan* as well, demonstrates a control of material which goes far beyond that found in pure science fiction. The time-travel theme is made by Vonnegut into more than just a motif; it is here illustrative of the fact that in science fiction there often lies the germ of the ability to communicate themes which have been thought not to belong to that genre. When Vonnegut uses time travel, he uses it in such a way that, interwoven as absurdity, it eventually yields a world view not confined to time travel per se, or even to the science-fiction world in which time travel as an idea was born. Instead, time travel, and other science-fiction motifs as well, have become in Vonnegut's work a *sign* of the absurd universe which lies about us and which Vonnegut is determined to call to his readers' attention, whether they like it or not. By the time he wrote *Slaughterhouse-Five*, Vonnegut's integration of science fiction with the literature of experience was so thorough that it became difficult for critics to determine just what the novel was. Is this novel science fiction, or is it not? The answer must surely be that if the mere presence of some of the elements of science fiction makes a work fall into that classification, then, yes, this is science fiction. If an author may be permitted to use the elements of science fiction because they suit his ends, without being placed in the "file drawer" that Vonnegut has occupied so unhappily for so long, then, no, *Slaughterhouse-Five* is not necessarily science fiction. It is the mature fusion of two types of literature into a new form, which has no name, and must be labeled, simply, "Vonnegut," since at this point he is its only practitioner.

If science fiction is ever to enter into the literary spectrum and stop being regarded as a poor relation of "true" literature, the fusion which Vonnegut has achieved must be recognized critically for what it is. The significance of Kurt Vonnegut as a science-fiction writer is simply that he is *not* a science-fiction writer in the accepted sense. He has gone beyond the form. There are many clever and articulate science-fiction writers, but they remain science fictionists. The fact that Kurt Vonnegut, Jr., is being taken seriously as an artist of this age, in spite of the fact that he has been labeled a science-fiction writer, is the key to his importance, both as a writer of science fiction and as a writer, period. When he uses the absurdity of time travel to reflect the absurdity of the universe in which Billy Pilgrim is bouncing around, Vonnegut defies classification.

The concretizing of abstract ideas has always been a major goal of art; perhaps the most abstract and important idea of all has been the question of the ultimate destiny of the human race. This has been a constantly reiterated theme of artists through the ages. In dealing with this motif, Vonnegut has most clearly illustrated his ability to integrate science fiction into the mainstream of literature. There is in his work a constant effort to project something of today as it must become if the human race continues into its insane self-created future. In *God Bless You, Mr. Rosewater*, during the recounting of one of Kilgore Trout's novels (which bears a striking resemblance, in the matter of plot, to "Welcome to the Monkey House"), a character expresses the wish to meet God. When asked why, he says that he wants to ask God a question, the answer to which he has never been able to find out down here. The question is, "What in hell are people for?" In *Slaughterhouse-Five*, Vonnegut places his hero in the position not of simply stumbling blindly toward destiny, but, because time is not conceived of here as linear, of having freedom of movement in time, just as he has in space. Yet again, ideas come to the forefront—ideas about the nature of time, the nature of space, and the nature of man—and always, always the question to be asked, again and again, what are people for?

Science fiction has been asking, for a couple of generations now, "What is the ultimate destiny of the human
race?" It is the same question. Only the answers have been
changed by Vonnegut; but it is the direction that change
is taking which indicates how fully Vonnegut understands
the question. Within this ultimate-destiny motif lie most of
the important questions that can be asked about life, about
man, about the absurd universe we live in. It is to Kurt
Vonnegut, Jr.'s credit that he is integrating two modes of
literature in order to ask anew the questions which form
the lifeblood of literary art. If anyone can pull science
fiction into the mainstream of literature, Vonnegut can. If
this cannot be done, then he will have shown us that it is
necessary that twentieth-century man at least draw from
that branch of literature that has come to exist because of
the scientific essence of the twentieth century. The role
that science has to play in life has been both denigrated
and glorified, but seldom has it been examined as Vonnegut examines it. From his pen come a startling number of
quasi-answers, answers on the order of "No damn cat, no
damn cradle." But these are better than the mere statement
that the universe is absurd. By now man knows that the
universe is absurd. Perhaps he may, however, let Kurt
Vonnegut explore the idea of absurdity further in terms of
time travel, space travel, man's ultimate destiny, and all
the motifs which fit his time so well because they grew
out of and were created within it.

NOTES TO CHAPTER 10

1. Isaac Asimov, "Forword I—the Second Revolution," *Dangerous Visions #1*, ed. Harlan Ellison (New York, 1967),
p. 7.

2. Leon Edel and Gordon N. Ray, "Foreword," *Henry James and H. G. Wells* (Urbana, Ill., 1958), p. 11. Materials concerning Wells's and James's disagreement as to the nature of fiction is based primarily upon this text. Specific quotations included in this study are from Wells's "The Contemporary Novel," from his *An Englishman Looks at the World,* and from "Digression About Novels," from his *Experiment in Autobiography.* Both selections are included in Edel and Ray's book, which is an excellent distillation of materials concerning the literary feud of James and Wells.

3. Jerome Klinkowitz, "Kurt Vonnegut, Jr., and the Crime of His Times," *Critique*, 12 (#3, 1971), 49–50.

Chapter 11

MOTHER NIGHT,
CAT'S CRADLE,
AND
THE CRIMES
OF OUR TIME

————— •◆• —————

JEROME KLINKOWITZ

KURT VONNEGUT, JR., through six novels and more than forty stories, has crafted for his readers an exceedingly mad world. He holds his own with the black humorists, matching Yossarians with Howard Campbells, Guy Grands with Eliot Rosewaters, and Sebastian Dangerfields with Malachi Constants. But unlike Joseph Heller, Vonnegut is prolific, tracing his vision through many different human contexts. He surpasses Terry Southern by striking all limits from human absurdity: destruction by nuclear fission is for Vonnegut the most passé of apocalypses. Moreover, he teases us with a Mod Yoknapatawpha County; "Frank Wirtanen" and "Bernard B. O'Hare" (originally characters in his third novel, *Mother Night*) and others appear again and again, always (as befits the modern county) in a maddening metamorphosis of roles. Favorite cities such as "Rosewater, Indiana" and "Ilium, New York" are storehouses for the paraphernalia of middle-class life which so delight Vonnegut, whose religion is one of cultural value rather than geographical place. But unlike Southern and Bruce Jay Friedman, who mock such culture in the sociosatiric mode of Evelyn Waugh (Southern scripted *The Loved One* for the movies), Vonnegut uses his roots more like John Barth uses Maryland: interest lies beneath the surface, and the surface itself is constantly changing. Vonnegut, in short, demands independent investigation. One finds at the end of Vonnegut's vision a "fine madness" indeed, but a madness at the same time more clinical and more cosmic than found in conventional black humor—or, indeed, nearly anywhere else.

Perhaps a reason for the long critical neglect of Kurt Vonnegut is that his vision is superficially akin to that of Orwell, Huxley, and others who have written dolefully of the mechanical millennium to come. His first novel, *Player Piano*, warns of the familiar *Brave New World* future, while the much-praised title story of *Welcome to the Monkey House*, with its Ethical Suicide Parlors and waning sentimental romanticism, recalls Evelyn Waugh's alternatives of "Love Among the Ruins" and *Scott-King's Modern Europe*. In Chapter Ten Karen and Charles Wood have shown how Vonnegut's material moves beyond the bounds of science fiction, the label used so long to restrain his recognition. But to justify a reputation for Vonnegut, one must also recognize the essential elements in his technique which surpass the efforts of a black humorist like Terry Southern, and understand the complexity of his vision.

Both technique and theme are well represented by two novels published well into his career: *Mother Night* and *Cat's Cradle*. In *Mother Night*, Vonnegut's panorama of the Nazi world is a black humorist's dream: all the stuff of middle-class life is present, but the people in the picture are not G. E. flaks or Indiana brewers but rather honest-to-goodness "criminals against humanity." Rudolph Hoess, Heinrich Himmler, and Adolf Eichmann himself (the book was published in 1961, when Eichmann was in the news) are presented to the reader, who gasps and giggles like a tourist on a Beverly Hills sightseeing bus. And Vonnegut exploits our fascination by giving us these men in their utter banality. This, of course, is orthodox black-humor technique, and signals Vonnegut's departure from the standard humanistic approach to the subject of the rise and fall of the Third Reich: in all of William L. Shirer's heavily documented book there is not a single Ping-Pong tournament, which is one of the things Vonnegut gives us.[1] But the absurdity of this world yields more than an affectatious glimpse behind the scenes, as Terry Southern offers in *Dr. Strangelove*. Life in Vonnegut's Nazi realm is more properly absurd: the hero, Howard W. Campbell, Jr., acts out an Ionesco drama as he broadcasts vital secrets to the Allies in coded gestures he cannot understand. Vonnegut toys with ironic *déjà-vu* as the documents of 1960's "White Christian Minutemen" are recognized as crafted a generation earlier by Howard Campbell when in the service of the Nazis. The morbid dance of life reaches its black-humor climax when no less than the neo-Nazi journalist Rev. Doctor Lionel Jason David Jones, D.D.S., D.D., the unfrocked Paulist Father Patrick Keeley, Robert Sterling

Wilson (the "Black Fuehrer of Harlem"), Russian agent Iona Potapov, Legion Post Americanism Chairman Lt. Bernard B. O'Hare, O.S.S. spy-maker Col. Frank Wirtanen, and various FBI agents and sundry nineteen-year-old Minutemen from New Jersey battle over the body and soul of Vonnegut's hero.

Neither does Vonnegut's absurd humor stop here. Terry Southern's *The Magic Christian* is equal in single absurdities; Vonnegut surpasses him by working in triplets. Campbell's wartime buddy Heinz Schildknecht is not merely comically robbed of his dearer-than-life motorcycle; on the second turn Heinz shows up as a gardener for a rich expatriate Nazi in Ireland, courting fame as an authority on the death of Hitler ("Hello out there, Heinz. . . . What were you doing in Hitler's bunker—looking for your motorcycle and your best friend?" [p. 89]), and on the third is revealed to have been a secret Israeli agent all the time, gathering evidence for Campbell's prosecution. Vonnegut's is a spiraling, madly rebounding absurdity. A hangman's noose suggestively placed in Campbell's apartment by the American Legion is not merely laughed at and discarded. Instead, "Resi put the noose in the ash can, where it was found the next morning by a garbageman named Lazlo Szombathy. Szombathy actually hanged himself with it— but that is another story" (p. 112). Double turn: Szombathy is despondent because as a refugee he is barred from practicing his profession of veterinary science. Triple turn: Szombathy is particularly despondent because he has a cure for cancer, and is ignored. Absurdity to the third power rules the entire world: not only is Campbell's dramatic work pirated and plagiarized by a looting Soviet soldier, but the best of the loot turns out to be Campbell's secret and sensitive love memoirs, which at once become the *Fanny Hill* of postwar Russia. Third turn: the soldier is caught and punished, but not for plagiarism: "'Bodov-skov had begun to replenish the trunk with magic of his own,' said Wirtanen. 'The police found a two-thousand-page satire on the Red Army, written in a style distinctly un-Bodovskovian. For that un-Bodovskovian behavior, Bodovskov was shot'" (p. 157). Other examples abound: Arndt Klopfer, official Reich chancellery portrait photographer, turns up in Mexico City as the country's greatest brewer. But not for long; he's really a Russian spy. We are teased with the knowledge that one of the world's greatest admirers of Lincoln's *Gettysburg Address* is Paul Joseph Goebbels. But *the* greatest admirer, literally brought to tears by the document, is Adolf Hitler. Triple turn: the most gleeful fan of Campbell's anti-Semitic broadcasts is Franklin Delano Roosevelt.

The triplet madness, besides being an ingenious technique, serves to introduce Vonnegut's more serious theme. George Kraft, alias Iona Potapov, becomes at one and the same time Howard Campbell's most sincere friend plus the agent who is working most seriously to engineer his exploitation, torture, and death in Moscow. Moreover (triplets again), Kraft is widely acknowledged as the best of modern artists ("surely the first man to understand the whole of modern art," according to a *Herald Tribune* review supplied by the Haifa Institute). Others besides Kraft-Potapov lead double lives. One of Campbell's Israeli prison guards is Arpad Kovacs, who spent the war as a Jewish spy among the S.S. in Germany. He boasts to Campbell:

"I was such a pure and terrifying Aryan that they even put me in a special detachment. Its mission was to find out how the Jews always knew what the S.S. was going to do next. There was a leak somewhere, and we were out to stop it." He looked bitter and affronted, remembering it, even though he had been that leak (p. 10).

Campbell himself, of course, had lived a double life for the years of World War II. He was, at the same time, *the best* Nazi radio propagandist and *the best* spy in the service of the Allies. He understands this apparently contradictory situation, even finding the clinical name for it: " 'I've always known what I did. I've always been able to live with what I did. How? Through that simple and widespread boon to modern mankind—schizophrenia' " (p. 136). Schizophrenia indeed seems the proper name for the madness devouring Vonnegut's world. When federal agents raid the basement quarters of the White Christian Minutemen, an incredulous G-man wonders how the professedly anti-Catholic and anti-Negro Reverend Jones can have as his two most loyal cohorts Father Patrick Keeley and Robert Sterling Wilson, the black Fuehrer of Harlem, the latter who announces plans for killing all whites. Campbell's explanation is worth seeing at length:

> I have never seen a more sublime demonstration of the totalitarian mind, a mind which might be likened unto a system of gears whose teeth have been filed off at random. Such a snaggle-toothed thought machine, driven by a standard or even a substandard libido, whirls with the jerky, noisy, gaudy pointlessness of a cuckoo clock in Hell.
>
> The boss G-man concluded wrongly that there were no teeth on the gears in the mind of Jones. "You're completely crazy," he said.
>
> Jones wasn't completely crazy. The dismaying thing about the classic totalitarian mind is that any given gear, though mutilated, will have at its circumference unbroken

sequences of teeth that are immaculately maintained, that are exquisitely machined.

Hence the cuckoo clock in Hell—keeping perfect time for eight minutes and thirty-three seconds, jumping ahead fourteen minutes, keeping perfect time for six seconds, jumping ahead two seconds, keeping perfect time for two hours and one second, then jumping ahead a year.

The missing teeth, of course, are simple, obvious truths, truths available and comprehensible even to ten-year-olds, in most cases.

The willful filing off of gear teeth, the willful doing without certain obvious pieces of information—

That was how a household as contradictory as one composed of Jones, Father Keeley, Vice-Bundesfuehrer Krapptauer, and the Black Fuehrer could exist in relative harmony—

That was how my father-in-law could contain in one mind an indifference toward slave women and love for a blue vase—

That was how Rudolf Hoess, Commandant of Auschwitz, could alternate over the loudspeakers of Auschwitz great music and calls for corpse-carriers—

That was how Nazi Germany could sense no important differences between civilization and hydrophobia—

That is the closest I can come to explaining the legions, the nations of lunatics I've seen in my time. And for me to attempt such a mechanical explanation is perhaps a reflection of the father whose son I was. Am. When I pause to think about it, which is rarely, I am, after all, the son of an engineer (pp. 168–70).

The key to Vonnegut's vision, however, is not merely this clinical diagnosis of the illness of an age. The traditional desire to maintain the integrity of self in the face of a too chaotic world has always been a schizophrenia of sorts.

Faced with the pressures of Nazi Germany, Campbell takes a solace not unusual in Western culture: he retreats first to art, and then to love. Crucial to this solace is that man have a self to flee to, a self which cannot be reached and abused by others. Like any fictive artist of the ages, Campbell offers "lies told for the sake of artistic effect." His self knows that on their deepest level his fictions are "the most beguiling forms of truth" (p. ix), but the surface is all art. Hence in the thirties, when Hitler's war machine is building, Campbell is the apparent escapist, scripting "medieval romances about as political as chocolate *éclairs*" (p. 26). When forced as a spy into the service of the Nazis, he finds refuge in parody and satire. "I had hoped, as a broadcaster, to be merely ludicrous" (p. 122). Campbell's second traditional refuge is that of love, where the escapist and even schizoid tendencies are more marked. From the terrors of daily social existence Vonnegut's hero flees to *Das Reich der Zwei*. "It was going to show how a pair of lovers in a world gone mad could survive by being loyal only to a nation composed of themselves—a nation of two" (p. 27). Its geography, he admits, "didn't go much beyond the bounds of our great double bed" (p. 33). In both artistic and emotional form, Campbell's theme becomes "Reflections on Not Participating in Current Events" (p. 92), and he honestly states that "My narcotic was what had got me through the war; it was an ability to let my emotions be stirred by only one thing—my love for Helga" (p. 36). Art and love are two traditional ways of coping with the chaos of the outside world. Come what may, the self should be inviolate, and it is here that Campbell places his hope.

Vonnegut's point, however, is that in this modern world the self can indeed be violated, and is so at every turn.

Campbell's love is the first casualty. Helga is captured on the Russian front, but this alone is no more than a challenge to Campbell's romantic imagination. He will nurture his grief and celebrate his melancholy. Modern espionage, however, not only mocks his grief, but uses him to do the mocking.

> This news, that I had broadcast the coded announcement of my Helga's disappearance, broadcast it without even knowing what I was doing, somehow upset me more than anything in the whole adventure. It upsets me even now. Why, I don't know.
>
> It represented, I suppose, a wider separation of my several selves than even I can bear to think about.
>
> At that climactic moment in my life, when I had to suppose that my Helga was dead, I would have liked to mourn as an agonized soul, indivisible. But no. One part of me told the world of the tragedy in code. The rest of me did not even know that the announcement was being made (p. 140).

Neither will history let his love rest. The intimate diary of his life with Helga is plagiarized and made into pornography, complete with fourteen plates in lifelike color. "That's how I feel right now," Campbell admits, "like a pig that's been taken apart, who's had experts find a use for every part. By God—I think they even found a use for my squeal" (pp. 155–56).

Art is no safer a refuge. Campbell had hoped, as a propagandist, to be satirically ludicrous—on the one hand, it would cover his self-respect, while on the other it might indeed, by *reductio ad absurdum*, bring down the Nazi regime in gales of laughter. "But this is a hard world to be ludicrous in," Campbell learns, "with so many human beings so reluctant to laugh, so incapable of thought, so eager to believe and snarl and hate. So many people wanted to believe me!" (p. 122).[2] At the end of the war Campbell is confronted with the awful possibility that his intended satire may have in fact prolonged the war. His high-ranking father-in-law confides, " 'I realized that almost all the ideas that I hold now, that make me unashamed of anything I may have felt or done as a Nazi, came not from Hitler, not from Goebbels, not from Himmler—but from you.' He took my hand. 'You alone kept me from concluding that Germany had gone insane' " (p. 75). Campbell reflects on the fate of his several selves: "The part of me that wanted to tell the truth got turned into an expert liar! The lover in me got turned into a pornographer! The artist in me got turned into an ugliness such as the world has rarely seen before" (p. 156). Throughout the book Campbell has been priding himself on his integrity. He has devoted a full chapter to the lunatic Reverend Doctor Jones "in order to contrast with myself a race-baiter who is ignorant and insane. I am neither ignorant nor insane" (p. 52). Unlike the trite and banal Eichmann, Campbell knew right from wrong, "the only advantage" being "that I can sometimes laugh when the Eichmanns can see nothing funny" (pp. 126–27). But the self, Campbell finally learns, offers no refuge. Art and love are impossibilities, themselves easily manipulated into cruel absurdities. The self is not inviolate; there is no place to hide.

To this point Vonnegut is on firm if traditional ground. Howard Campbell has in these terms learned no more than Winston Smith did in 1984, and Vonnegut's vision seems one with Wylie Sypher's: the loss of the self in modern art and literature (and love) is exactly what has happened to our hero.[3] Vonnegut, however, has more to say. His vision extends backward as well as to the fore. How has the

modern world come to be such a chamber of horrors?
Where lies the cause for the loss of the self? Vonnegut
answers that the very cause may be found in the traditional notion of the inviolate self. Because men have
abandoned all else and have selfishly fled to their selves as
the romantic center of the universe, when the self col-
lapses, everything, quite literally, is lost. This is what
Vonnegut's character finally recognizes. Campbell, after
all, does not follow through on his offer to surrender to the
Israelis and accept punishment for his crimes against humanity. At the last moment, on the eve of his trial, when in
fact conclusive evidence for his innocence has come with
the day's mail, he makes his decision: "I think that tonight
is the night *I* will hang Howard W. Campbell, Jr., for
crimes against *himself*" (p. 202, italics added). In spite of
all humanistic arguments to the contrary, Campbell sees
the absurd use that he has made of his self, and the evil
which has come of it. Vonnegut's indictment, in his own
signed headnote to the story, is no less severe: "This book
is rededicated to Howard W. Campbell, Jr., a man who
served evil too openly and good too secretly, the crime of
his times" (p. xii).

Mother Night remains, to date, Vonnegut's only book
with an explicitly stated moral: "We are what we pretend
to be, so we must be careful about what we pretend to be"
(p. v). The author has been clear in his condemnations:
art and love are selfish, false escapes. But if one is "careful," can there be a valid pretense? *Cat's Cradle,* Vonnegut's next novel, presents a tempting program. Its opening
disclaimer is also an imperative: "Nothing in this book is
true./Live by the *foma* that make you brave and kind and
healthy and happy" (p.[v]). "Foma" are the magic elements, correcting the rampant cowardices, cruelties, sick-

nesses, and sadnesses of *Mother Night*. A comparison to the "soma" of *Brave New World* is alarming but intentionally immediate: sounding similar, working similar, Vonnegut dares to confront us with something too good to believe: a pain pill for the ills of the world.

Mother Night presents the destructive pretenses that make modern life a nightmare; *Cat's Cradle*, however, offers *foma* as "*harmless* untruths" [italics added]. They are the key elements in the book's religion, Bokononism. Why is religion a valid pretense, whereas love and art are not? The answer lies with the peculiar state of modern man, and with his need for a unique religion. Other modern novelists, particularly Saul Bellow, have written of the "romantic over-valuation of the Self"[4] which most terrifyingly makes "each of us . . . responsible for his own salvation."[5] But Vonnegut's Bokononism is a religion after alienation, for it seeks a way for man to be comfortable in a world he no longer wishes to admit is his own. The "lies" of this particular religion are purgative, restoring man's happiness, balance, and comfort. Bokononism reorders our notion of the finite world so that we may accept it, rather than simply rebel against it in fruitless anger. It is the first step toward accommodating oneself to the schizophrenic reality given full treatment in *Slaughterhouse-Five*, as will be discussed by John Somer in Chapter Fourteen.

The danger that Vonnegut actively courts in *Cat's Cradle* is religion's becoming an opiate. His writer-narrator is told that "When a man becomes a writer . . . he takes on a sacred obligation to produce beauty and enlightenment and comfort at top speed" (p. 189). The writer accepts the methodology of religion by seeking the ultimate meaning of things. Bokononism cooperates by teaching that "humanity is organized into teams, teams that do

God's Will without ever discovering what they are doing. Such a team is called a *karass*" (p. 14). Therefore the writer tries to include in his book "as many members of my *karass* as possible," and "to examine strong hints as to what on Earth we, collectively, have been up to" (p. 16). If one sought the reason for the madly twisted life of Howard W. Campbell, Jr., the answer might be found in *Cat's Cradle:* "'If you find your life tangled with somebody else's life for no very logical reason,' writes Bokonon, 'that person may be a member of your *karass*'" (p. 14). Hence the writer studies the affairs of Dr. Felix Hoenikker, for, as his memorial states, "THE IMPORTANCE OF THIS ONE MAN IN THE HISTORY OF MANKIND IS INCALCULABLE" (p. 53).

Bokononism follows tradition in its eschatological imperative; it departs, however, when at the same time it calls any such search absurd:

> "In the beginning, God created the earth, and he looked upon it in His cosmic loneliness.
>
> "And God said, 'Let Us make living creatures out of mud, so the mud can see what We have done.' And God created every living creature that now moveth, and one was man. Mud as man alone could speak. God leaned close as man sat up, looked around, and spoke. Man blinked. 'What is the *purpose* of all this?' he asked politely.
>
> "'Everything must have a purpose?' asked God.
>
> "'Certainly,' said man.
>
> "'Then I leave it to you to think of one for all this,' said God. And He went away" (pp. 214–15).

The first axiom of this religion, then, is that if there is to be an ultimate meaning for things, it is up to man's art to find it. But as we know from *Mother Night,* his art can be selfish and escapist. Vonnegut's writer is at one point mis-

taken for a drug salesman, and is then encouraged to write
a book for "people who are dying or in terrible pain." The
writer suggests an improvisation on the Twenty-Third
Psalm, and is told "Bokonon tried to overhaul it" but
"found out that he couldn't change a word" (pp. 128–29).

Whether religion is an opiate, and whether the "consola-
tions of literature" are little more than the wares of drug
salesmen, must be decided by comparison with men's other
eschatological artifices. For consolation Felix Hoenikker
played games: one resulted in the chance invention of the
atom bomb, another in the creation of *ice-nine*. His daughter Angela's "one escape" is playing weirdly authentic
blues clarinet, but "such music from such a woman could
only be a case of schizophrenia or demonic possession" (p.
150), and from the lessons of *Mother Night* must be dismissed. Little Newt paints, but his works appear "sticky
nets of human futility hung up on a moonless night to dry."
Art lies, we are told again. Recalling the game of cat's
cradle his father played with him, Newt comments:

> "No wonder kids grow up crazy. A cat's cradle is noth-
> ing but a bunch of X's between somebody's hands, and
> little kids look and look at all those X's . . ."
> "And?"
> *"No damn cat, and no damn cradle"* (p. 137).

Newt is objecting that the cat's cradle has excluded the
real, or the finite. The necessary artifice is one which will
handle the finite on its own terms, without recourse to
"lies." Finite existence in San Lorenzo is depressingly futile, and so "the religion became the one instrument of
hope" (p. 143). McCabe and Bokonon, founders of the
Republic, "did not succeed in raising what is generally
thought of as the standard of living," the writer is told.

"The truth was that life was as short and brutish and mean as ever." But Vonnegut's world cannot remain Hobbesian; Bokononism provides a system whereby "people didn't have to pay as much attention to the awful truth. As the living legend of the cruel tyrant in the city and the gentle holy man in the jungle grew, so, too, did the happiness of the people grow. They were all employed full time as actors in a play they understood, that any human being anywhere could understand and applaud" (p. 144). The writer learns that "for the joy of the people, Bokonon was always to be chased, was never to be caught" (p. 178). Vonnegut speaks elsewhere in *Cat's Cradle* of "the brainless ecstasy of a volunteer fireman" (p. 157), anticipating the role Eliot Rosewater will find most comfortable in *God Bless You, Mr. Rosewater*. Here the idealized, sustained game is part of a "dynamic tension" which argues that "good societies could be built only by pitting good against evil, and by keeping the tension between the two high at all times" (p. 90). Not surprisingly, we learn that as a student in Episcopal schools Bokonon was "more interested in ritual than most" (p. 91).

Vonnegut's religion is a type unto itself: heretical, in fact, but to a particular purpose. Within the situation of San Lorenzo one finds both tragic and comic possibilities; it is the daily life which is tragic, however, while its religion is comic. Nathan Scott, in relating the comic to the religious, has remarked that only comedy can tell us "the whole truth."[6] When the whole truth is not told, when a salient element of reality is denied concrete existence, we have the heresy of Gnosticism, which posits "a God unknowable by nature . . . . and utterly incommensurable with the created order."[7] Vonnegut's impetus is in the opposite direction. The finite is granted a real existence, rather than being an imperfect shadow of some higher ideal. Pushed far enough, such doctrine would constitute the heresy of Manicheanism. The value of Bokononism, however, is that it makes possible what Scott terms the "cosmic *katharsis*," which involves "such a restoration of our confidence in the realm of finitude as enables us to see the daily occasions of our earth-bound career as being not irrelevant inconveniences but as possible roads into what is ultimately significant in life."[8] A Gnostic approach to the evils of San Lorenzo would indeed encourage a flight from "meaningless" finitude. But such flight would be hopeless, as Vonnegut demonstrated in *Mother Night*. Modern man, romantically placed at the center of the universe and responsible for his own salvation, cannot flee from evil, even into himself; for in himself he will find only evil's deepest source. Vonnegut's alternative in Bokononism is a recognition of the finite for what it is: an external repository of certain elements, some of which may be evil but none of which are egocentrically identified with Man. Wylie Sypher, whose discussion of the loss of the self coincides with the theme of *Mother Night*, makes a plea for a new fiction which is answered in *Cat's Cradle*. Sypher speaks of "our need for unheroic heroism" or "anonymous humanism"[9] which will relieve man of his untenable position as center of the universe, a position which the terrible amounts of evil wrought in the twentieth century have caused man to become alienated from his very self. Bokononism is a religion after alienation because it carefully removes evil from the self and deposits it in a finitude granted real existence, not a finitude vaguely (and Platonically) reflective of Ideal Man.

Bokononism is not an opiate, nor is it irresponsible. It is not a turning away at all, but rather an acceptance of the finite for what it is, as part of the whole truth. The single identified saint in *Cat's Cradle* is Julian Castle, who "forestalled all references to his possible saintliness by talking out of the corner of his mouth like a movie gangster" (p. 138). Castle heroically saves countless lives, but can also appreciate the grotesqueness of his situation; as Robert Scholes agrees, "an excess of the horrible is faced and defeated by the only friend reason can rely on in such cases: laughter."[10] If evil is securely located in a coexisting finitude, there is no compulsive need "to concentrate on [Castle's] saintly deeds and ignore entirely the satanic things he thought and said" (p. 140). Bokononism is one religion which accommodates the finite. In a whimsical manner, a psalmlike "Calypso" reminds us that "We do, doodley do . . . What we must, muddily must . . . Until we bust, bodily bust" (p. 216). And the last rites of this curious Church simply affirm, "I loved everything I saw" (p. 181).

The theme of *Cat's Cradle* is repeated in Vonnegut's later work, where, perhaps because of his growing prominence,[11] he writes more directly and even personally. To a new edition of *Mother Night* in 1966 Vonnegut added an introduction, speaking not as "editor" of the "American edition of the confessions of Howard W. Campbell, Jr." (p. ix), but as an individual who has had "personal experience with Nazi monkey business" (p. v). In *Slaughterhouse-Five* Vonnegut includes a great deal of autobiography and comment as the first chapter of his otherwise fictional work. Here he contrasts his anthropology courses at the University of Chicago, where he was taught that man is a benign creature, with his after-school work as a police reporter. The deliberately retrospective preface to *Welcome to the Monkey House* features the same duality;

recalling his brother's adventures with a newborn son and his sister's dignified death from cancer, Vonnegut states: "And I realize now that the two main themes of my novels were stated by my siblings: 'Here I am cleaning the shit off of practically everything' and 'No pain' (p. xiv). When in *Slaughterhouse-Five* Vonnegut's father accuses him that "you never wrote a story with a villain in it" (p. 7), we need not fear that Vonnegut has been an irresponsible joke-ster or even a blithe optimist. Indeed, Vonnegut's public pronouncement has been that he is "a total pessimist," and has been since the experiences of Dresden, Hiroshima, and Dachau.[12] Writing on the fall of Biafra, he admits that "joking was my response to misery that I can't do anything about,"[13] but he has also reminded us that "to weep is to make less the depth of grief."[14] The joking in Bokononism is not a palliative: instead it is a fundamental reordering of man's values, solving the problem which has made man uncomfortable as the center of the universe. Wylie Sypher decries egocentric romanticism, and charges that it has alienated man from himself; Vonnegut begs that we still trust "the most ridiculous superstition of all: that humanity is at the center of the universe,"[15] proving that to sustain such a position "all that is required is that we become less selfish than we are."[16] That selfishness, however, is strong enough to have spawned a heresy and determined man's expression in art. Shaping a new religion is no small achievement.

Despite their rouges' galleries of unpleasant incidents, both *Mother Night* and *Cat's Cradle* are finally optimistic works. Howard W. Campbell, Jr., commits not so many "crimes against humanity" as "crimes against himself," the latter which, once recognized, can be successfully and personally purged. *Cat's Cradle* goes a step farther by relieving man of his unbearable egocentric responsibility for the conditions of existence. Granted that the world can become absurd, and that any good life may be unliveable: at this point Vonnegut's man can responsibly bow out, having "the good manners to die" (p. 220), and with great composure and respectability "turn the humor back on the joker."[17] Modern life, for all its errors, has a great clarifying power in helping man find his proper place in the universe. Rightly positioned, the Vonnegut hero can honestly say of his life, "Everything was beautiful, and nothing hurt."[18]

NOTES TO CHAPTER 11

1. The respected German historian Klaus Epstein harshly criticized Shirer's *The Rise and Fall of the Third Reich* ("Shirer's History of Nazi Germany," *Review of Politics*, 23 [1961], 230–45) because of its "curious inability to understand the nature of a modern totalitarian regime" (p. 230); Epstein singles out Shirer's failure to study "the entire domestic history of wartime Germany" (p. 236) as a key to understanding the "defiance of self-interest and sanity" (p. 239).

2. *The Goebbels Diaries*, ed. Louis P. Lochner (New York: Doubleday, 1948), contain a fascinating comment on Campbell's closest real-life counterpart: "The English speaker, Lord Haw Haw, is especially great at biting criticism, but in my opinion the time for spicy debate is past. . . . During the first year of war the people still listen to the delivery; they admire the art and the spiritual qualities of the presentation. Today they want nothing but facts" (p. 227).

3. Wylie Sypher, *Loss of the Self in Modern Art and Literature* (New York: Random House, 1962).

4. Saul Bellow, "Recent American Fiction," lecture delivered under the auspices of the Gertrude Clarke Whittal Poetry and Literature Fund (Washington: Library of Congress, 1963). Reprinted in *Encounter,* 21 (November, 1963), 23.

5. Saul Bellow, *Dangling Man* (New York: New American Library, 1965 [first published in 1944]), p. 59.

6. Nathan Scott, "The Bias of Comedy and the Narrow Escape into Faith," *The Christian Scholar,* 44 (Spring, 1961), 20–21. Scott refers to Aldous Huxley's essay, "Tragedy and the Whole Truth."

7. Scott, p. 13.

8. Scott, p. 32.

9. See Sypher's last chapter, "The Anonymous Self: A Defensive Humanism," pp. 147–65.

10. Robert Scholes, *The Fabulators* (New York: Oxford, 1967), p. 43.

11. In the fall of 1965 Vonnegut began a two-year lectureship at the University of Iowa Writers Workshop, followed by a Guggenheim fellowship (1967–68) and a creative-writing post at Harvard University (1970–71).

12. Kurt Vonnegut, Jr., "Up Is Better Than Down" (commencement address at Bennington College, 1970), *Vogue* (August 1, 1970), pp. 54, 144.

13. Kurt Vonnegut, Jr., "Biafra," *McCall's* (April, 1970), p. 135.

14. *Vogue,* p. 144. He quotes *Henry VI, Part Three,* II, i. l. 85.

15. *Vogue,* p. 144.

16. *Vogue,* p. 145.

17. Scholes, p. 44.

18. *Slaughterhouse-Five,* p. 106.

Chapter 12

THE MODES OF VONNEGUT'S FICTION: OR, *PLAYER PIANO* OUSTS *MECHANICAL BRIDE* AND *THE SIRENS OF TITAN* INVADE *THE GUTENBERG GALAXY*

JAMES M. MELLARD

IF ONE WERE Marshall McLuhan, one would begin by saying something like this: "Kurt Vonnegut, Jr., is hanging ten on the crest of the new oral wave, surfing in the wake of the old pictorial"—something to match McLuhan's "Heidegger surf-boards along on the electronic wave as triumphantly as Descartes rode the mechanical wave," or "Peter Ramus and John Dewey were the two educational 'surfers' or wave-riders of antithetic periods."[1] But one shouldn't say such things about Kurt Vonnegut. It is hard to imagine such a shambling bear of a middle-aged man on a surfboard in the first place. In the second, surfboarding is really no appropriate image for the struggle Vonnegut has gone through to get beyond one literary mode —McLuhan's typographic and "pictorial"—and deeply into another, one McLuhan calls the electronic but that has its origin in popular oral tradition. The long, lean, tanned image of a California surfer may not quite fit Vonnegut, yet it nonetheless suggests that he plays a transitional role in modern letters. In the seven-year journey from *Player Piano* (1952) to *The Sirens of Titan* (1959), Vonnegut does indeed cross the aesthetic backwash between the pictorial old order and the oral-aural new. In the developments of those two books, Vonnegut charts all the territory he will later explore in *Mother Night* (1961), *Cat's Cradle* (1963), *God Bless You, Mr. Rosewater* (1965), and *Slaughterhouse-Five* (1969).

Player Piano presents to us the early conflict of modes in Vonnegut's work. The theme of this novel is rather precisely the theme of McLuhan's *The Mechanical Bride*, which, in an analysis of newspaper, comic strips, and advertisements, arrives at a "Folklore of Industrial Man." That folklore has two main themes: mechanics and sex. "Of these," writes Father Walter Ong, S.J., "perhaps mechanics is the more significant, for the sexual theme has always been present in mythologies and folklore and acquires its present tonality when it is disinfected of its natural symbolic force and given a present mechanical orientation."[2] In *Player Piano*, Vonnegut's primary interest is also the machine that absorbs the lives of the people of Ilium, New York, with the mechanical society that has assumed the machine's rigidity, and with the deterministic history that has become yet one more machine to grind down the

individual who would try to stop its "progress." The object
of the revolutionary plot worked out in the novel, therefore, is the overthrow of the machine, the breakup of the
mechanical society, and the movement beyond unilinear
history. The object of Vonnegut's literary technique in the
novel, similarly, is the overthrow of the accepted literary
conventions of visual imagery, continuous plotting, connected characterization, uniform point of view—all the
mechanical aspects of pictorialism associated with Henry
James and the mimetic novel.

Player Piano works out the antimachine theme in many
ways. There are simple declarations against the machine's
incursion into the lives of human beings. The book's protagonist, Paul Proteus, is the origin of some. After listening to an "old displaced conductor," "Paul wondered at
what thorough believers in mechanization most Americans
were, even when their lives had been badly damaged by
mechanization" (p. 219). After listening to a super-an-
nuated first sergeant tell tales of the Last War, Paul
shakes his head at the image of "poor bastards fryin' on
the electric fence, the proximity mines poppin' under 'em,
the micro-wave sentinels openin' up with the remote control machine-gun nests, and the fire-control system swivel-
ing the guns and flame-throwers around as long as anything was quiverin' within a mile of the place" (p. 220).
The sergeant's "absurd tale" of how he got his Silver
Star leads Paul to meditate:

> That, then, was the war he had been so eager to get into
> at one time, the opportunity for basic, hot-tempered, hard-
> muscled heroism he regretted having missed. There had
> been plenty of death, plenty of pain, all right, and plenty
> of tooth-grinding stoicism and nerve. But men had been

called upon chiefly to endure by the side of the machines, the terrible engines that fought with their own kind for the right to gorge themselves on men. Horatio on the bridge had become a radio-guided rocket with an atomic warhead and a proximity fuse. Roland and Oliver had become a pair of jet-driven computers hurtling toward each other far faster than the flight of a man's scream. The great tradition of the American rifleman survived only symbolically, in volleys fired into the skies over the dead in thousands of military cemeteries. Those in the graves, the front-line dead, were heirs to another American tradition as old as that of the rifleman, but once a peaceful tradition —that of the American tinker (pp. 220–21).

And, much later, over a nationwide television network, amidst questions from his prosecutor, intent on seeing him punished for treason, Paul says that machines "have exceeded the personal sovereignty willingly surrendered to them by the American people for good government. Machine and organization and pursuit of efficiency have robbed the American people of liberty and the pursuit of happiness" (p. 272). "The main business of humanity," he adds, "is to do a good job of being human beings . . . not to serve as appendages to machines, institutions, and systems" (p. 273). Such statements, while they represent the blunter instruments of Vonnegut's technique, do not convey the novel's central theme so well as the symbolizations of the machine's incursions.

The impact of machine technology upon individuals is more interestingly suggested in the way *Player Piano*, like the advertisements analyzed in *The Mechanical Bride*, humanizes machines and mechanizes humans. The almost human spectacle of welding machines, with "mechanical hands," "welding heads," "electric eyes," and gaping "jaws," arrests the imagination of Paul Proteus as it does that of McLuhan's magazine ad writer:

> Looking the length of Building 58, Paul had the impression of a great gymnasium, where countless squads practiced precision calisthenics—bobbing, spinning, leaping, thrusting, waving. . . . This much of the new era Paul loved: the machines themselves were entertaining and delightful (p. 8).

From precision gymnastics, a mechanized army in Paul's fancy, the machines move on to greater artistic accomplishments, to symphonic orchestrations to rival *The Grand Canyon Suite:*

> —*the Building 58 Suite.* It was wild and Latin music, hectic rhythms, fading in and out of phase, kaleidoscopic sound. He tried to separate and identify the themes. There! The lathe groups, the tenors: *"Furrazz-ow-ow-ow-ow-ow-ak! ting! Furr-azz-ow-ow* . . ." The welders, the baritones: *"Vaaaaaaa-zu-zip!"* And, with the basement as a resonating chamber, the punch presses, the basses: *"Aw-grumph! tonka-tonka. Aw-grumph! tonka-tonka* . . ." It was exciting music, and Paul, flushed, his vague anxieties gone, gave himself over to it (p. 10).

And then to *dance,* to a programmed Rockettes, a miniature Busby Berkeley choreography:

> Out of the corner of his eye, a crazy, spinning movement caught his fancy, and he turned in his delight to watch a cluster of miniature maypoles braid bright cloth insulation about a black snake of cable. A thousand little dancers whirled about one another at incredible speeds, pirouetting, dodging one another, unerringly building their snug snare about the cable. Paul laughed at the wonderful machines, and had to look away to keep from get-

ting dizzy. In the old days, when women had watched over the machines, some of the more simple-hearted had been found sitting rigidly at their posts, staring, long after quitting time (pp. 10–11).

In the concluding observation about the rigidly staring women, however, Vonnegut makes one see the other side of the coin, for if man in his imagination can humanize the machine, surely the machine, and all its avatars—organization, army, government—can mechanize man. That is what has happened to Paul's colleague, Baer, who "was possibly the most just, reasonable, and candid person he'd ever known" but who also was "remarkably machine-like in that the only problems he interested himself in were those brought to him, and in that he went to work on all problems with equal energy and interest, insensitive to quality and scale" (p. 168). That is what has happened to Paul's wife, Anita, and their marriage, which they honor by dutifully repeating "I love you" as if on an electronic circuit. That is what has happened to the ritual mating dance of sex; Paul can muse that his wife has "the mechanics of marriage down pat," and though her "approach was disturbingly rational, systematic, she was thorough enough to turn out a creditable counterfeit of warmth" (p. 16). Anita herself can complain, "All you need is something stainless steel, shaped like a woman, covered with sponge rubber, and heated to body temperature. . . . I'm sick of being treated like a machine!" (pp. 215–16).

The machine-sex image Anita conjures here is rather startlingly the one McLuhan employs in *The Mechanical Bride* to suggest the sensual relationship between man and his machines. It is also the pervasive image Vonnegut uses, on the one hand, between the Reeks and Wrecks (mass industrial man) and their machines, gadgets, gimmicks and, on the other, between the engineers and managers and the corporate system. The relationship between the organization man and the "anthropomorphic image of the corporate personality" is perfectly clear in the figure of Garth, Paul Proteus' competition for a top-management vacancy:

> Garth stood in relation to that image as a lover, and Paul wondered if this prevalent type of relationship had ever been given the consideration it deserved by sexologists. On second thought, he supposed that it had—the general phenomenon of a lover's devotion to the unseen—in studies of nuns' symbolic marriages to Christ. At any rate, Paul had seen Garth at various stages of his love affair, unable to eat for anxiety, on a manic crest, moved to maudlin near-crying at recollections of the affair's tender beginnings. In short, Garth suffered all the emotional hazards of a perennial game of she-loves-me, she-loves-me-not. To carry out directions from above—an irritating business for Paul—was, for Garth, a favor to please a lady (p. 112).

Ironically, Anita, if not Paul, gets a sexual satisfaction when the offer of the vacant position finally comes. Vonnegut writes frankly: "Anita slept—utterly satisfied, not so much by Paul as by the social orgasm of, after years of the system's love play, being offered Pittsburgh" (p. 116). But not even Paul, who sees momentarily that she is all he has, can get away from the linkage of lover, social and corporate position, and self-identity: "He felt oddly disembodied, an insubstantial wisp, nothingness, a man who declined to be anymore. Suddenly understanding that he, like Anita, was little more than his station in life, he threw his arms around his sleeping wife, and laid his head on the breast of his fellow wraith-to-be" (pp. 117–18).

The relationship between the mass-man and the machine is not quite so overtly sexual. But it becomes rather clearly so in the novel's final chapter, as it has in McLuhan's discussion, for instance, of a Buick advertisement, when the rank and file rebels begin to reconstruct an Orange-O machine that, in the vernacular of the gadgeteers, has become decidedly feminine—a "she" into which one pushes nickels and which lights up reassuringly when its needs are satisfied, a machine Vonnegut calls "an excretor of . . . blended wood pulp, dye, water, and orange-type flavoring . . . as popular as a nymphomaniac at an American Legion convention" (p. 292).

In *Player Piano*, Vonnegut brings together the varied motifs of his major theme in the pentathol induced truth-dream Paul Proteus has in his first actual encounter with the Ghost Shirt Society. Dreams traditionally are thought to tell the real truth, with or without truth serum, so not surprisingly Paul's dream, which combines both the musical and the choreographic motifs from early in the novel, gets at the crux of the complex relationship between husband and wife and man and organization. Interspersing questions from a "voice" and Paul's own giddy answers that deny any further conscious affiliation with the corporate image, Vonnegut gives us a balletic enactment of Paul's rejection of both his mechanical brides, the wife and the corporation, represented by Kroner and Shepherd:

> And in his dream, Paul danced powerfully, gracefully, to the hectic rhythms of the *Building 58 Suite*.
> "*Furrazz-ow-ow-ow-ow-ow-ak! ting!*" went lathe group three, and Paul leapt and spun among the machines, while, pink amid the gray machines in the building's center, Anita lay invitingly in a rainbow-colored nest of control wires. Her part in the dance called for her only to lie there

motionless, while Paul approached and fled, approached and fled in frenzied, random action.

＊　　＊　　＊

Kroner joined the ballet, ponderously, earthbound, with a methodical marching to the voices of the punch presses in the basement: *"Aw-grumph! tonka-tonka. Aw-grumph! tonka-tonka . . ."*
Kroner looked lovingly at Paul, caught him as he bounded past, and carried him in a bearlike embrace toward Anita. Paul squirmed free in the nick of time, and off he went again, leaving Kroner in tears, urging Anita to follow him into the out-of-doors.

＊　　＊　　＊

Shepherd, clumsily but energetically, entered the growing tableau from the basement, choosing as his theme the hoarse voices of the welders: *"Vaaaaaaa-zuzip! Vaaaaaaa-zuzip!"* Shepherd marked time with one foot, watching Paul's gyrations, another rejection of Kroner, another effort to coax the dead-panned Anita from her nest amid the machines. Shepherd watched with puzzlement and disdain, shrugged, and walked straight to Kroner and Anita. The three settled in the nest of wires, and together followed Paul's movements with baffled, censorious eyes (pp. 247–48).

These stylized movements, in which Paul Proteus gives up the one identity he can call his own, thus become a Ghost Dance, too, a choreography in honor of disembodiment, wispiness, nothingness. It also becomes a celebration of the essential self, a self that strives against physical limitations as the dancer strives with and against gravity. It celebrates an idealized identity that emerges clearly later on in Paul's revelatory vision of that "most ancient of road forks," one familiar "in folk tales the world over," where "the good guys and the bad guys, whether in chaps, breechclouts, serapes, leopardskins, or banker's gray pin-stripes, all separated" (p. 269). It celebrates Being, the ultimate *Record* for which James J. Lasher, the "enemy of the Devil," the "man of God," consciously fought the new Ghost Shirt rebellion and for which Paul Proteus was willing to fight as well. Ultimately, Paul's dream-dance celebrates the fully human, the notion that good things can come from dismal evil, that laudable benevolence can come from base motivations, and that exquisite beauty can come from refuse—"the most beautiful peonies I ever saw," said Paul, "were grown in almost pure cat excrement" (p. 275).

These themes in *Player Piano* are paralleled by Vonnegut's technical effort to break out of the single dimension of linear plot, continuous explanation, explicit characterization and the like, the literary effects of the Gutenberg Galaxy created by print technology. Vonnegut no doubt felt about Jamesian fiction what Paul was beginning to feel about his brave new world, that "it was an appalling thought, to be so well-integrated into the machinery of society and history as to be able to move in only one plane, and along one line" (p. 31). The Jamesian mode, that is, the *pictorial*, is a literary machine such as this one of society and history (to which surely its owes many debts): it is primarily visualist, explicit, uniform, and sequential. It prizes a "Fine Central Intelligence," a "Commanding Centre as a Principle of Composition," and the attempt "to give all the sense without all the substance or all the surface, and so to summarize or foreshorten, so to make values both rich and sharp, that the mere procession of items and profiles is not only, for the occasion, superseded, but is, for essential quality, almost 'compromised'—such a case of delicacy proposes itself at every turn to the painter of life who wishes both to treat his chosen subject and to confine his necessary picture."[3] It is above all a literate *prose* medium. What Vonnegut was seeking was another medium, one that would reverse these priorities of the unilinear prose picture. This "new" medium—as McLuhan says, "whether in the primitive past or the electronic present"—would be "non-literate," "implicit, simultaneous, and discontinuous." Vonnegut reveals some of these qualities in *Player Piano*.

The language of *Player Piano* is less and less literate as we move from beginning to end. It begins rather classically with the description of Ilium, New York, its division into three parts; it ends with surviving Reeks and Wrecks considering ways to get the Orange-O vending machine back in operation, a youngster asking for an eighth-horsepower electric motor—"Yep, if I had a decent little motor to go with what I got . . . I'll betch anything I could make a gadget that'd play drums like nothing you ever heard before" (p. 293)—and Finnerty, von Neumann, and Proteus pouring drinks from a whisky bottle, toasting a better world and "the record," and marching off to their capture at the hands of the corporate and governmental authorities. In between, Vonnegut begins to capture the speech of the masses in Homestead, the idiom of Alfy Tucci and Haycox, the ribald insouciance of the superannuated sergeant's absurd war story, the resonant *non*-language of the Shah of Bratpahr—"*Khabu bonanza-pak?*"; "*Takaru yamu brouha, pu dinka bu,*" and the like—as well as the polyphonic sounds of the machines, the "music" Paul hears in *the Building 58 Suite* "*Furrazz-ow-ow-ow-ow-ow-ak! ting! Furr-azz-ow-ow. . . .*" Vonnegut begins moreover, to include snatches of songs—*Ooooooooooooh, give me some men, who are stout-hearted men, who will fight for the right they adore"*—of poems, in the language of the Shah!

> "Allakahi baku billa,
> Moumi a fella man;
> Serani assu tilla,
> Touri serin a sam."

and in English:

> "Silver bells shall light my way,
> And nine times nine maidens fill my day,
> And mountain lakes will sink from sight,
> And tigers' teeth will fill the night" (p. 106).

There are several letters, such as the one to Ewing J. Halyard about his graduation deficiencies and the one from Halyard to Dr. Albert Herpers in which, five years previously, Halyard had complained about the conduct of Dr. Roseberry, the same Roseberry for whom Halyard must now complete the physical education deficiency for the degree he thought he had already secured. And Vonnegut includes, finally, such virtuoso performances as the "personnel card" of Edgar R. B. Hagstrohm, the statistically average Iliumite, the "keynote play" at the Meadows, and the absolutely superb catalog of "twinkling treasures" littering the streets of rebellion-torn Ilium:

> bits of air conditioners, amplidynes, analyzers, arc welders, batteries, belts, billers, bookkeeping machines, bottlers, canners, capacitors, circuitbreakers, clocks, coin boxes, calorimeters, colorimeters, computers, condensers, conduits, controls, converters, conveyers, cryostats, counters, cutouts, densitometers, detectors, dust precipitators, dishwashers, dispensers, dynamometers, dynamotors, electrodes, electronic tubes, exciters, fans, filers, filters, fre-

quency changers, furnaces, fuses, gages, garbage disposers, gears, generators, heat exchangers, insulators, lamps, loudspeakers, magnets, mass spectrometers, motor generators, motors, noisemeters, oscillographs, panelboards, personnel machines, photoelectric cells, potentiometers, pushbuttons, radios, radiation detectors, reactors, recorders, rectifiers, reducers, regulators, relays, remote controls, resistors, rheostats, selsyns, servos, solenoids, sorters, spectrophotometers, spectroscopes, springs, starters, strain-gages, switchboards, switches, tape recorders, tachometers, telemeters, television sets, television cameras, testers, thermocouples, thermostats, timers, toasters, torquemeters, traffic controls, transistors, transducers, transformers, turbines, vacuum cleaners, vacuum gages, vacuum tubes, venders, vibration meters, viscosimeters, water heaters, wheels, X-ray spectrogoniometers, zymometers . . . (pp. 290–91).

In displays such as these, Vonnegut begins to suggest that his real literary interests lie in the *nonliterary*, in the inarticulate, the subliterary. He begins to suggest, indeed, that his real mode will be more polyphonic than the conventional novel, more expansive in its range of human expression, more interested in the puns, alliteration, and aphorisms of vernacular speech, less concerned with sequential plot, developed and motivated character, coherent explanations. In short, the mode for which Vonnegut is searching through the wreckage of *Player Piano's* Ilium is the old popular oral mode of the storyteller expanded by the varied artifacts of print and electronic communications.

The finale of *Player Piano*, with its blaring PA systems, omnipresent TV equipment, and radio announcements of the progress of the Ghost Dance rebellion from places like Salt Lake City, Oakland, and Pittsburgh, thrust us back into the circular, tribal, and acoustical world of nonliterate man. The corporate and governmental structure the Ghost Shirt Society would displace is rectilinear, feudal, and visual—however much it plays at tribal values at the Meadows' sing-alongs, games, and symbolic central tree. But the Ghost Shirt rebels *institute* their tribal values in their organization, their secret meetings, and their symbol—the Indian shirt. And they intend to implement them by declassifying society and returning to a life style that would break down the lines between the social classes in Ilium, by desacralizing machines and returning *some* of them to the people as tools, and by resacralizing human life and returning to a harmony among people and objects, natural and artificial. The new media absorbed by society in the novel, whether the Ghost Shirt Society knows it, are likely to make the changes the society cannot forcibly institute: the incursion of audio and video in the lives of the people of Ilium will inevitably impel them back toward oral values, if McLuhan is right in the argument of *The Gutenberg Galaxy*. And whether Vonnegut knew it in 1952, his absorption of the content of the new media, which insists upon a raucous incursion of *sound* in *Player Piano* and a revivified metaphor of music as a unifying ideal, would inevitably push him into a new literary mode whenever he got around to writing another book. In contrast to the falsely literate, aristocratic sophistication of *Player Piano*, Vonnegut's new mode in *The Sirens of Titan* will be naïve, popular, nonliterate.

Naïve literature, according to Northrop Frye, is "primitive or popular, in the sense given those terms of an ability to communicate in time and space more readily than other types of literature."[4] For any writer the ability to communicate readily rests on several principles. One principle is that the language the writer employs will be comprehensible to a broad spectrum of people who have average fluency in it; another is that thought or meaning will be easily assimilated into the traditional values of culture; yet another is that plots in narrative will include traditional character types, traditional episodes, and traditional controlling structures. As Frye says, "The stream of literature . . . like any other stream, seeks the easiest channels first: the poet who uses the expected associations will communicate more rapidly." The easiest channel is that of pure convention, as Frye terms formulaic types such as the western, the detective, the gothic thriller, and the like. Most common in naïve literature, the purest conventions appear in "the fixed epithets and phrase-tags of medieval romance and ballad, in the invariable plots and character types of naïve drama, and, to a lesser degree, in the *topoi* or rhetorical commonplaces which, like other ideas in literature, are so dull when stated as propositions, and so rich and variegated when they are used as structural principles in literature."

The Sirens of Titan is *naïve* literature in every way possible, since it is a formulaic type (science fiction), employs formulaic characters, episodes, themes, properties, and settings, and is written in a remarkably simple style that, though not particularly formulaic, nevertheless includes evidence of formulaic epithets and phrase-tags. But *The Sirens of Titan* is also naïve *art*, and Vonnegut has managed to transcend the formula-ridden genre as he did with another formula, the Utopian-anti-Utopian novel, *Player Piano*. In his second novel, Vonnegut transcends the form by instilling life into its most transparent clichés, by reducing its formulas to absolute archetypes, and by elevating its trite metaphysical theme to the status of a believable eschatology.

Naïve literature that is also naïve art will validate the most pervasive aspects of culture. Since culture's most pervasive aspect is language and the values inherent in it, the one element naïve fiction *must* validate is its language, its style. *The Sirens of Titan* even more than *Player Piano*, therefore, must overcome many liabilities of style, for its very low threshold immediately admits all sorts of triteness, cliché, and stereotype. The book's epigraph is a stereotyped, almost formulaic statement about progress:

> "Every passing hour brings the Solar System forty-three thousand miles closer to Globular Cluster M13 in Hercules—and still there are some misfits who insist that there is no such thing as progress." —RANSOM K. FERN

The only difference between Fern's statement and any numbers of others we all have heard is the content referring to the Solar System and Globular Cluster M13 in Hercules; normally, the content of this grammatical position of the formula—in *Babbitt*, for instance—would include the name of a city, a state, a nation, or "the world," and some arbitrary fiscal goal. There is nothing *literary* or intrinsically valuable in Fern's comment, therefore. But Vonnegut gives it a certain formal value in *The Sirens of Titan* by allowing it to introduce, if only by implication, all the important themes of the work. Clustered around *progress*, then, are several related concepts, *time, history, eschatology,* that have to do with the question of the meaning of human life. Ransom K. Fern, like Vonnegut's American President who speaks (pp. 60–61) on "progerse," is only uttering, in the language *available* to him, a common notion, one that holds the most popular eschatological value of a technological culture.

The Sirens of Titan exhibits, then, considerable benevo-

lence toward what can only be called, in the new fictional
mode Vonnegut popularizes, the *artifacts of human expression*. Like the anthropologist who blesses every sliver,
shard, or remnant from a dead culture, Vonnegut manages
to cherish every banal utterance of his characters; while he
may not agree at all with its content, he knows full well the
potential depth of its meaning. For this reason, Vonnegut
may bring to this new mode of fiction any of the effects
(and values) of the old oral, aural, acoustic "literature"—
the naïve, popular mode of Homer, *Beowulf,* folk tale,
ballad. Where the uniform, visual, linear mode of the *novel*
either absorbs human utterance into a single uniform prose
style or draws a clear class line between styles, the mode
Vonnegut popularizes in *The Siren of Titan* absorbs, polyphonic, acoustic, and open forms into a mosaic of styles,
each of which controls its own autonomous existence. *The
Sirens of Titan* discovers most of its life, therefore, in the
many independent and varied artifacts of expression
known to an electronic age.

Consequently, while *The Sirens of Titan* is not of the
old pictorial mode, it can include as just one more of its
artifacts several explicit pictures—for instance, the painting
of Beatrice Rumfoord as a child—dressed all in white and
immaculate—presented clearly early on and then alluded
to several times later and the analogous photograph of the
three Sirens of Titan:

> Constant looked down at the photograph that had been
> ignored. He found that it was not a photograph of Miss
> Canal Zone's predecessor. It was a photograph that Rum-
> foord had slipped to him. It was no ordinary photograph,
> though its surface was glossy and its margins white.
> Within the margins lay shimmering depths. The effect
> was much like that of a rectangular glass window in the

surface of a clear, shallow, coral bay. At the bottom of that seeming coral bay were three women—one white, one gold, one brown. They looked up at Constant, begging him to come to them, to make them whole with love.

Their beauty was to the beauty of Miss Canal Zone as the glory of the Sun was to the glory of a lightning bug (p. 38).

These pictures are not merely the debris of expression washed up when Vonnegut dredges the channels of memory. In many ways such images—visual, audial, tactile, etc. —represent all that a man possesses. So much the worse for man if his cache, when confronted by a real human possession like Rumfoord's greatness, is so impoverished as that of the world's richest man, Malachi Constant:

Constant, who had offered his services to God as a messenger, now panicked before the very moderate greatness of Rumfoord. Constant ransacked his memory for past proofs of his own greatness. He ransacked his memory like a thief going through another man's billfold. Constant found his memory stuffed with rumpled, overexposed snapshots of all the women he had had, with preposterous credentials testifying to his ownership of even more preposterous enterprises, with testimonials that attributed to him virtues and strengths that only three billion dollars could have. There was even a silver medal with a red ribbon—awarded to Constant for placing second in the hop, skip, and jump in an intramural track meet at the University of Virginia.

Constant ripped open the seams of his memory, hoping to find a secret compartment with something of value in it. There was no secret compartment—nothing of value. All that remained to Constant were the husks of his memory—unstitched, flaccid flaps (pp. 21–22).

The wealth of a man, Vonnegut suggests, lies in his experience. If Constant's memories here become part of that experience for the reader, then a comment like that of Dr. Morris N. Castle, Director of Mental Health, Mars, is just as appropriate as another *experience:*

> "We can make the center of a man's memory virtually as sterile as a scalpel fresh from the autoclave. But grains of new experience begin to accumulate on it at once. These grains in turn form themselves into patterns not necessarily favorable to military thinking. Unfortunately, this problem of recontamination seems insoluble" (p. 106).

Vonnegut matches the textbookish banality of this statement with many others from figures, scholarly and otherwise, like Sarah Horne Canby (*Unk and Boaz in the Caves of Mercury*), Waltham Kittredge (*The American Philosopher Kings*), Martin Koradubian (article on the year One million A.D.), Dr. Maurice Rosenau (*Pan Galactic Humbug or Three Billion Dupes*), Beatrice Rumfoord (*The Beatrice Rumfoord Galactic Cookbook*) and Winston Niles Rumfoord (*The Winston Niles Rumfoord Authorised Revised Bible* and *The Winston Niles Rumfoord Pocket History of Mars*). Yet despite all its clinical sterility, Castle's statement *is* validated in Unk's (Malachi's) experience, for even after seven brain cleanings Unk can regain his identity through the verbal experience Vonnegut calls "Letter from an Unknown Soldier." That expression of experience, like one's memories, becomes one man's letter to himself.

There is no way to assess the value, then, of the artifacts of expression Vonnegut gives us. Like rocks brought back from the moon, these artifacts could help us understand untold histories if we could only reconstruct the experience represented in each—every word, phrase, sentence, however common. Literature "in its finest sense" (p. 132) can do this, as Unk's letter to himself attests, for it reconstructs those grains of experience through the words. In retrospect, one of the most moving passages in *The Sirens of Titan* is the short chapter four in which Vonnegut begins with a virtual nonsense chant:

> Rented a tent, a tent, a tent;
> Rented a tent, a tent, a tent.
> Rented a tent!
> Rented a tent!
> Rented a, rented a tent.
>
> —SNARE DRUM ON MARS

In the chapter's nine pages, this entire chant is repeated four times. By the end of the chapter this nonsense makes a perfectly sensible statement about freedom and bondage more powerfully than any oration. For those three words, representing the sounds of a single martial drummer, tell us what one man can be made to do under conditions not too far removed from the ordinary military experience: like Unk he may even murder his own best friend. The linguistic and experiential poverty of this ritualized chant therefore makes the best argument one can for the ultimate value Vonnegut posits in any human expression.

The way in which the naïve mode of *The Sirens of Titan* revitalizes what in other modes would be considered a verbal wasteland is well illustrated in Malachi Constant and Beatrice Rumfoord. Malachi and Bee, in the idiom of romantic adventure with which Vonnegut begins, are the "lovers" of *The Sirens of Titan*. A less promising romance could hardly be imagined, since not only is Beatrice already married to the man who seems to command Malachi's very existence, but the two are also polar opposites.

Malachi is the paradigm of the rich, dissipated profligate, one whose last riotous earthly party lasts fifty-six days. But Beatrice is as cold, austere, virginal as Malachi is sensual. Yet neither has a value except self-service. Beatrice has no shred of philosophy beyond the parody of Donne's sonnet she composes while a captive worker on Mars:

> *Break every link with air and mist,*
> *Seal every open vent;*
> *Make throat as tight as miser's fist,*
> *Keep life within your pent.*
> *Breathe out, breathe in, no more, no more,*
> *For breathing's for the meek;*
> *And when in deathly space we soar,*
> *Be careful not to speak.*
> *If you with grief or joy are rapt,*
> *Just signal with a tear;*
> *To soul and heart within you trapped*
> *Add speech and atmosphere.*
> *Every man's an island as in*
>   *lifeless space we roam.*
> *Yes, every man's an island:*
>   *island fortress, island home* (pp. 152–53).

Nor does Malachi have a philosophy beyond the comfortable banality available to the world's richest man, "I guess somebody up there likes me" (p. 7). What validates the language of Beatrice and Malachi is not the verbal artifact, but the experiences each accumulates like Castle's grains of sand. After their terrific, clearly *archetypal* sufferings—for Beatrice, rape, unwanted motherhood, warfare, alienation, and forced planetary cohabitation with her primal assailant, Malachi; for Malachi, impoverishment, animal assault, loss of memory and separation from family, murder of friend, ostracism, banishment from earth—they finally become lovers, though in a way presumably beyond the "bother" of the sensual; they become loving parents to a radically wayward son who at the end blesses them for their gift of life (p. 312); and ultimately they arrive at convictions diametrically opposed to their youthful attitudes. "The worst thing that could possibly happen to anybody," Beatrice says at the end, "would be to not be used for anything by anybody" (p. 310). Now she can thank Constant for using her, "even though I didn't want to be used by anybody" (p. 311). And Constant can admit to his friend, Salo—the little machine who, like Mal and Bee, achieves humanity—that Beatrice and he fell in love:

> "Only an Earthling year ago," said Constant. "It took us that long to realize that a purpose of human life, no matter who is controlling it, is to love whoever is around to be loved" (p. 313).

Blessed by a wife, a son, and a friend who loved him, Malachi validates those words, "Somebody up there likes me," that open the book. When they are repeated to him in his dying vision by his friend Stony Stevenson, Vonnegut suggests that between the novel's first and last words Malachi Constant has truly become a "faithful messenger," that between Alpha and Omega he has delivered the one message that we all have to deliver—a life. For Vonnegut the *Logos*, the word between Alpha and Omega, *is* life.

By accepting such expressive artifacts—all those sermons, prayers, speeches, letters, advertisements, chants, poems, doggerels, mnemonics, stories, tales, legends, scholarly extracts, photographs, paintings, statues, architecture, decorations—*The Sirens of Titan* invades the uniform, lineal, and merely visual universe of McLuhan's Gutenberg Galaxy. By investing all such artifacts with value, Vonnegut consecrates the verbal and physical objects, the furniture, of human existence. As a writer he becomes an "interior decorator," that most useful of artists as Vonnegut once called them in a speech. By such resacralizing he brings man back into the center of his existence, like the tribal man who exists in an acoustical enclosed space, unlike the punctual, civilized, literate man who exists in a vast linear universe that stretches perspectivistically and infinitely beyond him.

The values that Vonnegut validates in *The Sirens of Titan* are admittedly sentimental. But the *naïve* mode that Vonnegut revives is usually sentimental, since sentiment is a primitive emotion to which the popular audience can react as readily as it reacts to Vonnegut's narrative archetypes—the marvelous adventure of space travel, the perilous rescue on Mars, the scapegoat figures in Stony Stevenson and Malachi, the pastoral landscape on Titan. What a naïve mode such as Vonnegut's does is to reinstate popular sentimental values as commands—to love, to be courageous, to be kind. Robert Scholes has said that Vonnegut, as a black humorist, cannot employ the "rhetoric of moral certainty" found in the tradition of satire to which Vonnegut has also been allied. But if Vonnegut is a black humorist, he certainly does not suffer from the ethical unease Scholes attributes to that mode. As a popular writer in a naïve mode, Vonnegut employs not the rhetoric but the *sententiae* of moral certainty. At its highest the naïve mode Vonnegut has regenerated achieves what somewhere Northrop Frye has called the "aphoristic pinnacle of *sententiae*," though Vonnegut's aphorisms are appropriately hip to the new indeterminate world we have made:

"Don't truth me . . . and I won't truth you" (p. 212).

"I was a victim of a series of accidents, as are we all" (p. 229).

"Sooner or later, Chrono believed, the magical forces of the Universe would put everything back together again. "They always did" (p. 301).

"It was all so sad. But it was all so beautiful too" (p. 305).

From *Player Piano* to *The Sirens of Titan,* Vonnegut moves from a traditional mode, associated with a visual model of the world, to a new mode that begins to re-create an acoustic model. He also moves from an almost reflexive analysis of what McLuhan calls the major themes of mass culture, mechanics and sex, to a much more conscious, albeit fantastic, effort to create a world in which counter values can be revealed. In *The Sirens of Titan* Vonnegut has moved beyond technology (his *machine* is finally humanized), beyond sex (Malachi simply outgrows it and with his wife and son lives in a place where sex apparently is only for the birds, the giant Blue Birds of Titan), and arrived at the ideals, themes, and techniques he will then employ in *Mother Night, Cat's Cradle, God Bless You, Mr. Rosewater,* and *Slaughterhouse-Five.* With *The Sirens of Titan* Vonnegut finds his place in the literature of a post-Gutenberg world.

Vonnegut's place in contemporary fiction is discovered in the concept of the naïve. Most of the other major fiction writers are doing things similarly and have similar themes and preoccupations. Updike and Roth in novels like *Rabbit, Run* and *Portnoy's Complaint* mimic the vernacular idioms as well as—perhaps better than—Vonnegut. Barthelme, Coover, and Malamud have just as much interest in the elements of popular culture, if *Snow White, The Universal Baseball Association, J. Henry Waugh, Prop.,* or *The Natural* are our evidence. Barth and Barthelme, in *Lost in the Funhouse* and *Unspeakable Practices, Unnatural Acts,* have evinced a similar interest in "multimedia" forms and content. And surely either Borges or Nabokov has as great an interest in games, paradoxes, contradictory narrative postures, and cosmic riddles of existence. But all of these writers, in one way or another, suffer from what Barth, in *Lost in the Funhouse,* calls "paralyzing self-consciousness and the . . . weight of accumulated history."[5] These writers simply do not have the unselfconsciousness of the Vonnegut of the six novels to date. "Historicity and self-awareness," says Barth's alter ego, "while ineluctable and even greatly to be prized, are always fatal to innocence and spontaneity." Of all our fine contemporary writers, Vonnegut must be the one Barth would most like to become. Vonnegut up till now has prized neither historicity (though it is one of his *themes*) nor a mere post-Romantic self-awareness (though self-*knowledge* is another theme). Perhaps as a consequence, he has become the paradigm of the popular writer: he has availed himself of, at the same time he has made available, the most irreducible values, sentimental and sententious though they may be, of our contemporary mass culture. In the end, the very sophistication of the other writers sets them off from popular audiences, suggests indeed that they look down on the unsophisticated. But Vonnegut, in his naïve manner, shows that he goes among them, looks out on the world as the best of them do, and in fact *is* one of them. If that, for some critics, is his major fault, that no doubt is his greatest strength. That surely is why he is read at our cultural extremes by the new tribal love generation and by Middle America.

NOTES TO CHAPTER 12

1. *The Gutenberg Galaxy: The Making of Typographic Man* (New York: New American Library, 1969), pp. 295, 176.
2. "A Modern Sensibility," in *McLuhan: Hot & Cool,* ed. Gerald Emanuel Stearn (New York: New American Library, 1967), p. 93.
3. Henry James, *The Art of the Novel,* ed. R. P. Blackmur (New York: Charles Scribners' Sons, n.d.), p. xxiii.
4. *Anatomy of Criticism* (Princeton, N.J.: Princeton University Press, 1957), p. 367.
5. *Lost in the Funhouse: Fiction for Print, Tape, Live Voice* (New York: Bantam Books, 1969), p. 108.

Chapter 13

VONNEGUT'S FORMAL AND MORAL OTHERWORLDLINESS: *CAT'S CRADLE* AND *SLAUGHTERHOUSE-FIVE*

GLENN MEETER

K URT VONNEGUT IS often spoken of as a "guru," and his popularity is often related to his supposed religious "message." Yet the voice that speaks to us in his tales does not seem that of a prophet; the reader has no feeling of being seized and held and overpowered by something unearthly, like Coleridge's wedding guest when the Ancient Mariner seized him with his skinny hand and held him with his eye. The style is not exuberant or full of doom or poetic or rich. On the contrary, the narrator's voice is a very natural voice, a voice that seems, as a hostile reviewer put it, "programmed to be natural." In its use of the short sentence and short paragraph, the ordinary phrase or even cliché rather than metaphor, and casual direct address to the reader, it seems the voice of a man speaking to men, the voice of a man recollecting emotion in tranquillity.

One does not read far in Vonnegut, however, without discovering that despite the naturalness of the narrator's voice, he is not in the natural world. He is instead in a world of futuristic fantasy, a world where beings like Bokononists and Tralfamadorians are as natural as grass and trees. Vonnegut's narrator lacks the frenzy of Heller's in *Catch-22*, or the weirdness of Barth's in *Giles Goat-Boy*, and yet the world he evokes is as fantastic as anything in those books. Indeed it is more fantastic; it is harder to find real-life parallels to Tralfamadore than to Heller's World War II or Barth's cold-war campus. At the same time, Vonnegut's world is more "real" than these others. The naturalness of the narrator's voice gives us this feeling, but so do many details of setting. The names of Castro, Dresden, Hitler, and Stalin occur in *Cat's Cradle* and *Slaughterhouse-Five*, for example; but these real events and people are present in *Catch-22* and *Giles Goat-Boy* only as they are made metaphorical or allegorical.

In *Catch-22* the world of the Second War is captured in one microcosm, the United States Air Force. In *Giles Goat-Boy* the postwar world is allegorized, its main personages and events finding their parallels in the smaller world of a university campus. Here everything fantastic has its real-life or earthly counterpart. But in books like Vonnegut's *Sirens of Titan, Cat's Cradle,* and *Slaughterhouse-Five* there is a different alignment of fantasy and reality. The two are portrayed side by side, as if both are equally fantastic and equally real—Christianity and Bokononism, Tralfamadore and Dresden, the *Wall Street Journal* and the *Beatrice Rumfoord Galactic Cookbook*. Vonnegut's deadpan narrator is related to deadpan tall-tale narrators of all sorts from Swift's Gulliver to Twain's Jim Baker; but in Vonnegut's case the reader's pleasure is derived not only from the continued tension between tone and material (as in Swift and Twain) but, still more importantly, from the tension between two *kinds* of material, one fantastic and the other real.

Vonnegut's achievement in relating real and fantastic material may be summarized in a phrase which John Barth uses in discussing the work of Jorge Luis Borges: "the contamination of reality by dream."[1] Vonnegut like Borges has imagined an "alternative world" to which his stories allude; and like Borges he makes his fictions out of such allusions. *Cat's Cradle* might be described as a series of allusions to the imaginary *Books of Bokonon; Slaughterhouse-Five* makes of the Dresden fire-bombing massacre a kind of appendix to a discussion of Tralfamadorian notions of time and civilization.

Barth associates two special qualities with the "contamination of reality by dream," and they are both worth discussing in connection with Vonnegut. One quality is its effect on the reader; it reminds us of "the fictitious aspect of our own existence." In Vonnegut this effect is aided by the use of devices like the *regressus in infinitum:* in the opening pages of *Slaughterhouse-Five,* for example, he refers to his ceaseless, and fruitless, work on the "famous Dresden book" in terms of the song about Yon Yonson, which includes a song about Yon Yonson, "and so on to infinity." A similar device is the introduction of the author into his own work, which Vonnegut does indirectly, in *Slaughterhouse-Five,* in the person of Kilgore Trout, the science-fiction writer, and also directly: "That was I. That was me. That was the writer of this book." Another is the use of moral paradoxes, as when Bokonon advises the reader to live by *foma,* which are "useful lies," but also to "Close this book at once! It is nothing but lies!" Another is the reference to God himself as a maker of fictions, as when Bokonon is made to say, "God never wrote a good play in His life." These devices are used much more extensively, of course, by Borges, Nabokov, and others; Vonnegut is certainly a popularizer in that he uses them sparingly and easily.

The other quality which Barth mentions has to do with the causes of such fiction within the writer. This sort of fiction, Barth suggests, is the writer's response to "the felt ultimacies of our time," and particularly it is his response to the feeling that the novel, or narrative literature generally, or Western civilization itself, has run its course. One way to respond to a feeling that the novel is dead, says Barth, "is to write a novel about it"; and thus all the devices which remind us of the fictitious nature of our own existence may also be efforts by the author to use what seem to be exhausted artistic devices in order to create from them, paradoxically, a new work of art.

The notion that a writer mingles fantasy and reality in his work as a response to apocalyptical feelings seems especially appropriate to Vonnegut. All of his work could be said to form an apocalypse—that is, a writing about the end of the world. This is particularly true of *Cat's Cradle* and *Slaughterhouse-Five.* It is in these two books that we find most fully portrayed both his vision of the end and his response to that vision.

Vonnegut's books regularly have to do with cataclysmic events, like the war in *Mother Night,* the Dresden fire-bombing in *Slaughterhouse-Five,* and the freezing of the earth by "ice-nine" in *Cat's Cradle.* Somewhat less spectacularly, *God Bless You, Mr. Rosewater* deals with the end of the Rosewater fortune; but *The Sirens of Titan* and *Cat's Cradle* and *Player Piano* present Utopian societies which try to write an end to all previous history. The end of the United States is prophesied in *Slaughterhouse-Five* (it occurs in 1976)—although such prediction becomes academic in the light of *Cat's Cradle*'s worldwide freeze. There are in addition a good number of references to what by now are fairly standard indicators of apocalyptical feelings, like overpopulation and nuclear weapons. *Cat's Cradle* refers to a book about Hiroshima and another about the Second Coming; there is also a drink called End of the World Delight. But even in the absence of cataclysm, as Vonnegut reminds us in *Slaughterhouse,* there is always "plain old death." And death, as the Bokononist confesses when he takes his own life, means the destruction of the world. Much of *Slaughterhouse* is a litany for the dead and dying—including bacteria, Jesus, Jews, Germans, a glass of champagne, and the novel—all of these deaths followed by the ritual phrase "So it goes." In general Vonnegut's work reminds us of the truth of Bokonon's text, "It is never a mistake to say good-bye." And art, says Vonnegut, following Céline, is a "dance with death."

There are two ways of portraying the end of things in Vonnegut's work that are especially important and worth singling out. Taken together they show how the kind of fiction Vonnegut writes is related to the kind of religious "message" that is felt in his work. These are first of all the death of the novel, and secondly, linked with it, the passing of a sense of history and tradition.

Vonnegut enjoys playing with the idea of fiction as representing "truth" or "life" or "reality." The author's disclaimer to *The Sirens of Titan* reads, "All persons, places, and events in this book are real." "Nothing in this book is true," reads the parallel statement in *Cat's Cradle*—though the headnote goes on to develop the idea of the "useful fiction." *Slaughterhouse-Five* begins, "All this happened, more or less." This kind of playfulness is a familiar device in the deadpan narration—one thinks of Huck Finn's frequent references to the concept of truth in art—but in *Cat's Cradle* it becomes a major theme. The theme is truth and fiction, truth *against* fiction. The forces of science and government are shown together on the side of "truth," and art and religion are shown together on the side of "fiction." Those interested in truth (most notably Felix Hoenikker, father of the atom bomb and ice-nine, and his son Frank) are not interested at all in people; those who are interested in people, most notably Julian Castle, the Schweitzer-like jungle doctor, live by "harmless untruths," or *foma*—that is to say, they are Bokononists. In *Cat's Cradle* truth and art are separate; so are truth and love; so are truth and religion.

The point is that Vonnegut rejects both Western religion, with its insistence on God's acts in history, and the novel, the Western art form which more than any other finds meaning in history. The linkage of the two in *Cat's Cradle* can be seen in the book's plot, which is both a conversion story (from Christianity to Bokononism) and a parody of the *Bildungsroman*. It can also be seen in Bokononism itself, which is a parody both of the *Bildungsroman* and of religion: Bokononism provides a set of terms for a new religion, but they work equally well as terms of literary criticism for the novel. When we read of the narrator's search for his *karass*, or "team which does God's will without knowing it," we may interpret *karass* as "the elect" or "the chosen" or also as "the major characters." We may read the *vin-dit* (a "personal shove in the direction . . . of believing . . . that God Almighty had some pretty elaborate plans for me") as a "calling," or "leading," or also as a "foreshadowing." A *saroon,* or inner acquiescence to the demands of the *vin-dit,* can be "conversion" or "climax" or "anagnorisis." Both *saroon* and *vin-dit,* of course, bear some relation to the word "epiphany" as it is used in literature and religion. A *wampeter* or sacred object (the "pivot" of the *karass,* of which there are always two, "one waxing, one waning") may be thought of as "motif" or "symbol." A *wrang-wrang,* or one who steers someone away from a certain line of development by his own horrible example, does not have a near equivalent that I know of in either discipline; but it could prove useful to either, generating statements like, "Let Sodom be your *wrang-wrang,*" or "In *Tom Jones,* both Thwackum and Square serve as *wrang-wrangs.*" Whether we read the Bokononist terms as literary or religious, the point of the parody is the same: we recognize our conventions *as* conventions. We are made to see that meaning, in life or in art, is invented rather than discovered.

In *Slaughterhouse-Five* there are further suggestions of the futility of realism in fiction. The ninth chapter, for example, recounts a television discussion of the death of the novel (followed by the book's regular refrain for the dying, "So it goes") in which various critics make thinly veiled allusions to Styron's *Confessions of Nat Turner* as a rewrite of *Uncle Tom's Cabin,* and to Mailer's work as a script for his life, and speak of the novel's "function" in pornography, social training, and architecture (it provides spots of color against white walls)—after which Billy Pilgrim gives what

I take to be Vonnegut's own version of the new role of fiction, by describing his adventures in space and time travel.
He is "gently expelled during a commercial." Much of the
opening chapter is given over to Vonnegut's recounting of
his failures in handling the Dresden story "realistically," including a description of his mazelike multicolored outline
of causal and chronological sequences. In the fifth chapter
Billy Pilgrim and a friend, Eliot Rosewater (himself an intrusion from another Vonnegut fiction), are using literature to "re-invent themselves and their universe" and find
that science fiction is a "big help." "Rosewater said . . .
that everything there was to know about life was in *The
Brothers Karamazov* . . ." (including certainly the
legend of the Grand Inquisitor, who must have influenced
Vonnegut's benevolent, religion-creating tyrants, Rumfoord and Bokonon). Vonnegut concludes the incident,
however, by having Rosewater say, "But that isn't *enough*
any more." There is a nice parody of the realist's technique
also in the way the Tralfamadorians try to set up a perfectly typical human environment for the earthlings in
their zoo, using furniture "stolen from Sears in Iowa City,
Iowa." One is forced again to a recognition of realism as
artifice and convention by imagining Vonnegut, erstwhile
Iowa City resident, playing novelist by taking notes outside Sears' window, while the Sears window-dresser plays
the role of, say, Dreiser.

The book's most telling remark concerning Vonnegut's
own fiction occurs in the eighth chapter, when one of the
figures in the Dresden story, Edgar Derby, "becomes a
character"—that is, exerts his free will by making a speech
against an American traitor. (The traitor, Howard Campbell, is in turn another intrusion from a previous Vonnegut
fiction, *Mother Night*.) Even as the speech is made the

reader knows that Edgar Derby will soon be shot as a "plunderer" by Allied forces, being found after the Dresden massacre with a teapot in his hands. Vonnegut comments, "There are almost no characters in this story, and almost no dramatic confrontations, because most of the people in it are so sick and so much the listless playthings of enormous forces. One of the main effects of war, after all, is that people are discouraged from being characters." But all of Vonnegut's "characters" are the playthings of enormous forces, though they may not be listless or sick. If by "character" we mean one who finds meaning in his own life and acts on that meaning, then the term is limited (as Vonnegut seems to limit it here) to the realistic novel. And that may be a war novel as well as any other kind; the difference is not in subject but in vision.

Beyond the parodies of realism, there is in *Slaughterhouse-Five* the suggestion of a "new novel" or "anti-novel." Vonnegut calls it a Tralfamadorian novel, and his book's subtitle claims that it is just such a work. There is nothing new in his suggestion; as the Tralfamadorians stole their realism from Sears, they might have stolen a description of their antinovel from Joseph Frank's article "Spatial Form in Modern Literature."[2] Their books, the Tralfamadorians are recorded as saying in chapter five, contain "many marvelous moments seen all at one time"; they contain no sequences or causes or morals; they consist of "clumps of symbols," like groups of telegrams without any particular relationship—except that, when seen all at once, they produce an image of life "that is beautiful and surprising and deep." As for the sensibility which makes this sort of art possible, they might have stolen that from Ian Watt's *Rise of the Novel*—if they read it in reverse. For the Tralfamadorians there is no time, no causality, no free will. They see all moments at once, instead of, as we have been taught to see them, as points on a line. They are "Realists" in the medieval, not the modern sense. They are fatalists; they are machines and pride themselves on admitting it. In their lives and in their art they have escaped time and achieved what Joseph Frank called (speaking of all abstract art) "the eternal, ethereal tranquility of other-worldly existence." And so, to a great extent, has *Slaughterhouse-Five*.

One of the "felt ultimacies of our time" in Vonnegut's books is the death of the novel. The second, linked with it, is the passing of a sense of history, and the kind of religion based on that sense.

A regret for the loss of tradition, and with it a sense of historical purpose, has been common in Western literature at least since *The Waste Land*, and there is some of this regret in Vonnegut. At the beginning of *Cat's Cradle* there is a rather grim and mechanical Christmas party in the offices of General Forge and Foundry during which a scientist chortles that Christmas has been "dehydrated." In *Slaughterhouse-Five* we read that Billy Pilgrim's mother gave him a crucifix but no religion—because, "like so many Americans, she was trying to construct a life that made sense from things she found in gift shops." Later in the book Vonnegut uses Howard Campbell to make some highly satirical comments about the lack of community spirit, and particularly the self-hatred of the poor, among Americans. Satirical passages like these, whose portrayal of America as a merely secular agglomeration of individuals is familiar in writers like Eliot, Auden, and Waugh, is rare in Vonnegut. For the most part his work accepts the loss of tradition rather gladly as a fact, and even demands that it become a fact.

Vonnegut's work as a whole gives us a satiric version of

the sense of tradition and of God's movement in history; it shows the kind of faith which is built on that sense to be at best foolish and at worst demonic. Malachi Constant, the central figure of *Sirens of Titan,* makes some spiritual progress when he recognizes that God, far from "liking" him, as he once supposed, is indifferent to him; it is on this confession that Winston Niles Rumfoord attempts to build his church, the "Church of God the Utterly Indifferent." In *Cat's Cradle,* the human need for a sense of purpose and meaning finds an outlet through the belief in one's membership in a *karass,* or team that does God's will. Bokononism makes plain, however, that such a belief is *foma,* that is a harmless untruth or useful fiction. Furthermore the *karass* by definition "ignores national, institutional, familial, and class boundaries," and one can be sure of one's fellow *karass* members only after death. All earthly attempts to formalize the *karass* end in *granfalloon,* or false *karass,* "meaningless in terms of God's secret purposes." As examples of *granfalloon* Vonnegut cites Hoosiers, the Communist Party, the General Electric Company, and "any nation, anytime, anywhere." Examples of demonic *granfalloon* may be taken from the opening pages of *Mother Night,* in the names of the nations who have massacred one another in the Middle East. In *Slaughterhouse-Five* the results of demonic *granfalloonery* are displayed in the massacres perpetrated by Crusaders, Germans, and Americans, among others. All of this of course occurs in works of fiction which emphasize that they *are* fiction; but that Vonnegut takes the idea of the demonic *granfalloon* seriously is shown in an article he wrote on Biafra, in which he says "it is probably true that all nations are great and even holy *at the time of death*" (my italics), and concludes that those of us outside of Nigeria can not and should not take sides but "only deplore."[3]

Meaning, purpose, holiness (except possibly at the time of death) have nothing to do with nations and national history. Religion, Bokononism asserts, is on the side of art, lies, and humanity; by its nature it is subversive of nationhood and national history—not because of its prophetic stance toward questions of social justice, but, on the contrary, precisely because it is nonpolitical. "Pay no attention to Caesar," says Bokonon; "Caesar doesn't have the slightest idea what's really going on." This is a more radical separation of church and state than that suggested by the New Testament text; for Vonnegut any connection between politics and religion is a contradiction—compare his ironic reference to San Lorenzo's "Fort Jesus" in *Cat's Cradle*, and, in *Slaughterhouse-Five*, to the "services to Christianity" which are rendered by the Crusaders. Likewise the new version of the Christian gospel presented in *Slaughterhouse-Five* (in Kilgore Trout's "gospel from outer space") makes the Incarnation not a deliberate involvement of God in history but rather the opposite, an accident and an afterthought. Just how close Trout's gospel is to Luke's or Paul's, or to the actual development of the New Testament canon, is perhaps arguable; but it is certainly close to the Buddhist gospel of Salinger, in which the "fat lady in Iowa" is Christ. The net effect of Trout's gospel is to remove religion from purposeful action in history. In Trout's terms, the Christian gospel demands moral judgments about who should or should not be killed, decisions about who has "good connections"; the new gospel (God will "punish horribly anybody who torments a bum who has *no* connections") would tend to inhibit such judgments.

Finally for Vonnegut there is no meaning or purpose in history. God is not interested. *Deo volente* becomes, in *Slaughterhouse-Five*, "if the accident will." There is no such thing as Progress, or Providence, or Manifest Destiny. Vonnegut's own myth of history is given best in a vision which Billy Pilgrim has, in the fourth chapter of *Slaughter-house-Five*, of a war movie run backward. American planes, full of holes, corpses, and wounded bodies, take off backward from England; over France, German fighters heal their enemies and raise the dead by sucking bullets and shrapnel from them; over Germany, the bombers in turn heal their enemies by sucking up bombs and drying up flames; the bombs are shipped backward to America, where factories work night and day to dismantle them ("touchingly, it was mainly women who did this work"); their elements are shipped to specialists who hide them cleverly in the ground, in remote areas, so they can "never hurt anybody again." And then, in Billy's vision, the American airmen become innocent adolescents, Hitler becomes a baby, and all humanity conspires to produce a perfect couple in Paradise. History, in this vision, is sin; and the fall of man for Vonnegut is a fall from timelessness into history, as it is in heretical readings of *Paradise Lost*.

Vonnegut's vision of life and history has several features in common with the world view that Martin Buber has called Paulinism.[4] Paulinism as Buber describes it first arose when Judaism as a national faith was breaking up, when the holy land of Canaan had become only a part of the great empire of Rome; and it reappears in any period when individuals are estranged from their nation and its history. One feature of Paulinism is its vision of the enslavement of the cosmos by powers which are hostile to or indifferent to man. Vonnegut's vision of history, in *The Sirens of Titan*, as arranged by Tralfamadorians in order to communicate something about a missing part for a spaceship, is simply a more dramatic rendering of the view taken in *Cat's Cradle* and *Slaughterhouse*, where history is an accident or a joke. A second feature of Paulinism is the problematic nature of the law: in Paul, the moral law revealed to man by God is recognized as opposed to the law which God established in creation. Similarly in *Slaughterhouse-Five* Vonnegut tells us that the Tralfamadorians, though they can foresee evils, particularly wars, are powerless to stop them; and that past, present, and future are "among the things" which Billy Pilgrim can do nothing about. Throughout *Slaughterhouse-Five* Vonnegut's language emphasizes this vision of the world by using Newtonian terms for humans (they "flow" like liquid, or "expel fluid" like machines) and organic terms for the nonhuman (light "seeks to escape," and bubbles of air seek to climb out of a glass). Those who try to follow the moral law are either pathetic or futile, like Edgar Derby "becoming a character," or evil themselves, like all those who commit massacres for what they feel are righteous causes. A third common feature is man's response to his condition of enslavement. In Paul it is conversion; and conversion is effected by belief in a mediator and his action in history. In Vonnegut there is no mediator (unless he be the bringer of the message, Billy or Bokonon), and there is no action upon history, whose facts remain the same. But there is a conversion, a "belief," which is a new perspective, a new way of seeing things called Bokononism or Tralfamadorianism. Billy's job as spiritual optometrist is to provide the spectacles for a new, converted vision. Conversion to Bokononism and Tralfamadorianism brings results similar to Paul's conversion to Christianity: Bokononism gives a sense of purpose, Tralfamadorianism gives belief "that we will all live forever, no matter how dead we may sometimes seem to be." And it provides Billy Pilgrim with an epitaph which is in its way as affirmative as Paul's "I have fought the good fight," though it is less militant: "Everything was beautiful, and nothing hurt."

If we ask, then, what is the "religion" of Vonnegut's work, the answer would seem to be that it is Paulinism—more completely Pauline even than Paul's, in that it is still further removed from history. We can make such a statement, however, only by ignoring the ordinary, common-sense reading of, say, *Cat's Cradle* and the Epistle to the Romans, which tells us that the difference between Paul's Paulinism and Vonnegut's is immense. We may say, as does Howard Mumford Jones, in *Belief and Disbelief in American Literature,* that there is no literature without religion; we may say, as does Walter Ong, in *The Barbarian Within,* that the voice of a literary work is a summons to belief. But such statements leave us with the further question as to the difference between the religion of literature and that of religion itself. The difference between Vonnegut and Paul is partly, but only partly, one of content. We may try to explain the other differences historically, as differences appropriate to a primitive and a sophisticated age. In terms of Northrop Frye's succession of literary modes, Paul belongs to an age of myth, Vonnegut to an age of irony—the precursor, as Frye sees it, to another age of myth.[5] But the major difference is surely that between religion and literature, or between religion and art, as modes of expression. "Between religion's 'this is,'" Frye says, "and poetry's 'but suppose *this* is,' there must always be some kind of tension, until the possible and the actual meet at infinity." Presumably the tension may exist *within* a writer as well as between writers. One thinks of such modern writers as Blake, or Dostoevsky, or Kafka, or Nietzsche, as examples.

But Vonnegut more clearly than these others belongs on the side of fiction and poetry—more clearly because his playful insistence that fiction is today's religion directs our attention precisely to the difference between "this is" and "suppose this is." It is exactly the difference between *foma* and gospel. The voice of fiction, his fiction certainly, is not so much a summons to belief as an invitation to suspend disbelief. One entertains a faith, in Vonnegut's work, rather than submitting to it.

The artist risks less than the prophet, commits himself less fully. It is less dangerous to create than to reveal. "If you took a bunch of people out into the desert and the world didn't end, you'd come home shamefaced," says John Barth; "but the persistence of an art form doesn't invalidate work created in the comparable apocalyptic ambience. That's one of the fringe benefits of being an artist instead of a prophet."

Still, if one entertains a faith long enough he may finally submit to it. The artist's faith based on "as if" may be a necessary predecessor to the religious faith based on "must be." Vonnegut recently preached Bokononism and Tralfamadorianism to the college graduates of 1970. To the graduates of Bennington College he said, "I beg you to believe in the most ridiculous superstition of all: that mankind is at the center of the universe, the fulfiller or frustrator of the grandest dreams of God Almighty." This is Bokononism, saved from being prophecy only by the one word, "superstition." As for Tralfamadorianism, Vonnegut advised the graduates of another school not to save the world but to "go swimming and sailing and walking, and just fool around."[6]

NOTES TO CHAPTER 13

1. John Barth, "The Literature of Exhaustion," in *The American Novel Since World War II,*" ed. Marcus Klein (New York: Fawcett, 1969), pp. 267–79.
2. Joseph Frank, "Spatial Form in Modern Literature," reprinted from *Sewanee Review* (Spring, Summer, and Fall, 1945), in *Criticism: The Foundations of Modern Literary Judgment,* eds. Mark Schorer, Josephine Miles, and Gordon McKenzie (New York: Harcourt, Brace, 1948), pp. 379–92.
3. "Biafra: A People Betrayed," *McCall's,* April 1970, pp. 68–138.
4. Martin Buber, *Two Types of Faith* (1951), trans. Norman P. Goldhawk, Harper Torchbook edition (New York: Harper and Row, 1961).
5. Northrop Frye, *Anatomy of Criticism* (Princeton: Princeton University Press, 1957).
6. "Vonnegut's Gospel," *Time,* June 29, 1970, p. 8.

Chapter 14

GEODESIC VONNEGUT;
OR,
IF BUCKMINSTER FULLER
WROTE NOVELS

JOHN SOMER

IN THE FIRST CHAPTER of *Slaughterhouse-Five,* Vonnegut says, "I would hate to tell you what this lousy little book cost me in money and anxiety and time. When I got home from the Second World War twenty-three years ago, I thought it would be easy for me to write about the destruction of Dresden, since all I would have to do would be to report what I had seen. And I thought, too, that it would be a masterpiece or at least make me a lot of money, since the subject was so big." He goes on to say, however, that

221

"not many words about Dresden came from my mind then —not enough of them to make a book, anyway." He persisted over the years, nevertheless, to struggle with his memory of Dresden, and when anyone would ask him what he was working on he replied "that the main thing was a book about Dresden" (pp. 2–3). It took him twenty-three years and six novels to write his "lousy little book," and it did cost him much "money and anxiety and time."

Vonnegut found it difficult to write about the bombing of Dresden because it contradicted everything he was brought up to believe in; and it happened at an age, twenty-two, when a man's beliefs are most vulnerable. He grew up during the Depression, in hard times, but if we can believe the nostalgic stories of those who lived through them, those hardships united people rather than divided them. This certainly seems to have been the case in Vonnegut's home and neighborhood in Indianapolis. In an intellectual, cultural, humane, but atheistic environment, Vonnegut was taught to believe in the perfectibility of man, in the marvels of science and technology, and he was taught that he should assume a role in the creation of a "brave new world." His early heritage was reinforced when he studied chemistry in college, where he was taught to believe in the predictability of the material universe. He was brought up to believe that science and technology would ennoble man and advance civilization, but in the war Vonnegut discovered that the opposite could also be true. He watched science and technology debase man, saw it magnify his brutishness, not his compassion. He watched science and technology destroy, in fourteen hours, a thousand-year-old city, a symbol of man's cooperation, a monument to his nobility. He saw the "fairy-land" city of Dresden reduced to its essential chemical properties, saw man's "artificial thing" reduced to its "natural" state. Vonnegut watched his dream of progress feed its "light's flame with self-substantial fuel,/Making a famine where abundance" once lay.

Kurt Vonnegut could not rush home and knock out a masterpiece about the destruction of Dresden because his real subject was the destruction of Kurt Vonnegut, Jr. The little dream Vonnegut took with him to war was not founded upon the rubble of insanity, absurdity, and irrationality that he experienced in the Second World War. His dream was founded on order, stability, and justice. It was founded on what Dresden symbolized. And when Dresden evaporated, so too did Vonnegut's dream. Kurt Vonnegut could have responded to the annihilation of his "self" in many ways. He could have returned to the United States and pretended that Dresden had never happened, but he had too much integrity for that. He could have returned home and cynically thrown himself into the despair and futility of the world he had just discovered, but he had too much courage for that. Instead, he returned with determination to rebuild his dream, a dream that would enable him to go on living as a pacifist, as a humane and compassionate man. But this time the dream would have to be large enough to encompass Dresden and its horrible realities. It would have to be founded on the world as he now saw it, insane and brutal, but it would have to transcend its foundation and point the way to his father's brave new world.

VONNEGUT'S SEARCH FOR A HERO

Because Vonnegut's existential problems find their way into his art, his struggles to return from his annihilation, to survive the return, and to communicate what he had learned are clearly mirrored in his novels, specifically in his attempt to create a hero who could survive with dignity in an insane world. In *Player Piano*, Vonnegut created his first "hero," Paul Proteus, who is perhaps no better than a protagonist. When Paul discovers the insanity that man has wrought, he responds to it in kind. He wants to destroy it with violence. The ensuing revolution is sheer anarchy. Paul has no more control over the political events than he has over his own mind. He eventually realizes that his dissatisfaction with his society and consequent revolt were merely a spiteful attack upon his father, the chief architect of *Player Piano*'s technological nightmare. Thus he learns nothing more significant about the conduct of man than his need for sincere belief, and has nothing, other than this, to offer in the end.

Malachi Constant, the hero of *The Sirens of Titan,* is Vonnegut's next attempt at creating a hero capable of facing the terrors of Dresden. Malachi, "the richest American —and a notorious rakehell," is chosen as a messiah by Tralfamadore to begin saving mankind from the anxieties that Tralfamadore itself originally imposed upon Earthlings. The salvation Tralfamadore plans for Malachi is begun by Winston Niles Rumfoord but finished by Salo, the Tralfamadorian messenger stranded on Titan. Salo, through his example, teaches Malachi to embrace the schizophrenic condition imposed on Earthlings by Tralfamadore and to find in its last, catatonic state of withdrawal the only reparation Tralfamadore can make to Earth. Tralfamadore, after interjecting its punctual notion of time into Earthlings' minds and destroying their innocent living of cyclical time, can only offer the timeless world of the schizophrenic to the beleaguered Earthlings, can only offer them an illusion of their former innocence. As a result, Malachi learns on Titan to look into his soul rather than to the heavens for an answer to the human condition. Malachi, the savior of the world, dies, however, when he returns to Earth, and *The Sirens of Titan* ends with his frustrating and sentimental dream. In this, his second novel, Vonnegut discovered an answer to Dresden, but he did not yet know how to apply it. Winston Niles Rumfoord's discovery that "everything that ever has been always will be, and everything that ever will be always has been" (p. 26) lies inert in the novel, separate from its aesthetic resolution. In order to exorcise Dresden with his new vision, Vonnegut had to rid himself of his youthful notions of romanticism and liberalism, to acquire a context for Rumfoord's theory of time, and to isolate and to define the aesthetic problem raised by Dresden.

In *Mother Night* Vonnegut dismisses romanticism, with its anthropocentric notion of guilt, as a valid response to Dresden and announces the proper role of the imagination: "We are what we pretend to be, so we must be careful about what we pretend to be" (p. v). Howard Campbell, Jr., the protagonist of the novel, is given the opportunity to become an "authentic Hero" by Colonel Frank Wirtanen, given the opportunity to sacrifice himself nobly for the good of mankind by being a spy for "God's" side. Campbell eventually accepts Wirtanen's offer and becomes, for the Nazis, a propaganda specialist, whose speeches contain coded messages for the Allied forces. In order to live with himself, he turns his speeches into satirical attacks on the enemy. His wit betrays him, however, and his clever satires are taken literally by the Nazis. Consequently, he actually strengthens the forces of "evil." Unlike Proteus, Campbell has some insight into his situation, but it is far from the cosmic perspective of Malachi Constant. Campbell is aware that schizophrenia is "a simple and widespread boon to modern mankind" (p. 136) but is unable to avail himself of its healing properties. A born romantic, he is unable to accept his alter ego, his satirical mask. He remains true to his romantic illusion of his "self" but false to the insanity he sees around him. He naïvely assumes that he is morally superior to the world and therefore the only one who can be held accountable for its crimes. He says of himself that he "served evil too openly and good too secretly" (p xii). When he is tried for war crimes after the war, he is proven innocent of the charges brought upon him by Israel, but he executes himself because in his own mind he is guilty. Campbell's suicide, however, is essentially a futile act for in no way is human life improved by his death. It remains simply an affirmation of an ego obsessed with its own cosmic importance. Campbell's notes do not issue from an "authentic Hero," but from the underground voice of Dostoevsky's antihero. While Campbell learns much about the world, he fails to establish a rapport with it. He cannot stand the prospect of being free to return to an insane world, to an insanity that he also shares. He prefers a senti-mental, banal, and self-pitying farewell: "Goodbye, cruel world!", underscored with *"Auf wiedersehen?"*, the irony of which this master satirist probably overlooked.

In *Cat's Cradle* Vonnegut dismisses liberalism, with its anthropocentric notion of duty, and dramatizes the prin-ciple of Dynamic Tension, a state of careful and propor-tioned alignment of stresses that creates a geodesic dome of balanced forces, forces so arranged that they contain one another's energies. Jonah, the narrator and protagonist, fares better than Campbell. Again this is a story written after the fact, but this time the narrator has acquired some understanding of himself as well as the rest of mankind. He is a Bokononist and knows that no one man can assume the responsibility for the end of the world. Before his conversion to Bokononism, however, he is a liberal named John who, though vulgar and crass in his personal life, aspires to write a great book about the bombing of Hiroshima and improve Christian life on Earth. As one liberal force in the novel bent upon eliminating evil from the world, John is fate's pawn and the novel's catalyst that quickens the collapse of the geodesic social structure the insane Bokonon has established on San Lorenzo, a collapse that coincides with the end of John's world. Dr. Felix Hoenikker, the novel's playful scientist and major liberal force, discovers, upon the request of the military, a way to eliminate the evil of mud from the Earth. Hoenikker's invention, ice-nine, clear the path of soldiers, but it also creates a vacuum that is quickly filled by a far greater evil, one that in the hands of his irresponsible children destroys even mankind, or the "sitting-up mud" as Vonnegut calls it. The geodesic wisdom that Jonah acquires through his catastrophic experience as John is not only manifest in the novel, but is articulated by Bokonon: "good societies could be built only by pitting good against evil, and by keeping the tension between the two high at all times" (p. 90). As a result, Vonnegut acquired, in Bokonon's geodesy, the context for Rumfoord's theory of time. His final task was to isolate the aesthetic problem raised by Dresden.

In *God Bless You, Mr. Rosewater* Vonnegut finally confronted Dresden. When his hero, Eliot Rosewater, sees the imaginary fire storm devouring Indianapolis, he goes insane and sees the "inner core of white" in the flames. Upon his recovery, he discards his liberal sense of duty, his romantic guilt, and lives. *God Bless You, Mr. Rosewater* is structured unlike most of the earlier novels, in that it does not begin after the fact, but at the beginning, which allows Vonnegut to document Eliot's spiritual growth. Vonnegut's history of Eliot's growth is complete except for one year— the year of Eliot's insanity when he discovers the answer to his life. This gap in Eliot's life and in the novel underlines the technical problem that Vonnegut has been concerned with all along. He has not only been trying to enlighten his heroes to their role in a universe devoid of spiritual values, but he has been trying to define the void in contemporary man's life and trying to create a symbol, a literary device that could manifest an answer to this problem. With Eliot he almost succeeded. He created a hero who understands that the universe touches man in accidental ways, a hero who responds affirmatively to the insanity epitomized by the Dresden fire-bombing, and a hero who survives his return to the everyday world. Vonnegut needed one thing more, however—a literary device capable of manifesting the process that his hero must experience if he is to achieve a vision of reality that could encompass the implications of Dresden without surrendering to utter despair. It took him four more years to unite Rumfoord's theory of time and Bokonon's theory of dynamic tension into a structural principle for his Dresden book. It took him four years to dramatize the gap in Rosewater's life, the gap that defined the problem of contemporary man and its answer, four years to conceive his schizophrenic manner of writing, an aesthetic that could re-create and nurture a hero destroyed by Dresden.

On the title page of *Slaughterhouse-Five* Vonnegut announces that the book is written "SOMEWHAT IN THE TELEGRAPHIC SCHIZOPHRENIC MANNER OF TALES OF THE PLANET TRALFAMADORE." Midway through the novel he gives a clue to the "manner" of Tralfamadorian tales. They are something like telegrams. A Tralfamadorian explains to Billy Pilgrim, the hero of the novel, that

'each clump of symbols is a brief, urgent message—describing a situation, a scene. We Tralfamadorians read them all at once, not one after the other. There isn't any particular relationship between all the messages, except that the author has chosen them carefully, so that, when seen all at once, they produce an image of life that is beautiful and surprising and deep. There is no beginning, no middle, no end, no suspense, no moral, no causes, no effects. What we love in our books are the depths of many marvelous moments seen all at one time' (p. 76).

An excellent example that illustrates the schizophrenic manner of narration occurs in Chapter Three. Because there is no "particular relationship between all the messages," we may begin anywhere in the chapter. A good place to begin is after Billy has been captured. He and other prisoners are herded into a stone cottage to rest. There Billy falls asleep on the shoulder of a rabbi. In the next paragraph, Billy is in his optometrist's office back in Ilium, sleepily reading, only to be scared out of his wits by the noon whistle. In the following paragraph, he has been startled awake by a guard's kick and told to resume the march. During the march, the Germans decide to take some propaganda pictures exposing the pitiful state of the American soldier. To give spice to the film, they simulate an actual capture. Billy, chosen to be the star of the film, is thrown into shrubbery from which he emerges, "his face wreathed in goofy good will," and is then captured by the resourceful and brave Germans. His goofy smile, of course, is not caused by his second capture in 1944 but by the luxuriant feel of his Cadillac in 1967. He is on his way to a Lions Club luncheon where a major in the Marines is going to explain America's great war in Vietnam. After the luncheon, Billy goes home to take a nap, where he is awakened by a doorbell. Looking out the window, Billy sees a cripple at his door, another one across the street, and a new Buick Riviera containing the man who had hired the cripples to sell worthless magazine subscriptions. Billy is genuinely moved and begins to cry, only to realize in the next paragraph that his tears are caused by the winter wind in Luxembourg in 1944.

After his second capture, Billy "had been seeing Saint Elmo's fire, a sort of electronic radiance around the heads of his companions and captors. It was in the treetops and on the rooftops of Luxembourg, too. It was beautiful." Billy's group is joined then by more captives, forming a "Mississippi of humiliated Americans." The result of these carefully arranged messages—this collection of banalities, horrors, and ironies—is that "Billy found the afternoon stingingly exciting. There was so much to see—dragon's teeth, killing machines, corpses with bare feet that were blue and ivory" (pp. 48–56). Billy had arrived at "an image of life that is beautiful and surprising and deep." He had seen the "depths of many marvelous moments . . . all at one time." Vonnegut's manipulation of messages has produced here in Billy what Vonnegut hopes *Slaughterhouse-Five* will produce in its readers as they experience the schizophrenic manner of narration. Thus, after a tortuous journey through six novels, Vonnegut has finally created a hero who can survive with dignity in an insane world. His search for this character has ultimately forced him, however, to create an aesthetic that radically altered the structure and texture of his sixth novel. More important, though, his schizophrenic manner draws attention to and challenges a *tradition* of the novel never before acknowledged.

VONNEGUT AND THE SPATIAL-FORM TRADITION

Vonnegut's schizophrenic manner is actually a new name for a literary technique already described and defined by Joseph Frank in "Spatial Form in Modern Literature" (1945).[1] According to Frank, cultures that find themselves in harmony with their environment produce naturalistic art. That is to say, paintings are organized according to space and novels according to time. But in times of cultural upheaval when men feel threatened by their environment, they produce a "non-naturalistic abstract" art. Narration, for example, abandons its traditional structural principle of chronological time and adopts space as a structural principle. Narrative events no longer follow one another in logical sequence, but are arranged according to spatial patterns in the novel, patterns which not only allow two events to occur simultaneously, but attempt to manifest the simultaneity in the texture of the narrative. While Frank concerned himself with modern literature, the spatial-form principles serve as the basis for a tradition of the novel reaching back to Laurence Sterne's *The Life and Opinions of Tristram Shandy* (1760, 1767). Consequently, to fully appreciate Vonnegut's refinements of this tradition with his schizophrenic manner, we must review the thrust and development of this tradition from as far back as the eighteenth century, and consider the direction it has taken in the work of at least one of Vonnegut's contemporaries, Alain Robbe-Grillet.

The origin of the spatial-form tradition lies in the distinction Descartes made between the *res extensa* and the *res cogitans,* or, as Coleridge would later call them, the objective and the subjective worlds. The spatial-form tradition was a champion of *res cogitans;* it emphasized man's inner life and, in essence, declared that subjective reality was the only reality worth studying. The mainstream of the novel, which for convenience we may place in the temporal-form tradition, affirmed *res extensa* and treated the world as the new science told man he experienced it. These novels, in the mainstream, unfolded themselves lineally, according to the orderly and rational plan of Newtonian mechanics.

In the beginning the spatial-form tradition was minor, but its first artistic manifestation was grand—Sterne's *Tristram Shandy.* Sterne, through the persona of Tristram, wove within his narrative an incredible montage of events and experiences. Tristram's story follows no logical pattern, but jumps about at the mercy of an erratic memory. It is generally conceded now that Sterne's rambling method was firmly grounded in Locke's theory that the mind is essentially illogical and associates thoughts at random. *Tristram Shandy,* then, is both an argument for and a manifestation of Locke's and Sterne's conception of man's inner life. It protests against the scientific assumption that the intellect is man's principal faculty and that his experiences of life are orderly and logical. Even though *Tristram Shandy* stands opposite the mainstream of its day, a tradition in which authors freely interrupted the flow of the narrative to comment upon their characters, Sterne, as author, lurks behind Tristram and controls his discourse. Sterne's attempt to render the inner mind, then, is informed by a very real presence of the author's voice. By the time the spatial-form tradition emerged in the late nineteenth and early twentieth centuries as the dominant tradition, all traces of the author's voice had vanished. The temporal-form tradition, with its chummy relationship between author and reader, had lived a long and vigorous life but suffered an abrupt death. Ernest Hemingway delivered the coup de grace with his scathing parody in 1926, *The Torrents of Spring*.

In the spatial-form tradition, however, the author eliminated his *own* voice from his novel when the tradition evolved into its psychological or stream-of-consciousness phase. The events and contributions involved in this transformation are common knowledge to students of the modern novel. Writers such as Turgenev, Chekhov, Dostoevsky, and Dujardin heralded the change by their experiments in plot outline and explorations into the inner man. In Henri Bergson and William James, writers found the philosophical footing they needed to push their movement to its culmination in the works of Woolf, Joyce, and Faulkner. We need cite only one example to illustrate the import of this evolution, the Benjy section of Faulkner's *The Sound and the Fury* (1929). The hand of the author is there, but his voice is gone. Benjy is not a persona for Faulkner. George Moore's "melodic line," Henry James's "impressionism," and Joseph Conrad's narrations slowly evolved into the objective rendering of the subjective world in Joyce and Faulkner. It was about this time that some critics started talking about the "death of the novel." Such thinkers always underestimate the ingenuity of man, however, and this time they missed the subtle changes present in the spatial-form tradition as it began to leave its psychological phase and experience a rebirth in its lyrical phase, a phase thoroughly studied by Ralph Freedman in *The Lyrical Novel* (1963). The lyrical novelists, sensing that the psychological novelists had already compromised Descartes's philosophical basis for the spatial-form tradition by objectifying the subjective world, returned to their origins and emerged subjectifying the objective world.

The lyrical phase may have begun in the following way. As the psychological novelist attempted to capture the working of the *res cogitans* as it related to the *res extensa,* he used events and objects from the *res extensa* to serve as "objective correlatives" for the state of mind he wished to render. In his effort to find the exact "symbols" and to arrange them in the most effective order, he discovered that this mode of narration could accomplish more than the act of signifying the contents of men's minds or the way in which they worked internally. He found that this mode could also signify the epistemological act. Freedman says "the contribution of lyrical fiction has been this peculiar way of looking at perception." Elaborating on this statement, he says that "the engagements of a knowing self in the world are the novel's mark of distinction. But the novelist has many different ways at his disposal to express this relationship. He can ask how a hero relates to the historical process, to environment and ideas; he can inquire into the reciprocal relations of man and society, man and man. But novels can also ask these questions differently: how does the mind know its world? What is the functional relationship between the inner and the outer? What is the relationship of awareness of knowledge to human conduct and choice?" He concludes that the latter "way of looking at perception" is "the dominant mood in the lyrical novel."[2] In effect, then, "narrator and protagonist combine to create a self in which experience is fashioned in imagery."[3] The result is that the protagonist is a mask for the novelist as he weaves objective facts and events to manifest his vision, just as Tristram was a mask for Sterne. The distinction, however, between a lyrical novelist and Sterne is clear and significant. Sterne's mask represents his voice and his mind. The mask of a lyrical novelist, on the other hand, represents his act of knowing the objective world. "In this way," says Freedman, "perceived objects become manifestations of the poet's spirit—features of his self-portrait—as they are portrayed symbolically in the form of art. The 'object' is the catalyst through which a finite, individual self is transmuted into an infinite, aesthetic self." Ultimately, the lyrical novelist "*distorts* the universe or dissolves it into hallucination or dream in which its 'true' (infinite and organic) nature is revealed. Thus, the magic or spiritual awareness unfolds a picture of infinite reality which is hidden to the ordinary glance."[4]

The implications of the lyrical novel are twofold. First, it defends the individual from depersonalization as vigorously as did Sterne or the stream-of-consciousness writers, but the lyrical novelist approaches the problem in a different way. Unlike the psychological novelist, he does not use the objective world to portray the mind, but instead uses the mind to portray the world. Thus, while the lyrical novelist champions the individual, he is finally driven by impulse to know the *res extensa*. Second, this impulse, then, gives new direction to the spatial-form tradition and leads it into its phenomenological phase where in Robbe-Grillet the lyrical "I" becomes literally an "eye."

VONNEGUT AND ROBBE-GRILLET

Alain Robbe-Grillet's career curiously parallels Vonnegut's. In the first place, they both wrote novels with "gaps" in them. We have already discussed Eliot Rosewater's blank year; Robbe-Grillet confronted somewhat the same artistic difficulty in *The Voyeur* (1955). Like Vonnegut, he was also writing about a schizophrenic, a man who in his crisis commits a horrible crime, a crime that Robbe-Grillet represents by a "blank page." In *In the Labyrinth* (1959), he filled the gap in *The Voyeur* just as Vonnegut filled the gap in *God Bless You, Mr. Rosewater* with *Slaughterhouse-Five*. It is in the contrast between these two novels, *In the Labyrinth* and *Slaughterhouse-Five*, then, that the battle lines between these two contenders for the future direction of the spatial-form tradition becomes clear.

In his discussion of *In the Labyrinth*, Bruce Morrissette notes the structural key to the novel. "The narrative 'presence,' " says Morrissette, "who says 'I' in the first line . . . never again refers to himself until the end, when a 'my' is followed by the final word 'me.' "[5] The rest of the novel is concerned with objects in the *res extensa*. The lyrical impulse to know the objective world has reached such an extreme here that the "objective correlatives" seem to signify only themselves. This assumption is not really valid, as Roland Barthes points out. "Robbe-Grillet," he says, "requires only one mode of perception: the sense of sight." As a consequence, for Robbe-Grillet "the object is no longer a common-room of correspondences, a welter of sensations and symbols, but merely the occasion of a certain optical resistance."[6] Thus the gathering of objects from the *res extensa* serves now only to manifest an "eye." The great tradition of the spatial-form narrative that began as a champion of the individual now finds itself seemingly in the embarrassing position of destroying the individual. When Robbe-Grillet filled his blank page, he filled it with a blank character, a character that exists only as three pronouns. First the author removed himself from the novel in

the stream-of-consciousness phase, and now, in the phenomenological phase of the spatial-form tradition, he
seems to have removed even the character from the novel.

Vonnegut's experiments in the spatial-form tradition
are radically different from Robbe-Grillet's. When Vonnegut filled the gap in *God Bless You, Mr. Rosewater,* he did
not fill it with another gap, a blank character as did Robbe-
Grillet; he filled it with a character, Billy Pilgrim, and, like
Sterne, he filled it with the author's voice, but he went
even further; he filled it with himself, Kurt Vonnegut, Jr.
The gap, we must understand, symbolizes the problem of
contemporary man—his spiritual void. All Robbe-Grillet
did in *In the Labyrinth* was define the gap, the problem,
with greater precision than he did in *The Voyeur.* Vonnegut, on the other hand, not only defines the problem in
Slaughterhouse-Five, but offers a solution to it that is consistent with man's cultural and spiritual evolution at this
point in history. His solution is the geodesic principle of
dynamic tension, which is manifested in the structural,
textural, and existential relationships between the author
and his character. Vonnegut shows us how to thrive in a
world epitomized by Dresden, and becomes consequently
the ultimate champion of the individual and the spatial-
form tradition. He is humanistically, if not also aestheti-
cally, superior to Robbe-Grillet.

Vonnegut and Robbe-Grillet differ in their treatment of
the spatial-form tradition because of their respective in-
terpretations of modern science. Robbe-Grillet's destruction of his character, reducing him to an "eye" surrounded
by objects that offer him "optical resistance," is actually an
attempt to save the individual, to defend him from the
terrors that post-Einsteinian science has created. In *Loss of
the Self in Modern Literature and Art,* Wylie Sypher

stresses "that in every modern heroism there must be a degree of self-obliteration."[7] He says that new novelists such as Robbe-Grillet apply the law of entropy and allow their characters to be "absorbed into a field."[8] Robbe-Grillet, Sypher argues, fuses "the personality of his characters . . . with their environment."[9] In effect, then, Robbe-Grillet is responding to the problem raised by modern science, the almost impossible task of experiencing initiation in the post-Einsteinian world. His contribution to the spatial-form tradition actually does not contradict its long tradition of defending the individual from the *res extensa* but is simply responding to a new science in a way that on the surface appears to be viable. But even a casual glance at the cosmic implications of the work of Albert Einstein and R. Buckminster Fuller, as interpreted by Guy Murchie, the immediate influence on Vonnegut,[10] makes it clear that modern physics has made it impossible for man to initiate himself, to be reborn, to lose himself in the phenomenological world—in fact, in anything outside of himself except the time-space continuum, whether it be animals, plants, stars, or modern literature and art.

VONNEGUT AND THE FOURTH DIMENSION

We have already noted that a geodesic dome is an apt illustration of Vonnegut's principle of dynamic tension, a state of careful and proportioned alignment of stresses that creates an artificial dome of balanced forces. As Guy Murchie points out, Einstein's theory that inertia is the "*universal* aspect of gravity" and that gravity is the "*local* aspect of inertia" is also an illustration of dynamic tension. Because Einstein argued that both inertia and gravity are "relative geometric properties," he concluded, as Murchie says, "that the earth no longer need strain centrifugally or schizophrenically against the tension of solar gravitation but instead could float in complete relaxation along her natural track, her private geodesic line through space-time."[11] This last illustration not only clarifies the principle of dynamic tension in the abstract, but indicates why man needs and fears this principle in the concrete. To understand this paradox, we must look at another of Murchie's examples:

> Suppose, for example, that you were born and brought up (or down) in a falling elevator, or more realistically, in my orbiting space station. In such a vehicle, an apple does not fall and, if you had never heard of the phenomenon of falling, it would take a great effort of imagination to visualize and understand the strange world of a planet's surface where a wholesale molecular bombardment is always pushing "upward" so hard that loose things like apples seem to want to go "downward." It would sound absurd to be told that in fact the only reason your apple inside the vehicle does not "fall" is that the whole vehicle including yourself is already "falling." Yet from the outside we know that this is true—at least relatively speaking. We can see at last that the state of falling is the normal state of bodies in the universe—of all free, whole bodies at any rate—and that it is only the denser sub-regions (like a planetary surface) containing tiny captive crumbs (like you) that must undergo the frustration of not being allowed their full response in unhindered falling.[12]

The terror that man found in the fourth dimension of space-time is now clear: "the state of falling is the normal state of bodies in the universe" except, that is, for earth-bound "captive crumbs" such as human beings. By magnifying the initiatory realm to cosmic proportions, man exposed himself to his first ingrained fear, an instinct, the fear of falling. The rite of initiation, then, leaped beyond such acts as circumcision as practiced by primitive tribes,[13] leaped beyond the annihilation of the "self" in the world of plants, animals, and stars, and stood poised on the brink of the fourth dimension. Until man loses his inherent fear of falling, he cannot make the leap into the "normal state of bodies in the universe" and experience the ultimate initiation. It is unlikely, however, that man will ever achieve his "normal state" for both physical and emotional reasons. In the first place, such small creatures as human beings would have to position themselves far away from the Earth in order to exist in harmony with it. Secondly, man has been conditioned, through a million years of experience, to accept gravity as a normal state. It seems unlikely that he could easily discard this conditioning.

Consequently, man must realize, along with Malachi Constant, that an answer to the world created by modern science lies not in the *res extensa,* but in his ability to become what he pretends to be. Because he cannot leap into the time-space continuum and escape the "strain" of cultural schizophrenia—the division of man into intellect and intuition—he must artificially reduce the strain and consciously create a geodesic harmony within himself, a harmony that reflects, but does not manifest, the harmony of the spheres. As Vonnegut considers in *Player Piano,* man must do those "artificial things" which distinguish him "from the rest of the animals" (p. 270), and create his own initiation rite. Such a task is not as difficult as it first appears. In fact, in an epistemological sense, man has always done just that. What is an initiation, if not the absorption, the annihilation of the ego in a vision of reality that the ego had created in the first place? Certainly the task was not arbitrary with the hunter, the plant gatherer, and the star gazer, but an organic part of their world experiences. We are different from such primitive societies in that the world we are consciously aware of exceeds the vision of the naked eye. The world of primitive man was circumscribed by the horizon. Ours is microscopically small and telescopically large, and consequently useless to us at the moment for a basis of initiation. The world we are consciously aware of is too intangible, too frightening for us to surrender ourselves to it. So Vonnegut bids us turn our backs on the universe and look inside ourselves for a basis of initiation, a means of squarely facing Dresden. He bids us to harmonize our schizophrenic halves, to synchronize our rational awareness of punctual time with our intuitive living of (what Henri Bergson calls) pure duration, to create an existential state of dynamic tension within ourselves, a psychic geodesic dome free of gravity, an illusion of reality in which we can immerse and lose our ego. Vonnegut bids us to create an artificial rite of initiation.

VONNEGUT'S INNOVATIONS

Such naked ideas, however, interest philosophers and theorists. Artists must in some way manifest their ideas to give form to their literary efforts. Artists, as Vonnegut says in *The Sirens of Titan*, must create a literature that makes us "courageous, watchful, and secretly free" (p. 132). They strive to create forms that man can intuit and experience in his earthbound way; and yet these forms, to Vonnegut, must also help man transcend his limitations and be reborn. Consequently, Vonnegut has striven to amplify Malachi Constant's dream and to fill the gap in Eliot Rosewater's life by using his principles of schizophrenic time-lessness and dynamic tension as the structural frame for *Slaughterhouse-Five*—a frame that can support the strands of the cat's cradle as they weave the fabric of his schizophrenic manner, a manner that manifests his initiatory rite and demonstrates the proper use of western man's schizophrenic nature.

Naturally, Vonnegut's singular response to modern science required him to introduce revolutionary techniques into the spatial-form tradition. Again, the best place to begin a study of Vonnegut's schizophrenic manner is with his treatment of Billy Pilgrim's story. Vonnegut shares one trait with his predecessors and contemporaries in that his spatial, rather than temporal, arrangement of events is informed by epistemology. However, unlike the psychological novelists, Vonnegut is not interested in learning about the workings of the mind; unlike the lyrical novelists, he is not interested in how the mind knows the *res extensa;* unlike the phenomenological novelists, he is not interested in discovering the truth in external reality. Rather, he is concerned with discovering "an image of life that is beautiful and surprising and deep." The historical urgency epitomized by the Dresden firestorm has forced Vonnegut to seek an immediate answer and not more questions.

The answer is manifested in Billy Pilgrim. Billy has come "unstuck in time" and been miraculously granted an abrupt and easily attained beatific vision of reality. Billy's erratic movements through time and *Slaughterhouse-Five* are not instigated by his mental turbulence, although they do symbolize this turbulence, but are instigated by an "accident" in the physical world. Thus, Billy is different from all other heroes in the spatial-form tradition. The structure of this novel—its erratic sequence of events—is not merely a symbol of Billy's inner state, but an objective fact. Because Vonnegut uses time travel, a stock-in-trade item of the science-fiction novelist, as his device to elevate Billy, he has shifted the entire basis of the spatial-form tradition. His technical treatment of Billy is informed by the *res extensa,* not the *res cogitans.* This startling innovation at once gives Vonnegut enormous mobility as a novelist, but it also challenges the reader at every point. As a result, Vonnegut needs his optometrist, Billy Pilgrim, to help the reader see a deep, surprising, and beautiful image of life. While this image was easy for Billy to attain, Vonnegut, his creator, had to work hard for it, as our discussion of his first five novels indicates. Billy is the direct descendant of the stumbling Paul Proteus, the foolish Howard Campbell, and the "humane" John. It is more important, however, that he is the direct descendant of Malachi Constant, the hero who found the answer but could not bring it back to Earth, and Eliot Rosewater, the hero who brought back the spirit of renewal but failed to show us how and where he found it. Billy makes none of the mistakes of Proteus, Campbell, and John, and he combines the virtues of Constant and Rosewater. This sudden elevation of Billy, however, must have been one of the most difficult decisions that Vonnegut faced in writing *Slaughterhouse-Five.* His solution of miraculously freeing Billy from the restriction of punctual time, at first glance, may even appear a mistake. Certainly it does try our willing suspension of disbelief.

Working with this problem, some readers must find consolation in the short third paragraph of Billy's story: "He says." That paragraph is the narrator's comment on Billy's statement that he is free of time. It seems to imply that the narrator is dubious of Billy's story and that the reader should be also. It seems to imply that the narrator and the reader are in on a great joke: Billy is actually insane and his time travels are really hallucinations. But that implication is simply not valid. Billy experiences three hallucinations in his story and the narrator carefully distinguishes them from Billy's time travels. For example, just before Billy is captured by the Germans, he stands on the ice of a frozen creek and dreams that he is ice skating in "dry, warm, white sweatsocks." The narrator says, "Billy Pilgrim was having a delightful hallucination. . . . This wasn't time-travel" (p. 42). Clearly Vonnegut denies us the right to translate Billy's bizarre experiences into terms that are rationally acceptable to us. Just as in *The Sirens of Titan* Malachi Constant does not personify "wrong-headedness" but symbolizes it (p. 225), Billy does not personify *insanity* but symbolizes it. We must accept Billy's freedom in time as a fact within the fictional world of *Slaughterhouse-Five,* no matter how much it strains our willing suspension of disbelief, if we are to taste the fruits of Vonnegut's twenty-three years of labor. Billy's coming unstuck in time is an innovative technique that enables Vonnegut to condense his hard-won wisdom into a single symbol, albeit an extremely complex one. Billy's miraculous initiation into a deep understanding of the universe parallels the torturous journey that Malachi Constant took. Vonnegut's immediate benefit of condensing Malachi's initiation into one symbol is that he could begin *Slaughterhouse-Five* where *The Sirens of Titan* left off. He did not have to redramatize the lengthy schizophrenic process of initiation in *Slaughterhouse-Five* but could begin immediately on the business at hand, showing the benefits of a schizophrenic initiation. The result was not only a short book, but more important, a sharply focused one.

Because Billy is unstuck in time, he not only acquires wisdom and returns with it to his normal life, but he continues to oscillate freely between the worlds of enlightenment and everyday life. On one hand, he marries the boss's fat daughter, makes piles of money selling frames for glasses to the workers at the General Forge and Foundry Company in Ilium, and drives about in his Cadillac, which is plastered with banal political stickers. On the other hand, because he ricochets erratically and uncontrollably within an enclosed sphere of punctual time, he has acquired an overview of life, a memory of both the past and the future, a vision that enables him to live in this world and yet transcend it at the same time. Thus, he lives in a world superior to that of Earthlings but obviously inferior to that of Tralfamadorians who, in *Slaughterhouse-Five*, exist in the fourth dimension. Billy, then, does not possess a pure vision of reality but an approximation of it, an illusion that conforms so closely to the fourth dimension that Billy experiences a beatific vision, an illusion created by the dynamic tension between his two worlds.

The most important result of Billy's geodesic experience is his understanding that man has been too concerned with mortality and has misunderstood the true nature of time, that mortality is actually immortality, and that man's few years are actually an eternity.[14] In the second letter Billy writes to mankind he says:

> The most important thing I learned on Tralfamadore was that when a person dies he only *appears* to die. He is still very much alive in the past, so it is very silly for people to cry at his funeral. All moments, past, present, and future, always have existed, always will exist. The Tralfamadorians can look at all the different moments just the way we can look at a stretch of the Rocky Mountains,

for instance. They can see how permanent all the moments are, and they can look at any moment that interests them. It is just an illusion we have here on Earth that one moment follows another one, like beads on a string, and that once a moment is gone it is gone forever.

When a Tralfamadorian sees a corpse, all he thinks is that the dead person is in bad condition in that particular moment, but that the same person is just fine in plenty of other moments. Now, when I myself hear that somebody is dead, I simply shrug and say what the Tralfamadorians say about dead people, which is "So it goes" (p. 23).

Consequently, Billy, who like Vonnegut has lived through the destruction of Dresden, knows the moment of the bombing was structured, knows "it had to be done." " 'It was all right,' " says Billy. " '*Everything* is all right, and everybody has to do exactly what he does. I learned that on Tralfamadore' " (p. 171).

Because of his transcendental vision that nullifies guilt and anxiety, Billy feels sorry for Earthlings. He has spent his normal life prescribing glasses for people, and when he decides to tell the world the truths he knows, he begins "prescribing corrective lenses for Earthling souls. So many of those souls were lost and wretched, Billy believed, because they could not see as well as his little green friends on Tralfamadore" (p. 25). He does not respond to the world like the conventional hero, a James Bond, and destroy evil, conquer it, and banish it from the universe, nor does he wither under the pressure into an anti-hero whose ineffectual acts help no one, not even himself. Instead, he reacts like the schizophrenic hero that he is, a hero both of this world and apart from it, a hero falling on his geodesic line: he begins teaching man how to find his own geodesic principle. He dies as he lives, assured of his vision, standing before a huge audience under a geodesic dome preaching his wisdom, predicting his own imminent death, refusing protection, and closing his speech with these words, "Farewell, hello, farewell, hello," while an insane Paul Lazzaro aims a high-powered laser gun at his forehead. When Billy Pilgrim dies the narrator says, "So Billy experiences death for a while. It is simply violet light and a hum. There isn't anybody else there. Not even Billy Pilgrim is there." He goes on to say that Billy then "swings back into life again, all the way back to an hour after his life was threatened by Lazzaro—in 1945" (p. 122–24). Billy is right. Mortality is immortality; time is eternity; the finite is infinite; man is his own salvation. Thus Billy weaves his way through time, creating a mosaic pattern in this spatial-form novel, moving slowly and artfully so that his movements create "an image of life that is beautiful and surprising and deep," moving carefully under the deft hand of Vonnegut, the narrator, whose first word, "Listen," echoes and re-echoes through the erratic corridors of Billy's schizophrenic passage through time.

While Billy's spastic movements in time symbolize the shamanistic possibilities of schizophrenia to create an artificial fourth dimension, a realm of initiation accessible now to man, Billy's relationship to the narrator structures this book and demonstrates the technical significance of dynamic tension. *Slaughterhouse-Five* is a framed novel; that is, a story within a story—or, more accurately, a fictive story within an autobiography. Consequently, this is not a mere framed story, but an innovation that strains the conventions of both the spatial and temporal-form traditions and even brings them together into a technical and structural relationship of dynamic tension. What we would unthinkingly call preface and epilogue, Vonnegut calls Chapter One and Chapter Ten of a book called *Slaughterhouse-Five, or The Children's Crusade*.

Hence, Vonnegut's innovations in the spatial-form tradition are consistent and progressive. He shifts the basis of the tradition from the subjective world to the objective, then surrounds his novel, a product of the imagination, that is the subjective world, with an autobiography, a series of events from the objective world. His next logical step is to interject the narrator of the objective world into the subjective world, so that the literary perspectives of the *res extensa* and the *res cogitans*, the presence of the author and the absence of the author, could establish a harmonious relationship of dynamic tension. This innovation allows Vonnegut to establish three points. First, it shows that the narrator, or Vonnegut, was a comrade-in-arms with Billy. Second, it shows that the narrator and Billy are united in some spiritual way. Third, it forms a pattern that shows Vonnegut and his objective world easing themselves into Billy's fictive world where they can mutually identify with one another and create an illusionary, imaginative, and artificial equilibrium of dynamic tension.

When the inner story begins, the narrator has full command of the story. He first calls for our attention: "Listen." Then he describes Billy's unusual predicament, briefly summarizes Billy's life up to the time of his first public statements, draws Billy's story out of this brief biography, and, finally, flashes back to Billy's first time travel. At that point, Vonnegut surrenders apparent control of the narrative to the whims of Billy's life experiences, and the story unravels itself according to the conventions of the spatial-form tradition and Billy's erratic time travel. Occasionally, Vonnegut interrupts the spatial flow to place himself at Billy's side, to identify with him, or to remind the reader of his presence. For example, just before the flying saucer comes late at night to pick up Billy, he receives a phone call from a drunk whose breath Billy could almost smell, a breath like "mustard gas and roses" (p. 63). We are, of course, reminded of Vonnegut's habit of telephoning late at night when he is drunk with "breath like mustard gas and roses" (p. 4). Vonnegut's phone call into his novel has no effect on Billy and his story, but it does remind the reader that somewhere behind Billy's story lurks a consciousness that, like fate itself, is seeking Billy out.

Occasionally the narrator asserts his full prerogatives and leaps into the narrative. Despite Hemingway's abuse of this posture in *The Torrents of Spring*, Vonnegut leaps back into the eighteenth-century temporal-form tradition, and almost like Fielding has a chummy chat with the reader about the astonishing connotations of the word "motherfucker" to the sensibility of a white man in the year 1944 and about the appropriateness of the book's epigraph to Billy's crying jags. In Chapter Eight, when Kilgore Trout, Vonnegut's favorite mask, enters the novel, the narrator assumes temporal control of the story instead of following Billy around in time. At first, it may appear that Vonnegut, the novel's intellect, is making a frantic and desperate attempt either to enter the frozen, still world of art in order to escape the vicissitudes of life, or to immerse himself in the erratic fluidity of Billy, a figment of Vonnegut's own intuition. But neither is the case as Vonnegut's fourth and last innovation in the spatial-form tradition indicates.

Vonnegut not only plays havoc with the spatial-form tradition by introducing a narrator who lives in the *res extensa* and controls events in the novel through the manipulation of the *res extensa,* but he once again defies the very foundation of the spatial-form tradition by outlining the profile of Billy's essential story in chronological order. Billy is captured, sent to Dresden, experiences the bombing, lives through it, and sees its results. That is the story as the narrator sees it, but not as Billy lives it, and thus we arrive at the crux of the book. It is split-minded, schizophrenic. Vonnegut and Billy can never fuse into oneness. *Slaughterhouse-Five* is composed of equal parts of autobiography and fiction, of Vonnegut and Billy, of body and soul, of consciousness and unconsciousness, of intellect and intuition, of punctual time and schizophrenic time, and of spatial and temporal narrative devices. Thus, Vonnegut has technically acknowledged the indelible cleft in Western man's psyche. The challenge he has accepted in *Slaughterhouse-Five* is not to destroy or suppress one part of the mind or the other, nor is he naïve enough to assume that he can fuse them into an organic whole. His technical problem is to synchronize the two parts of the book, bring their conflicting times, rhythms, together so both plots may reach a simultaneous climax and create a structural dynamic tension, a book that can fall on a geodesic path through its readers' minds. It is as though Vonnegut were placing *Tristram Shandy* and *Tom Jones* within two covers, telling each story, and resolving them simultaneously. In Vonnegut's canon the solution to the individual's plight in the contemporary world is not to push the spatial-form tradition further from the temporal-form tradition as does Robbe-Grillet, but to bring them closer, so they may suggest man's only key to his unique, earthbound, schizophrenic nature—the geodesic harmony of dynamic tension.

VONNEGUT RE-INVENTED

Thus, in his schizophrenic manner, Kurt Vonnegut discovers a means of re-inventing himself and his universe. The principle of dynamic tension informs not only the fabric and structure of the novel, but it also informs the existential relationship between Vonnegut and his transcendent hero, Billy Pilgrim. This relationship dramatizes Vonnegut's rite of initiation. We have already defined the rite of initiation as the absorption of the ego by a concept of reality that the ego itself has created, and we have observed the frightening aspects of the Einsteinian world that frustrate such a traditional process. As a result of man's inherent fear of the fourth dimension, Vonnegut's rite of initiation is not founded on the notion of annihilation by absorption but on the notion of creation by synchronization. Just as Vonnegut, in his twenty-second year, picked his way through the rubble of Dresden, Billy Pilgrim, toward the end of *Slaughterhouse-Five*, picks his way through the squalid ruins of a pornographic shop and finds there the inarticulate wisdom of Kilgore Trout, one of Vonnegut's masks, finds his "impossible hospitable world." Just as Vonnegut, twenty years later, is struggling to leave his autobiography and to enter his own fictive world to seek Billy out, Billy is pursuing Vonnegut in the guise of Trout with the same relentless tenacity. Both the intellect and the intuition are struggling to march to the same beat, striving to arrive simultaneously at the same image. At the end of *Slaughterhouse-Five* both Vonnegut and Billy, caught in different time dimensions, are synchronized by space, Dresden, and by "an image of life that is beautiful and surprising and deep," an image of an enclosure, vehicles of transportation, an image of the male womb,[15] or rebirth. Separated by time, their souls can never really touch; cast in the schizophrenic culture, they remain divided. Consequently, they erect an artificial realm of eternity, schizophrenic timelessness, the path of the intuition, where they can be delivered, reborn into maturity by synchronizing their souls. In *Cat's Cradle* the faithful of Bokononism illustrate the principle of dynamic tension in their ritual of *boko-maru*, this *shadow* of ancient and complete rituals. The participants, sitting facing each other, shoes off, feet raised, each clasping his own ankles, "giving himself the rigidity of a triangle," press the "soles of their bare feet together" (p. 131), forming a geodesic relationship. What at first glance appears to be a very weak pun, "sole-soul," becomes the crux of Vonnegut's vision. In Vonnegut's schizophrenic world men will never touch souls because they are all trapped, cut off. But they must accept second best and touch soles; they must perform "artificial things," invent rituals if they are to survive. They must make life an art form.

With the invention of his schizophrenic manner, Kurt Vonnegut, Jr., created the technical perspective that he needed to exorcise the distracting and consuming cloud of Dresden, to resolve the aesthetic problems he discovered in *The Sirens of Titan*, and to re-invent himself and his universe in his "lousy little book" that sings like the crystal goblet of the schizophrenic planet Mercury. With the resolution of his twenty-three years of labor in *Slaughterhouse-Five*, Vonnegut could return with equanimity and confidence to the themes of *God Bless You, Mr. Rosewater* as evidenced by his new novel *Breakfast of Champions*. Whatever Vonnegut accomplishes after this point in his career, however, will be deeply informed by the success of his struggle with *Slaughterhouse-Five*. Because his moral confrontation with Dresden was steady and persistent throughout his career, the affirmation of life, vibrating in this climactic novel is based not on self-deception but upon the greatness of the human spirit confronted by great adversity. More important, though, the integrity of this affirmation signals the aesthetic strength and freedom of Vonnegut's vision, a vision that captures the essential spiritual dilemma of contemporary man and represents an enduring contribution to his literary heritage and to man's quest for "wonderful *new* lies."

NOTES TO CHAPTER 14

1. *Criticism,* eds. Mark Schorer *et al.* (New York: Harcourt, Brace and Co., 1948), pp. 379–92.
2. *The Lyrical Novel* (Princeton: Princeton University Press, 1963), p. 272.
3. Freedman, p. 31.
4. Freedman, p. 21.
5. Bruce Morrissette, "Surfaces and Structures in Robbe-Grillet's Novels," trans. Richard Howard, *Two Novels by Robbe-Grillet,* ed. Richard Howard (New York: Grove Press, Inc., 1965), p. 8.
6. Roland Barthes, "Objective Literature: Alain Robbe-Grillet," trans. Richard Howard, *Two Novels by Robbe-Grillet,* ed. Richard Howard, p. 13.
7. New York: Random House, 1962, p. 161.
8. Sypher, p. 134.
9. Sypher, p. 120.
10. See Kurt Vonnegut, Jr., "Excelsior! We're Going to the Moon! Excelsior," *The New York Times Magazine,* July 13, 1969, p. 11.
11. *The Music of the Spheres* (Cambridge: Houghton Mifflin, 1961), p. 571.
12. Murchie, p. 568.
13. Joseph Campbell, *The Hero with a Thousand Faces* (New York: World Publishing Co., 1956), pp. 137–39.
14. Vonnegut said on page eleven of his article "Excelsior" that the following passage from Guy Murchie's *The Music of the Spheres* strongly influenced one of his books: "I

sometimes wonder whether humanity has missed the real point in raising the issue of mortality and immortality— whether perhaps the seemingly limited time span of an earthly life is actually unlimited and eternal—in other words, whether mortality itself may be a finite illusion, being actually immortality and, even though constructed of just a few 'years,' that those few years are all the time there really is, so that, in fact, they can never cease" (p. 589).

15. As Joseph Campbell points out, the *male womb* "sounds the leitmotif of the Greek mysteries of the initiatory second birth" (p. 142). The most popular "enclosure" he notes is the "worldwide womb image of the belly of the whale" (p. 90).

Appendix

THE VONNEGUT BIBLIOGRAPHY

———————

JEROME KLINKOWITZ,
ASA B. PIERATT, JR.,
AND STANLEY SCHATT

I. NOVELS

Player Piano

New York: Charles Scribner's Sons, 1952.

Toronto: S. J. Reginald Saunders, 1952.

London: Macmillan, 1953, 1955, 1967.

New York: Bantam Books, 1954 (retitled *Utopia 14*).

London: Mayflower, 1962.

Munich: Heyne, 1964 (*Das Höllische System,* trans. Wulf H. Bergner).

Rome: Piacenza, 1966 (*La Società Della Camicia Stregata,* trans. Roberta Rambelli).

New York: Holt, Rinehart and Winston, 1966.

New York: Avon Books, 1967, 1970.

Moscow: Molodaya gvardiya, 1967 (*Utopija 14,* trans. M. Bruh-nov).

London: Panther, 1969.

Amsterdam: Meulenhoff, 1969.

Brazil: Editora Artenova Ltda., 1971.

New York: Delacorte/Seymour Lawrence, 1971.

Hungary: Artijus, 1971.

New York: Delta-Dell, 1972.

The Sirens of Titan

New York: Dell, 1959, 1966, 1970.

Boston: Houghton Mifflin, 1961.

Paris: DeNoël, 1962 (*Les Sirènes de Titan,* trans. Monique Theis).

London: Victor Gollancz, 1962, 1967.

Toronto: Thomas Allen, 1962.

London: Corgi, 1964.

Rome: Piacenza, 1965 (*Le Sirene di Titano,* trans. Roberta Rambelli).

London: Hodder-Fawcett, 1967.

Amsterdam: Meulenhoff, 1968.

Copenhagen: Stig Vendelkaers Forlag, 1971.

New York: Delta-Dell, 1971.

New York: Delacorte/Seymour Lawrence, 1971.

Mother Night

New York: Fawcett, 1961 [Printed February, 1962].

New York: Harper & Row, 1966 [including an Introduction by the author, incorporated into later editions].

New York: Avon Books, 1967, 1970.

London: Jonathan Cape, 1968.

Milan: Rizzoli, 1968 (*Madre Notte,* trans. Luigi Ballerini).

Brazil: Editora Artenova Ltda., 1971.

New York: Delacorte/Seymour Lawrence, 1971.
New York: Delta-Dell, 1972.

Cat's Cradle

New York: Holt, Rinehart & Winston, 1963.
London: Victor Gollancz, 1963.
New York: Dell, 1965, 1970.
Toronto: S. J. Reginald Saunders, 1964.
New York: Dell, 1965, 1970.
London: Penguin, 1965.
Milan: Rizzoli, 1968 (*Ghiaccio-Nove,* trans. Roberta Rambelli).
Tokyo: Hayakawa Shobô, 1968 (*Neko No Yurikago,* trans. Itô Norio).
Hamburg: Hoffman und Campe, 1969.
Copenhagen: Stig Verdelkaers, 1969 (*Da verden gik under,* trans. Arne Herløv Petersen).
France: Edition du Seuil, 1970.
Czechoslovakia: Mlada fronta, 1970.
Spain: Editorial Novaro, 1970.
Moscow: Holodaya gvardiya, 1970 (*Kolybel' dlya Koshki,* trans. Rita Rait-Kovalyova).
Amsterdam: Meulanhoff, 1971.
New York: Delacorte/Seymour Lawrence, 1971.

God Bless You, Mr. Rosewater

New York: Holt, Rinehart & Winston, 1965.
Toronto: Holt, Rinehart & Winston, 1965.
London: Jonathan Cape, 1965.
Barcelona: Grijalbo, 1966 (*Dios Le Bendiga, Mr. Rosewater,* trans. Amparo García Burgos).
New York: Dell, 1966, 1970.
London: Panther, 1967, 1969.
Gütersloh: Bertelesmann, 1968 (*Gott Segne Sie, Mr. Rosewater,* trans. Joachim Seyppel).
New York: Delta-Dell, 1968.

Oslo: Gyldendal, 1971 (*Perler for svin eller Gud vel singne Dem, Mr. Rosewater*, trans. Arne Herløv Petersen).
New York: Delacorte/Seymour Lawrence, 1971.

Slaughterhouse-Five

New York: Delacorte/Seymour Lawrence, 1969.
Finland: Messrs Tammi, 1969.
Tokyo: Hayakawa Shobo, 1969.
Sweden: P. A. Norstedt, 1969.
Hamburg: Hoffman und Campe, 1969.
Stockholm: P. A. Norstedt, 1971.
Italy: Mondadori, 1969.
Barcelona: Editorial Grijalbo, 1970.
France: Edition du Seuil, 1969.
Copenhagen: Gyldendal, 1970.
London: Jonathan Cape, 1969.
Amsterdam: Meulenhoff, 1970 (*Slachthuis vijf, of De Kinderkruistacht*, trans. Else Hoog).
Poland: Panstwowy Instytut Wydawniczy, 1970.
New York: Delta-Dell, 1970.
Moscow: *Novyi Mir*, 3 (1970), 78–132; 4 (1970), 148–178 (*Boinya nomer pyat', ili krestovyi pokhod detei*, trans. Rita Rait-Kovalyova).
Oslo: Gyldendal, 1970.
Hungary: Artijus, 1971.
Brazil: Editora Artenova Ltda., 1971.
New York: Dell, 1971.

II. COLLECTIONS OF STORIES AND SHORT WORKS:

Canary in a Cat House

New York: Fawcett, 1961.
Contents and Original Publication:
"Report on the Barnhouse Effect." *Collier's*, 125 (February 11, 1950), 18–19, 63–65.

"All the King's Horses." *Collier's*, 127 (February 10, 1951, 14–15, 46–48, 50.

"D. P." *Ladies' Home Journal*, 70 (August, 1953), 42–43, 80–81, 84.

"The Manned Missiles." *Cosmopolitan*, 145 (July, 1958), 83–88.

"The Euphio Question." *Collier's* 127 (May 12, 1951), 22–23, 52–54, 56.

"More Stately Mansions." *Collier's*, 128 (December 22, 1951), 24–25, 62–63.

"The Foster Portfolio." *Collier's*, 128 (September 8, 1951), 18–19, 72–73.

"Deer in the Works." *Esquire*, 43 (April, 1955), 78–79, 112, 114, 116, 118.

"Hal Irwin's Magic Lamp." *Cosmopolitan*, 142 (June, 1957), 92–95.

"Tom Edison's Shaggy Dog." *Collier's* 131 (March 14, 1953), 46, 48–49.

"Unready to Wear." *Galaxy Science Fiction*, 6 (April, 1953), 98–111.

"Tomorrow and Tomorrow and Tomorrow" (orig: "The Big Trip Up Yonder"). *Galaxy Science Fiction*, 7 (January, 1954), 100–110.

Welcome to the Monkey House

New York: Delacorte/Seymour Lawrence, 1968.

Hamburg: Hoffman und Campe, 1969.

London: Jonathan Cape, 1969.

Sweden: Norstedt, 1969.

Tokyo: Hayakawa Shobo, 1970.

Czechoslovakia: Odeon, Natodni, 1970.

Amsterdam: Algemene Uitgeverij Meulenhoff, 1970.

New York: Dell, 1970.

New York: Delta-Dell, 1970.

Brazil: Editora Artenova Ltda., 1971.

Contents and Original Publication:

"Where I Live" (orig: "You've Never Been to Barnstable?"). *Venture-Traveler's World,* 1 (October, 1964), 145, 147–49.

"Harrison Bergeron." *Magazine of Fantasy and Science Fiction,* 21 (October, 1961), 5–10.

"Who Am I This Time" (orig: "My Name Is Everyone"). *Saturday Evening Post,* 234 (December 16, 1961), 20–21, 62, 64, 66–67.

"Welcome to the Monkey House." *Playboy,* 15 (January, 1968), 95, 156, 196, 198, 200–201.

"Long Walk to Forever." *Ladies' Home Journal,* 77 (August, 1960), 42–43, 108.

"The Foster Portfolio." In *Canary in a Cat House* (as *CCH,* below).

"Miss Temptation." *Saturday Evening Post,* 228 (April 21, 1956), 30, 57, 60, 62, 64.

"All the King's Horses." In *CCH.*

"Tom Edison's Shaggy Dog." In *CCH.*

"New Dictionary" (orig: "The Latest Word"). *New York Times Book Review,* October 30, 1966, pp. 1, 56.

"Next Door." *Cosmopolitan,* 138 (April, 1955), 80–85.

"More Stately Mansions." In *CCH.*

"The Hyannis Port Story" (written 1963, not previously published).

"D. P." In *CCH.*

"Report on the Barnhouse Effect." In *CCH.*

"The Euphio Question." In *CCH.*

"Go Back to Your Precious Wife and Son." *Ladies Home Journal,* 79 (July, 1962), 54–55, 108, 110.

"Deer in the Works." In *CCH.*

"The Lie." *Saturday Evening Post,* 235 (February 24, 1962), 46–47, 51, 56.

"Unready to Wear." In *CCH.*

"The Kid Nobody Could Handle." *Saturday Evening Post,* 228 (September 24, 1955), 37, 136–37.

"The Manned Missiles." In *CCH*.
"Epicac." *Collier's*, 126 (November 25, 1950), 36–37.
"Adam." *Cosmopolitan*, 136 (April, 1954), 34–39.
"Tomorrow and Tomorrow and Tomorrow." In *CCH*.

III. PUBLISHED PLAYS:

Between Time and Timbuktu, or Prometheus–5 (New York: Delacorte/Seymour Lawrence, 1972; New York: Delta-Dell, 1972).
"Fortitude." *Playboy*, 15 (September, 1968), 99–100, 102, 106, 217–18.
Happy Birthday, Wanda June (New York: Delacorte/Seymour Lawrence, 1971; New York: Delta-Dell, 1971).
"The Very First Christmas Morning." *Better Homes and Gardens*, 40 (December, 1962), 14, 19–20, 24.

IV. UNCOLLECTED STORIES:

"Ambitious Sophomore." *Saturday Evening Post*, 226 (May 1, 1954), 31, 88, 92, 94.
"Any Reasonable Offer." *Collier's*, 129 (January 19, 1952), 32, 46–47.
"Bagombo Snuff Box." *Cosmopolitan*, 137 (October, 1954), 34–39.
"The Boy Who Hated Girls." *Saturday Evening Post*, 228 (March 31, 1956), 28–29, 58, 60, 62.
"Brief Encounters on the Inland Waterway." *Venture-Traveler's World*, 3 (October/November, 1966), 135–38, 140, 142.
"Custom-Made Bride." *Saturday Evening Post*, 226 (March 27, 1954), 30, 81–82, 86–87.
"Find Me a Dream." *Cosmopolitan*, 150 (February, 1961), 108–11.
"Lovers Anonymous." *Redbook*, 121 (October, 1963), 70–71, 146–48.

"Mnemonics." *Collier's,* 127 (April 28, 1951), 38.

"A Night for Love." *Saturday Evening Post,* 230 (November 23, 1957), 40–41, 73, 76–77, 80–81, 84.

"The No-Talent Kid." *Saturday Evening Post,* 225 (October 25, 1952), 28, 109–10, 112, 114.

"The Package." *Collier's,* 130 (July 26, 1952), 48–53.

"Poor Little Rich Town." *Collier's,* 130 (October 25, 1952), 90–95.

"The Powder Blue Dragon." *Cosmopolitan,* 137 (November, 1954), 46–48, 50–53.

"A Present for Big Nick." Argosy, December 1954, pp. 42–45, 72–73.

"Runaways." *Saturday Evening Post,* 234 (April 15, 1961), 26–27, 52, 54, 56.

"Souvenir." *Argosy,* December 1952, pp. 28, 76–79.

"Thanasphere." *Collier's,* 126 (September 2, 1950), 18–19, 60, 62.

"This Son of Mine . . ." *Saturday Evening Post,* 229 (August 18, 1956), 24, 74, 76–78.

"2BRO2B." *Worlds of If,* January 1962, pp. 59–65.

"Unpaid Consultant." *Cosmopolitan,* 138 (March, 1955), 52–57.

V. POETRY:

"Carols for Christmas 1969: Tonight If I Will Let Me." *New York Times Magazine,* December 21, 1969, p. 5.

VI. ARTICLES AND REVIEWS:

"Biafra: A People Betrayed." *McCall's,* 97 (April, 1970), 68–69, 134–38.

"Closed Season on the Kids." Rev. of *Don't Shoot—We Are Your Children,* by J. Anthony Lukas, *Life,* 70 (April 9, 1971), 14.

"Deadhead Among the Diplomats." Rev. of *The Triumph* by John Kenneth Galbraith, *Life*, 64 (May 3, 1968), 14.

"Der Arme Dolmetscher." *Atlantic Monthly*, 196 (July, 1955), 86–88.

"Don't Take It Too Seriously." Rev. of *Prize Stories 1966: The O. Henry Awards* edited by Richard Poirier and William Abrahams. *New York Times Book Review*, March 20, 1966, pp. 1, 39.

"Everything Goes Like Clockwork." Rev. of *Once a Greek . . .* by Friedrich Duerrenmatt, *New York Times Book Review*, June 13, 1964, p. 4.

"Excelsior! We're Going to the Moon! Excelsior." *New York Times Magazine*, July 13, 1969, pp. 9–11.

"The Fall of a Climber." Rev. of *Any God Will Do* by Richard Condon. *New York Times Book Review*, September 25, 1966, pp. 5, 42.

"Foreword." *Transformations*, by Anne Sexton. Boston: Houghton Mifflin, 1971, pp. vii–x.

"The Happiest Day in the Life of My Father." *American Academy of Arts and Letters. Proceedings. 1971.*

"Headshrinker's Hoyle on Games We Play." Rev. of *Games People Play* by Eric Berne, *Life*, 58 (June 11, 1965), 15, 17.

"Hello Star Vega, Do You Read Our Gomer Pyle?" Rev. of *Intelligent Life in the Universe* by S. I. Shklovskii and Carl Sogan, *Life*, 61 (December 9, 1966), R3 (Regional).

"The High Cost of Fame," *Playboy*, 18 (January, 1971), 124.

"Infarcted! Tabescent!" Rev. of *The Kandy-Colored Tangerine-Flake Streamline Baby* by Tom Wolfe. *New York Times Book Review*, June 27, 1965, p. 4.

"Introduction." *Our Time Is Now: Notes from the High School Underground*, ed. John Birmingham (New York: Praeger, 1970), pp. vii–x (expanded from "Times Change" below).

"Let the Killing Stop." *The Register*, October 23, 1969 (speech at Barnstable High School on Cape Cod).

"Money Talks to the New Man." Rev. of *The Boss* by Goffredo Parise. *New York Times Book Review*, October 2, 1966, p. 4.

"The Mysterious Madame Blavatsky." *McCall's,* 97 (March, 1970), 66–67, 142–144.

"Oversexed in Indianapolis." Rev. of *Going All the Way* by Dan Wakefield, *Life,* 69 (July 17, 1970), 10.

"Physicist, Purge Thyself." *Chicago Tribune Magazine,* June 22, 1969, pp. 44, 48–50, 52, 56.

"Reading Your Own." *New York Times Book Review,* June 4, 1967, p. 6.

"Reflections On My Own Death," *The Rotarian,* May 1972, p. 24.

"Science Fiction." *New York Times Book Review,* September 5, 1965, p. 2, rpt. in Francis Brown, ed., *Page Two* (New York: Holt, Rinehart, and Winston, 1969), pp. 117–20.

"The Scientific Goblins Are Gonna Git Us." Rev. of *Unless Peace Comes* edited by Nigel Calder, Life, 65 (July 16, 1968), 8.

"Second Thoughts on Teacher's Scrapbook." Rev. of *Up the Down Staircase* by Bel Kaufman, *Life,* 59 (September 3, 1965), 9–10.

"Teaching the Unteachable." *New York Times Book Review,* August 6, 1967, pp. 1, 20.

" 'There's a Maniac Loose Out There.' " *Life,* 67 (July 25, 1969), 53–56.

"Times Change." *Esquire,* 73 (February, 1970), 60.

"Topics: Good Missiles, Good Manners, Good Night." *New York Times,* September 13, 1969, p. 26.

"Torture and Blubber." *New York Times,* June 30, 1971, p. 41.

"The Unsaid Says Much," Rev. of *Absent Without Leave* by Heinrich Böll. *New York Times Book Review,* September 12, 1965, pp. 4, 54.

"Up Is Better Than Down." *Vogue,* August 1, 1970, pp. 54, 144–45.

"War as a Series of Collisions." Rev. of *Bomber* by Len Deighton, *Life,* 69 (October 2, 1970), 10.

"Well All Right." *Cornell Daily Sun,* November 4, 1971, p. 4 (reprints two samples of Vonnegut's student writing).

"Why They Read Hesse." *Horizon,* 12 (Spring, 1970), 28–31.

"Yes, We Have No Nirvanas." *Esquire*, 69 (June, 1968), 78–79, 176, 178–79, 182.

VII. INTERVIEWS AND RECORDED REMARKS:

ABRAMSON, MARCIA. "Vonnegut: Humor With Suffering." *The Michigan Daily* (Ann Arbor), January 22, 1969, p. 2.

BANKS, ANN. "Symposium Sidelights." *Novel: A Forum on Fiction*, 3, No. 3 (Spring, 1970), 208–11.

BOSWORTH, PATRICIA. "To Vonnegut, the Hero Is the Man Who Refuses to Kill." *New York Times*, October 25, 1970, sec. 2, p. 5.

BRYAN, C. D. B. "Kurt Vonnegut, Head Bokononist." *New York Times Book Review*, April 6, 1969, pp. 2, 25.

CASEY, JOHN. "Kurt Vonnegut, Jr.: A Subterranean Conversation." *Confluence*, 2 (Spring, 1969), 3–5.

DUNLAP, FRANK. "God and Kurt Vonnegut, Jr. at Iowa City." *Chicago Tribune Magazine*, May 7, 1967, pp. 48, 84, 86, 88.

GUSSOW, MEL. "Vonnegut Is Having Fun Doing a Play." *New York Times*, October 6, 1970, p. 56.

HEFFERNAN, HAROLD. "Vonnegut Likes a Change of Scenery." *Star-Ledger* (Trenton, New Jersey), June 8, 1971, p. 26.

HENKLE, ROGER. "Wrestling (American Style) with Proteus." *Novel: A Forum on Fiction*, 3, No. 3 (Spring, 1970), 197–207.

HICKEY, NEIL. " 'Between Time and Timbuktu.' " *TV Guide*, 20 (March 11, 1972), 24–26.

JOHNSON, A. "Authors and Editors." *Publishers' Weekly*, 195 (April 21, 1969), 20–21.

KRAMER, CAROL. "Kurt's College Kult Adopts Him as Literary Guru at 48." *Chicago Tribune*, November 15, 1970, sec. 5, p. 1.

MAHONEY, LAWRENCE. " 'Poison Their Minds with Humanity.' " *Tropic: The Miami Herald Sunday Magazine*, January 24, 1971, pp. 8–10, 13, 44.

MC CABE, LORETTA. "An Exclusive Interview With Kurt Vonnegut, Jr." *Writers Yearbook—1970*, pp. 92–95, 100–01, 103–05.

OKRENT, DANIEL. "A Very New Kind of WIR." *The Michigan Daily* (Ann Arbor), January 21, 1969, pp. 1–2.

————. "The Short, Sad Stay of Kurt Vonnegut, Jr." *The Michigan Daily* (Ann Arbor), January 25, 1969, p. 2.

REASONER, HARRY. "60 Minutes." 3 (September 15, 1970), CBS News Transcript, 14–17.

SAAL, ROLLENE W. "Pick of the Paperbacks." *Saturday Review*, 53 (March 28, 1970), 34.

SCHENKER, ISRAEL. "Kurt Vonnegut, Jr., Lights Comic Path of Despair." *New York Times*, March 21, 1969, sec. 1, p. 41.

SCHOLES, ROBERT. "A Talk With Kurt Vonnegut, Jr." *The Vonnegut Statement*, ed. Jerome Klinkowitz and John Somer (New York: Delacorte/Seymour Lawrence, 1973).

SHEED, WILFRID. "The Now Generation Knew Him When." *Life*, 67 (September 12, 1969), 64–66, 69.

TAYLOR, ROBERT. "Kurt Vonnegut." *Boston Globe Sunday Magazine*, July 20, 1969, pp. 10–12, 14–15.

THOMAS, PHIL. "Growing Sales Puzzle Writer." *Ann Arbor News*, December 12, 1971, p. 41.

TODD, RICHARD. "The Masks of Kurt Vonnegut, Jr." *New York Times Magazine*, January 24, 1971, pp. 16–17, 19, 22, 24, 26, 30–31.

TROY, CAROL. "Carol Troy Interviews Kurt Vonnegut." *Rags*, March 1971, pp. 24–26.

UNGER, ART. "Kurt Vonnegut, Jr./Class of 71." *Ingenue*, December 1971, pp. 14–18.

WOLF, WILLIAM. "Kurt Vonnegut/Still Dreaming of Imaginary Worlds." *Insight: Sunday Magazine of the Milwaukee Journal*, February 27, 1972, pp. 15–18.

(unsigned). *Publishers' Weekly*, March 22, 1971, pp. 26–27.

(unsigned). "We Talk To . . . Kurt Vonnegut." *Mademoiselle*, August, 1970, p. 296.

(unsigned). "Vonnegut's Gospel." *Time*, 95 (June 29, 1970), 8.

VIII. SPECIAL VONNEGUT NUMBERS OF SCHOLARLY JOURNALS:

"Vonnegut," *Critique*, 12 (#3, 1971); essays and a bibliography by Max Schulz, Leonard Leff, Jerome Klinkowitz, and Stanley Schatt (individually cited below).

"Kurt Vonnegut, Jr.: A Symposium," *Summary*, 1 (#2, 1971); pictorial and critical essays by Jill Krementz, Robert Scholes, Robert Kiely, David Hayman, Armin Paul Frank, Brian W. Aldiss, Tony Hillman, and "An Ancient Friend of His Family" (individually cited below).

IX. CRITICAL ESSAYS AND BOOKS ABOUT VONNEGUT:

ALDISS, BRIAN W. "Guru Number Four." *Summary*, 1 (#2, 1971), 63–68.

BELLAMY, JOE DAVID. "Kurt Vonnegut for President: The Making of an Academic Reputation." *The Vonnegut Statement*, ed. Jerome Klinkowitz and John Somer (New York: Delacorte/Seymour Lawrence, 1973).

BESTUZHEV-LADA, I. "Kogda lishim stanovitsya chelovechestvo" ("When Mankind Becomes Superfluous"), foreword to *Utopija 14* (*Utopia 14*, translated from the retitled Bantam edition of *Player Piano* by M. Bruhnov) (Moscow: Molodaya gvardiya, 1967), pp. 5–24.

BODTKE, RICHARD. "Great Sorrows, Small Joys: The World of Kurt Vonnegut, Jr.: *Cross Currents*, 20 (Winter, 1970), 120–25.

BRYAN, C. D. B. "Kurt Vonnegut on Target." *New Republic*, 155 (October 8, 1966), 21–22, 24–26.

BRYANT, JERRY H. *The Open Decision* (New York: Free Press, 1970), pp. 303–24.

CARSON, RONALD. "Kurt Vonnegut: Matter-of-Fact Moralist." *Listening*, 6 (Autumn, 1971), 182–95.

CIARDI, JOHN. "Manner of Speaking." *Saturday Review*, 50 (September 30, 1967), 16, 18.

COOK, BRUCE. "When Kurt Vonnegut Talks—and He Does—The Young All Tune In." *National Observer*, October 12, 1970, p. 21.

DEMOTT, BENJAMIN. "Vonnegut's Otherworldly Laughter." *Saturday Review*, 54 (May 1, 1971), 29–32, 38.

DIEHL, DIGBY. "And Now the Movies." *Showcase/Chicago Sun-Times*, February 28, 1971, p. 2.

ENGEL, DAVID. "On the Question of Foma: A Study of the Novels of Kurt Vonnegut, Jr." *Riverside Quarterly*, 5 (February, 1972), 119–128.

FIEDLER, LESLIE A. "The Divine Stupidity of Kurt Vonnegut." *Esquire*, 74 (September, 1970), 195–97, 199–200, 202–04.

FRANK, ARMIN PAUL. "Where Laughing Is the Only Way to Stop It From Hurting." *Summary*, 1 (#2, 1971), 51–62.

GOLDSMITH, DAVID. *Kurt Vonnegut: Fantasist of Fire and Ice* (Popular Writers Series Pamphlet #2) Bowling Green, Ohio: Bowling Green University Popular Press, 1972).

GOSS, GARY L. "The Selfless Billy Pilgrim." *Buffalo Spree*, 5 (Fall, 1971), 34–35, 44–45, 47, 52–53, 60–61.

HARRIS, CHARLES B. *Contemporary American Novelists of the Absurd* (New Haven: College & University Press, 1971), pp. 51–75.

HASSAN, IHAB. "Fiction and Future: An Extravaganza for Voice and Tape." *Liberations* (Middletown, Connecticut: Wesleyan University Press, 1971), pp. 193–94.

HAUCK, RICHARD BOYD. *A Cheerful Nihilism* (Bloomington, Indiana: Indiana University Press, 1971), pp. 237–45.

HAYMAN, DAVID. "The Jolly Mix: Notes on Techniques, Style and Decorum in *Slaughterhouse-Five*." *Summary*, 1 (#2, 1971), 44–50.

HILDEBRAND, TIM. "Two or Three Things I Know About Kurt Vonnegut's Imagination." *The Vonnegut Statement*, ed.

Jerome Klinkowitz and John Somer (New York: Delacorte/ Seymour Lawrence, 1973).

HILLEGAS, MARK. "Dystopian Science Fiction: New Index to the Human Situation." *New Mexico Quarterly*, 31 (1961), 238–49.

HILLMAN, TONY. "Hooked." *Summary*, 1 (#2, 1971), 69–72.

KAEL, PAULINE. "Current Cinema." *New Yorker*, 46 January 23, 1971), 76–78.

KAZIN, ALFRED. "The War Novel: From Mailer to Vonnegut." *Saturday Review*, 54 (February 6, 1971), 13–15, 36.

KENEDY, R. C. "Kurt Vonnegut, Jr." *Art International*, 15 (May, 1971), 20–25.

KIELY, ROBERT. "Satire as Fantasy." *Summary*, 1 (#2, 1971), 41–43.

KLINKOWITZ, JEROME. "Kurt Vonnegut, Jr., and the Crime of His Times." *Critique*, 12 (#3, 1971), 38–53.

———. "Kurt Vonnegut, Jr.: The Canary in a Cathouse"; "*Mother Night, Cat's Cradle*, and the Crimes of our Time"; "Why They Read Vonnegut." *The Vonnegut Statement*, ed. Jerome Klinkowitz and John Somer (New York: Delacorte/ Seymour Lawrence, 1973).

———, and Somer, John. "The Vonnegut Statement." *The Vonnegut Statement* (New York: Delacorte/Seymour Lawrence, 1973).

KNIGHT, DAMON. *In Search of Wonder* (Chicago: Advent Publishers, 1967), pp. 166–67, 236–37.

KREMENTZ, JILL. "Pictorial." *Summary*, 1 (#2, 1971), between pp. 34–35.

LAWRENCE, SEYMOUR. "A Publisher's Dream." *Summary*, 1 (#3, 1971), 73–75.

LEFF, LEONARD. "Science and Destruction in Vonnegut's *Cat's Cradle*." *Rectangle*, 46 (Spring, 1971), 28–32.

———. "Utopia Reconstructed: Alienation in Vonnegut's *God Bless You, Mr. Rosewater*." *Critique*, 12 (#3, 1971), 29–37.

LEWIS, FLORA. "A Writer Of and For the Times." *Chicago Sun Times*, January 5, 1971, p. 22.

MAY, JOHN R. "Vonnegut's Humor and the Limits of Hope." *Twentieth Century Literature*, 18 (January, 1972), 25–36.

MC NELLY, WILLIS E. "Science Fiction: The Modern Mythology." *America*, September 5, 1970, pp. 125–27.

MEETER, GLENN. "Vonnegut's Formal and Moral Otherworldiness: *Cat's Cradle* and *Slaughterhouse-Five*." *The Vonnegut Statement*, ed. Jerome Klinkowitz and John Somer (New York: Delacorte/Seymour Lawrence, 1973).

MELLARD, JAMES M. "The Modes of Vonnegut's Fiction: Or, *Player Piano* Ousts *Mechanical Bride* and *The Sirens of Titan* invade *The Gutenberg Galaxy*." *The Vonnegut Statement*, ed. Jerome Klinkowitz and John Somer (New York: Delacorte/Seymour Lawrence, 1973).

OLDERMAN, RAYMOND M. *Beyond the Waste Land* (New Haven: Yale University Press, 1972), pp. 187–219.

ORLOVA, R. "O romane Kurta Vonneguta" ("On Kurt Vonnegut's Novel"), afterword to *Boinya nomer pyat', ili krestovyi pokhod detei*, translated from *Slaughterhouse-Five* by Rita Rait-Kovalyova; *Novyi Mir*, 4 (1970), 179–80.

PAGETTI, CARLO. "Kurt Vonnegut, tra fantascienza e utopia." *Studi Americani* (Roma), 12 (1966), 301–22.

PALMER, RAYMOND C. "Vonnegut's Major Concerns." *Iowa English Yearbook*, No. 14 (Fall, 1969), pp. 3–10.

RANLEY, ERNEST W. "What Are People For?" *Commonweal*, 94 (May 7, 1971), 207–11.

RITTER, JESS. "Teaching Kurt Vonnegut on the Firing Line." *The Vonnegut Statement*, ed. Jerome Klinkowitz and John Somer (New York: Delacorte/Seymour Lawrence, 1973).

SAMUELS, CHARLES THOMAS. "Age of Vonnegut." *New Republic*, 164 (June 12, 1971), 30–32.

SCHATT, STANLEY. "The Whale and the Cross: Vonnegut's Jonah and Christ Figures." *Southwest Quarterly*, Winter, 1971, pp. 29–42.

———. "The World of Kurt Vonnegut, Jr." *Critique*, 12 (#3, 1971), 54–69.

SCHOLES, ROBERT. "Afterword." *The Sounder Few*, ed. R. H. W.

Dillard, *et al.* (Athens, Georgia: University of Georgia Press, 1971), pp. 186–91.

———. "Chasing a Lone Eagle." *Summary*, 1 (#2, 1971), 35–40. Reprinted in *The Vonnegut Statement*, ed. Jerome Klinkowitz and John Somer (New York: Delacorte/Seymour Lawrence, 1973).

———. "Fabulation and Satire." *The Fabulators* (New York: Oxford University Press, 1967), pp. 35–55.

———. "'Mithridates, He Died Old': Black Humor and Kurt Vonnegut, Jr." *The Hollins Critic*, 3 (October, 1966), 1–12. Reprinted in *The Sounder Few*, ed. R. H. W. Dillard, *et al.* (Athens, Georgia: University of Georgia Press, 1971), pp. 173–185.

SCHRIBER, MARY SUE. "You've Come a Long Way, Babbit! From Zenith to Ilium." *Twentieth Century Literature*, 17 (April, 1971), 101–06.

SCHULZ, MAX. "The Unconfirmed Thesis: Kurt Vonnegut, Black Humor, and Contemporary Art." *Critique*, 12 (#3, 1971), 5–28.

SEELYE, JOHN. "What the Kids Are Reading." *New Republic*, 163 (October 17, 1970), 23–26.

SKORODENKO, V. "O bezumnom mire; puzitsii khudozhnika" ("On the Irrational World and the Position of the Artist"), afterword to *Kulybel' dyla Koshki*, translated from *Cat's Cradle*, by Rita Rait-Kovalyova; Moscow: Molodaya gvardiya, 1970, pp. 212–33.

SOMER, JOHN. "Geodesic Vonnegut; Or, If Buckminster Fuller Wrote Novels." *The Vonnegut Statement*, ed. Jerome Klinkowitz and John Somer (New York: Delacorte/Seymour Lawrence, 1973).

TANNER, TONY. "The Uncertain Messenger: A Study of the Novels of Kurt Vonnegut, Jr." *Critical Quarterly*, 11 (Winter, 1969), 297–315. Reprinted in Tanner's *City of Words* (New York: Harper & Row, 1971), pp. 181–201.

TURNER, SUSAN M. "Life Is Sure Funny Sometimes . . . and Sometimes It Isn't . . . A Guide to Understanding Kurt

Vonnegut, Jr., *or* The Fool's Guide to Confusion *or* A Shot in the Dark *or* What Vonnegut Means to Me (this week anyway)." *The Thoroughbred* (University of Louisville), 2 (Spring, 1971), 43–46.

WAKEFIELD, DAN. "In Vonnegut's *Karass*." *The Vonnegut Statement*, ed. Jerome Klinkowitz and John Somer (New York: Delacorte/Seymour Lawrence, 1973).

WALSH, CHAD. *From Utopia to Nightmare* (New York: Harper & Row, 1962), pp. 85–88.

WEALES, GERALD. "What Ever Happened to Tugboat Annie?" *The Reporter*, 35 (December 1, 1966), 50, 52–56.

WOOD, KAREN AND CHARLES. "The Vonnegut Effect: Science Fiction and Beyond." *The Vonnegut Statement*, ed. Jerome Klinkowitz and John Somer (New York: Delacorte/Seymour Lawrence, 1973).

(unsigned). "An Account of the Ancestry of Kurt Vonnegut, Jr., by an Ancient Friend of His Family." *Summary*, 1 (#2, 1971), 76–118.

(unsigned). "Forty-six and Trusted." *Newsweek*, March 3, 1969, p. 79.

(unsigned). "New Creative Writers." *Library Journal*, June 1, 1952, p. 1007.

X. DOCTORAL DISSERTATIONS:

GOLDSMITH, DAVID HIRSH. "The Novels of Kurt Vonnegut, Jr." Bowling Green State University, 1970.

OLDERMAN, RAYMOND MICHAEL. "Beyond the Waste Land: A Study of the American Novel in the Nineteen-Sixties." Indiana University, 1969.

SCHATT, STANLEY. "The World Picture of Kurt Vonnegut, Jr." University of Southern California, 1970.

SOMER, JOHN. "Quick-Stasis: The Rite of Initiation in the Novels of Kurt Vonnegut, Jr." Northern Illinois University, 1971.

WEINSTEIN, SHARON ROSENBAUM. "Comedy and Nightmare: The Fiction of John Hawkes, Kurt Vonnegut, Jr., Jerzy Kosinski, and Ralph Elison." University of Utah, 1971.

XI. BIBLIOGRAPHIES:

BURNS, MILDRED BLAIR. "Books by Kurt Vonnegut." *The Hollins Critic*, 3 (October, 1966), 7. Updated in *The Sounder Few: Selected Essays from The Hollins Critic*, ed. R. H. W. Dillard, George Garrett, and John Rees Moore (Athens, Georgia: University of Georgia Press, 1971), pp. 192–93.

KLINKOWITZ, JEROME, AND PIERATT, ASA B., JR. *Kurt Vonnegut, Jr.: A Descriptive Bibliography and Annotated Secondary Checklist* (London: The Nether Press, 1972).

KLINKOWITZ, JEROME, PIERATT, ASA, AND SCHATT, STANLEY. "The Vonnegut Bibliography." *The Vonnegut Statement,* ed. Jerome Klinkowitz and John Somer (New York: Delacorte/Seymour Lawrence, 1973).

SCHATT, STANLEY, AND KLINKOWITZ, JEROME. "A Kurt Vonnegut Checklist." *Critique,* 12 (#3, 1971), 70–76.

XII. NEWSPAPER AND MAGAZINE REVIEWS:

Player Piano

ARMSTRONG, LOUISE. *Saturday Review,* 49 (May 14, 1966), 44.
FABUN, DON. *San Francisco Chronicle,* August 29, 1952, p. 15.
FLEISCHER, L. *Publishers' Weekly,* January 30, 1967, p. 113.
FRANKLIN, H. B. *Southern Review,* 3 [n.s.] (Autumn, 1967), 1036–1049.
GOLDKNOPF, DAVID. *New Republic,* 127 (August 18, 1952), 19.
HENDERSON, R. W. *Library Journal,* 77 (August, 1952), 1303.
HICKS, GRANVILLE. *New York Times,* August 17, 1952, p. 5.
HILTON, JAMES. *New York Herald Tribune Book Review,* August 17, 1952, p. 5.

KORMAN, SEYMOUR. *Chicago Sunday Tribune*, August 24, 1952, p. 2.

LEE, CHARLES. *Saturday Review*, 35 (August 30, 1952), 11.

MERRIL, J. *Fantasy and Science Fiction*, November, 1966, p. 62.

PETERSEN, C. *Books Today*, 4 (March 26, 1967), 9.

PICKREL, PAUL. *Yale Review*, 42 (Autumn, 1952), 20.

SHEPPARD, R. Z. *Life*, 60 (April 8, 1966), 15.

STURGEON, T. *National Review*, 18 (May 17, 1966), 478.

(unsigned). *Booklist*, September 1, 1952.

(unsigned). *Kirkus*, 20 (June 1, 1952), 330.

(unsigned). *National Observer*, 5 (May 23, 1966), 23.

(unsigned). *New Yorker*, 28 (August 16, 1952), 88.

The Sirens of Titan

PETERSEN, C. *Books Today*, 3 (December 4, 1966), 34.

———. *Books Today*, 4 (January 15, 1967), 9.

———. *Books Today*, May 7, 1967, p. 9.

(unsigned). *Times (London) Literary Supplement*, 15 (June 15, 1967), 543.

Mother Night

ARMSTRONG, LOUISE. *Saturday Review*, 49 (May 14, 1966), 44.

BANNON, B. A. *Publishers' Weekly*, 182 (February 28, 1966), 94.

CLARK, J. J. *Best Sellers*, 26 (May 15, 1966), 79.

GORAN, L. *Books Today*, 31 (July 31, 1966), 6.

GRANT, M. K. *Library Journal*, 91 (June 1, 1966), 2882.

GREENBURG, J. *Denver Quarterly*, Summer, 1966, pp. 119–20.

KITCHING, J. *Publishers' Weekly*, 189 (February, 1966), 183.

PETERSEN, C. *Books Today*, 4 (April 23, 1967), 10.

SAAL, ROLLENE. *Saturday Review*, 53 (March 28, 1970), 34.

SCHICKEL, RICHARD. *Harpers*, 232 (May, 1966), 103.

SMITH, WILLIAM JAMES. *Commonweal*, 84 (September 16, 1966), 592–94.

(unsigned). *Choice*, 3 (Summer, 1966), 524.

(unsigned). *Kirkus*, 34 (February, 1966), 207.

(unsigned). *Life*, 60 (April, 1966), 15.

(unsigned). *National Observer,* 5 (May, 1966), 23.
(unsigned). *Publishers' Weekly,* March 6, 1967, p. 78.
(unsigned). *Time,* 87 (April 29, 1966), 122.
(unsigned). *Virginia Quarterly Review,* 42 (Summer, 1966), xc.

Cat's Cradle

BRIEN, ALAN. *Spectator,* 211 (August 2, 1963), 158–59.
LASKI, M. *Observer,* August 22, 1965, p. 21.
SOUTHERN, TERRY. *New York Times Book Review,* June 2, 1963, p. 20.
(unsigned). *Best Sellers,* October 1, 1965, p. 274.

God Bless You, Mr. Rosewater

ALLSOP, K. *Spectator,* October 29, 1965, p. 554.
COLEMAN, J. *Observer,* October 24, 1965, p. 28.
DOLBIER, M. *New York Herald Tribune,* April 5, 1965, p. 21.
DUCHENE, A. *Manchester Guardian,* November 25, 1965, p. 11.
FREMONT-SMITH, E. *New York Times,* April 9, 1965, p. 35M.
GRADY, R. F. *Best Sellers,* 25 (May 1, 1965), 68.
HICKS, G. *Saturday Review,* 48 (April 3, 1965), 19.
KILPATRICK, C. E. *Library Journal,* 90 (April 15, 1965), 1935.
KNICKERBOCKER, CONRAD. *Life,* 58 (April 9, 1965), 6, 10.
LEVIN, MARTIN. *New York Times Book Review,* April 25, 1965, p. 41.
MADDOCKS, MELVIN. *Christian Science Monitor,* May 6, 1965, p. 9.
MERRIL, J. *Fantasy and Science Fiction,* July, 1965, p. 78.
MORGAN, EDWIN. *New Statesman,* 70 (October 29, 1965), 658.
PETERSEN, C. *Books Today,* 4 (May 7, 1967), 9.
———. *Book World,* 2 (November, 1968), 21.
PRICE, R. G. *Punch,* November 17, 1965, p. 741.
TALBOT, DANIEL. *Sunday Herald Tribune Book Week,* April 11, 1965, p. 6.
(unsigned). *Booklist,* July 15, 1965, p. 1057.
(unsigned). *Kirkus,* February 1, 1965, p. 128.

(unsigned). *New Yorker*, 41 (May 15, 1965), 216.

(unsigned). *Times (London) Literary Supplement* (November 11, 1965), p. 1007.

(unsigned). *Time*, May 7, 1965, p. 112.

Welcome to the Monkey House

BLACKBURN, SARA. *Nation*, 207 (September 23, 1968), 286.

KING, LARRY L. *New York Times Book Review*, 73 (September 1, 1968), 4.

LEVITAS, M. *New York Times*, 117 (August, 1968), 35.

MADDOCKS, MELVIN. *Life*, 65 (August, 1968), 8.

NICOL, CHARLES. *Atlantic*, 222 (September, 1968), 123.

REEDY, GERARD. *America*, 119 (September 14, 1968), 190.

RHODES, RICHARD. *Book World*, 2 (August 18, 1968), 4.

SOKOLOV, R. A. *Newsweek*, 72 (August 19, 1968), 84.

(unsigned). *Christian Science Monitor*, 61 (December 5, 1968), 23.

(unsigned). *Kirkus*, 36 (June, 1968), 664.

(unsigned). *Publishers' Weekly*, 193 (June, 1968), 127.

(unsigned). *Time*, 92 (August 30, 1968), 68.

Slaughterhouse-Five

ADAMS, PHOEBE. *Atlantic Monthly*, 223 (April, 1969), 146.

CAIN, SEYMOUR. *Christian Century*, 86 (August 13, 1969), 1069.

COFFEY, WARREN. *Commonweal*, 90 (June 6, 1969), 347.

CRICHTON, J. M. *New Republic*, 160 (April 26, 1969), 33.

HARPER, HOWARD M., JR. *Contemporary Literature*, 12 (Spring, 1971), 223–26.

HICKS, GRANVILLE. *Saturday Review*, 52 (March 29, 1969), 25.

LARDNER, SUSAN. *New Yorker*, 45 (May 17, 1969), 145.

MENKEN, NANCY. *Library Journal*, 94 (December 15, 1969), 4624.

O'CONNELL, SHAUN. *American Scholar*, 38 (Autumn, 1969), 718–22.

PRESCOTT, PETERS. *Look*, April 1, 1969, p. 10.

REED, JOHN. *Christian Science Monitor,* April 17, 1969, p. 15.

RICHARDSON, JACK. *New York Review of Books,* 15 (July 2, 1970), 7–8.

ROBINSON, W. C. *Library Journal,* 94 (March 1, 1969), 1021.

ROWLEY, PETER. *Nation,* 208 (June 9, 1969), 736.

SCHOLES, ROBERT. *New York Times Book Review,* April 6, 1969, p. 1.

SHEED, WILFRID. *Life,* March 21, 1969, p. 9.

STERN, DANIEL. *Book World,* April 13, 1969, p. 7.

(unsigned). *Best Sellers,* 29 (April 15, 1969), 31.

(unsigned). *Newsweek,* 73 (April 14, 1969), 122.

(unsigned). *Time,* 93 (April 11, 1969), 106.

Happy Birthday, Wanda June

KERR, WALTER. *New York Times,* October 18, 1970, Sec. 2, pp. 1, 18.

NOVICK, JULIUS. *Village Voice,* October 15, 1970, pp. 52, 54.

OLIVER, EDITH. *New Yorker,* 46 (October 17, 1970), 143–45.

SAINER, ARTHUR. *Village Voice,* October 15, 1970, pp. 53, 63.

(unsigned). *Newsweek,* 76 (October 19, 1970), 123.

(unsigned). *Time,* 96 (October 19, 1970), 74.

CONTRIBUTORS' NOTES

———— ·•◆•· ————

JEROME KLINKOWITZ has written on novelists from Hawthorne's day to the present for such journals as *Critique, Modern Fiction Studies, Chicago Review,* and *Studies in the Novel.* He teaches at the University of Northern Iowa, and is co-editor of *Innovative Fiction* (Dell, 1972).

JOHN SOMER has edited *Literature and Rhetoric, Literary Experience,* and, with Jerome Klinkowitz, *Innovative Fiction.* He is Assistant Professor of English at Kansas State Teachers College.

JESS RITTER's firing line is San Francisco State College; author of *Beyond Survival,* he is a frequent contributor to *Rolling Stone.*

ROBERT SCHOLES is Professor of English at Brown University, where he helps edit *Novel: A Forum on Fiction.* Oxford University Press has published his *The Nature of Narrative* (with Robert Kellogg) and *The Fabulators.*

DAN WAKEFIELD, whose books include *Island in the City, Revolt in the South, The Addict, Between the Lines,* and *Supernation at Peace and War,* has also written a best-selling novel, *Going All the Way.* Although his permanent home is Boston, he has recently been working in Hollywood, California.

JOE DAVID BELLAMY, an M.F.A. graduate of the University of Iowa Writers Workshop, teaches at St. Lawrence University in New York. His magazine, *The Falcon,* regularly features interviews with contemporary writers, and Mr. Bellamy's own interviews, stories, and poetry have appeared in *The Atlantic Monthly, Chicago Review,* and *The Wisconsin Review.*

TIM HILDEBRAND has edited *Mandala: A Magazine of Satire, Speculation & Supereality* from outposts in Madison, Wisconsin, and Iowa City, Iowa. He is completing an anecdotal novel, *Fables of Rotwang,* portions of which have appeared in small magazines.

KAREN AND CHARLES WOOD have taught in the Science Fiction Workshop of Illinois Valley College, and are presently editing the papers of author Willard Motley.

JAMES M. MELLARD writes frequently on modern novelists, and is the author of *Four Modes: A Rhetoric of Modern Fiction.* He is Associate Professor of English at Northern Illinois University.

GLENN MEETER'S stories have appeared in *Redbook* and *The Atlantic Monthly;* he has also written a booklet on Bernard Malamud and Philip Roth for the William Eerdmans series, *Contemporary Writers in Christian Perspective.*

ASA B. PIERATT, JR., once a student of political science, is preparing a full descriptive bibliography of Vonnegut's novels

for The Nether Press of London, England. He is an Assistant
Professor at the University of New Haven.

STANLEY SCHATT teaches at the University of Houston, and is
preparing a study of Vonnegut for the Twayne United States
Authors Series.

INDEX

281

INDEX

INDEX